One Hundred Years
of the
MANX ELECTRIC RAILWAY

Keith Pearson

*L*eading *E*dge™
press and publishing

Published by Leading Edge Press & Publishing Ltd, The Old Chapel, Burtersett, Hawes, North Yorkshire, DL8 3PB. ☎ (0969) 667566

A CIP Catalogue record for this book is available from the British Library.

ISBN -0 948135 38 7

Edited by Stan Abbott
Design and Type by Leading Edge Press & Publishing Ltd
Colour reprographics by Impression, Leeds
Printed and bound in Great Britain by Ebenezer Baylis and Son Ltd, Worcester

... for EKP

About the author

Keith Pearson was born in Manchester in 1929 and much enjoyed his native city's tramways when, as a schoolboy passenger, he travelled to what was then the Burnage High School, served by one of the city's two reserved track routes! Later war years saw him at Ulverston Grammar, coincidentally functioning as bellringer at Holy Trinity, Colton where (it later emerged) the Snaefell line's George Noble Fell had been baptised 95 years earlier!

From 1945, increasingly frequent visits to the Isle of Man saw the beginning of his studies of the Island's tramways, by 1952 pursued in parallel with professional studies in automobile and agricultural engineering at the Chelsea College. He then became a full time engineering lecturer, first at Chelsea and (following further studies at Bolton Training College) in East Anglia and Preston, where he retired from a Senior Lecturer post in 1987.

A personal involvement with museum tramcars began in 1951 with the rescue of a Douglas Southern Electric tramcar of 1896. Substantial "involvements" continued over succeeding years with the help of a small group of friends. This has included the restoration of a Douglas cable car and the major part of a Dundee steam trailer car, both by G F Milnes.

Other interests include music, architecture and horology.

Edward Hopkinson

John Hopkinson

The involvement of the brothers Edward and John Hopkinson in the creation of the tramway from Douglas to Laxey in 1893-4 is a major element in the history of electric traction in Great Britain. Dr Edward Hopkinson (pictured about 1897) was born in Manchester on May 28, 1859 — he was a product of Owen's College (later the Victoria University of Manchester) and Emmanuel College, Cambridge. He obtained a BSc, DSc and MA (Cantab) and enjoyed membership of the Institutes of Civil, Mechanical and Electrical Engineers. His pioneering role is summarised in the text of this book.

Dr John Hopkinson (pictured about 1892) was also Manchester-born (July 27, 1849). Like Edward, he attended Owen's College — he was a DSc, and was (from 1878) a Fellow of the Royal Society, having been a Scholar at Trinity. His premature death, aged 49, in a tragic family climbing accident cut short a brilliant career. His work in connection with the mechanical generation of electricity was of particular importance.

It will be realised how powerful a team the brothers represented — the one, Edward, a practical exponent, the other a brilliant theoretician.

Foreword

by

The Hon. Sir Charles Kerruish OBE, CP, LL.D
President of Tynwald

It is a great pleasure for me to respond to the author's invitation to contribute a foreword to his welcome, authoritative and timely account of our tramway system. Timely in that its issue coincides with the Manx Electric Railway's Centenary and I am convinced it will provide an invaluable source of information, not only to railway enthusiasts but also to all Manx people who have an interest in the evolution of this part of our heritage.

Having had a lifetime relationship with this railway, first travelling by MER to my local school, the Dhoon, at Glen Mona in the 1920s, and in more recent times since 1946, as the politician representing the Sheading of Garff, the constituency which is the heartland of the railway, I can vouch for the book's authority and believe it will prove to be "guide, philosopher and friend" to all who are interested in the operation of railway systems large or small.

In this book, Keith Pearson gives life and significance to the saga of our railway. His dedicated and detailed research adds enormously to our store of knowledge and in my judgement it is a work worthy of its subject. There can be no higher praise.

Prologue

The Island, 1892

WHEN IN 1893-4 THE ISLAND BECAME THE location for the most ambitious British electric traction scheme to date, the combination of local circumstances was perhaps at its most favourable. The Island had long ago left behind the 18th century twilight of the Athol lordships and instead was riding on the crest of a wave of tourist-generated prosperity, particularly since 1887. Its government was more flexible than its mainland counterpart and the obstacles which would surely have obstructed a similar mainland enterprise were thus largely absent. It seems certain, for example, that the success of the Manx lines "unlocked the door" for schemes like the Blackpool and Fleetwood tramway, albeit four years later. By the 1890s, the visitor base had spread substantially across the social spectrum, the villa-owning well-to-do (who came over for virtual summer residence, servants and all) being now well outnumbered by those who filled the ever-expanding rows of "boarding establishments".

In Douglas, older premises towards the back of the town (some going back to the 1840s) were soon to feel the loss of patronage as the fashionable promenade locations expanded year by year. This circumstance had a part to play in the construction of the town's cable tramway in 1895-6.

Expansion during the Loch governorship was particularly rapid. By 1892, as part of this economic growth the Island had acquired excellent steamer services, a large (for its size) steam railway system (constructed 1873-86) and, in particular, a promenade horse tramway at Douglas. From a fleet of three cars at opening in 1876 this had, by 1892, grown to operate a fleet of 29 and was carrying more than 800,000 passengers a year. Forming its northern terminus (and itself a major attraction) was Derby Castle, by now one of the several large-scale entertainment complexes whose somewhat Crystal Palace-influenced architecture made their buildings dominant features of the Douglas Bay panorama of the time.

However, from here northwards there extended nearly 20 miles of ruggedly beautiful landscape still sans railway. The harbour and mining village of Laxey formed the near mid-point of this coastline, with the still growing town of Ramsey as its northern limit. Laxey's boom era as a centre of lead mining was drawing to a close — the several surveys for steam lines described in Appendix 1 must have gained much of their impetus from this activity. Now, however, the wish to expand tourism perhaps had first place in railway development aspirations. The excellent Manx Northern could offer a 70-minute Ramsey-Douglas timing but it followed a roundabout route…

Now, almost 100 years later, let our story begin…

MER crest 1894-1950
The major roundel was 11ins in diameter

Contents

Illustrations: 1992 acknowledgements

In the case of the following major contributors their initials are used: S Broomfield; John C Cooke; D G Coakham; P Hammond; Manx Electric Railway (currently Isle of Man Railways); Mather & Platt (Machinery) Ltd. (Weir Pumps Ltd); National Tramway Museum.

In all other cases 'credits' are ascribed by name. Every effort has been made to ensure correct attribution—notice of any inadvertent error would be appreciated. The Author is grateful to the many people concerned for their continued assistance.

List of Illustrations

*   One half of the machine is depicted
**   Only one of the cars is winter service equipped
***   Both p82 illustrations refer to later text areas

Introduction

The author's original book, Isle of Man Tramways, published in 1970, began with the introduction which appears below, accompanied by Mr J C Cooke's map. Its content and sentiments have required little alteration, and will perhaps be seen to be echoed in the "postscript" added to form a direct link to the new parts of the work represented by the final chapters. Acknowledgements which appear at the end of the text have equal validity. Sadly, the 25-year interval means that many of those named are now deceased, but it is felt that their contribution should still be "on record". The help received over the last two years from present-day Manx friends has been no less than generous and valuable — the "electric railway" continues to enjoy the services of loyal and enthusiastic staff whose continued friendship makes an Island visit something special.

Part One

IN THE MID-SUMMER OF 1945, THE WRITER set sail for what was then, to him, a miniature new world — the Isle of Man. The particular attraction of its transportation was at once felt, and from this, and the friendliness and enthusiasm of operating and administrative staffs, has grown this book. Though primarily an account of the tramway undertakings, it is also to some extent a history of the Island's growth as a resort, and of its latter-day difficulties, and the writer hopes that Manx readers will show the same indulgence to a mainlander's examination of their affairs as they did towards his many queries.

The Isle of Man lies a little to the north of centre of the Irish Sea, and is geologically rather similar to England's Lake District, which at one point is only 30 miles away. The Island's mountainous slate backbone (rising to 2,034 feet at Snaefell) shelters a rather gentler limestone country in the south-east, while the far north consists of a remote plain extending to the Point of Ayre. The Island's greatest length is 33^1/$_4$ miles, the width 12^1/$_2$. The ever-present sea gives vegetation of a greenness only parallelled in the west of Ireland, a scenic resemblance furthered by the structural simplicity of the older Manx cottages. The towns are of moderate size; Douglas with around 18,800 inhabitants (1961) contrasts with Ramsey's 3,700, Peel's 2,500, and four others all with fewer than 2,000. The Island's total population in 1961 was 48,150.

Its people, and the near-extinct Manx language, are of complex origins. Rich in prehistoric remains, the Island also played a major part in the events of Celtic Christianity. From its 13th century status as part of the Kingdom of Norway, through successive Scottish and English overlordships, its history was continuously unsettled until it passed to the Dukes of Athol in the early 18th century. The Athol regime did little to improve the Island economically, smuggling being a dominant means of livelihood. But from 1829 the Isle of Man was once more brought under the English Crown and a more ordered economy evolved, at first centred on the herring industry and an improved agriculture, and later on the expanding holiday trade. The governorship of Sir Henry Brougham Loch, from 1863, marked the start of the most rapid period of evolution, in which the writer's fellow Mancunians (of past generations) played a major part. The Island's tramways were at once the product and the means of the tourist industry's growth and are an essential part of that industry today.

The Island has sustained in its Tynwald "court" the oldest unbroken Parliamentary tradition in the world. The lower house, the Keys, dates in its present elected form from 1866, and with its corresponding Legislative Council (the upper house) has exercised a marked influence on the status of the Island's tramways. Inspections of the new lines were made at the behest of the Governor, originally by men resident on the Island (as in 1876), but later by borrowing the inspecting engineer-officers of the mainland Board of Trade. The term "Act" in this book refers in every case to an Act of Tynwald.

No effort has been made to cover the history of the Island's steam railways, already well described in works by the late Ian Macnab and, more recently, by J I C Boyd.

Part Two, 1992

When completing the text of Isle of Man Tramways some 25 years ago, the events of 1893 were already beyond living recollection. Twenty years earlier still, when initial research commenced, older Manxmen and Manxwomen still lived, who were able to offer invaluable personal witness. These late Victorian islanders were invariably courteous and helpful to the (then) relatively junior author and they are here remembered with pleasure for their unfailing kindness.

My present publisher and I were confronted with a number of choices, but we came to concur that our best service to current readers would be rendered, initially, by an account of the "Manx Electric" group of lines alone. Modern printing has enabled an enhanced quality of photographic illustration and some improvement has also been made to black and white illustrative material — where better photographs have been found these are included so as to "freshen" the book still further.

The Upper Douglas Cable Tramway and that tramway extraordinaire, the lamented Southern Electric, both celebrate their centenary in 1996 and the writer hopes to see this occasion commemorated in print in a similar manner to the present volume... then, perhaps, the "Douglas Bay Tramway".

Changes in the text from that of 1979 are primarily those needed to avoid back reference to events before 1892-3, with the addition of corrections where errors have been discovered in the original text (these were relatively minor). The section dealing with events since that date attempts the difficult task of avoiding a procession of minor details without omitting events of real substance. The two rival enthusiast societies have published quarterly magazines over the period from 1973/4 to the present. These, in combination, chronicle most major events, though with varying editorial overtones! The Light Rail Transit Association's *Modern Tramway* has also continued to report on the Island events, usually more or less annually. Engineering judgments by the author relate to his past employment in mechanical engineering education and are, hopefully, objective.

The Island of the 1990s is much changed from its apparent self as of the late Sixties — its population has grown (inside planned guidelines) to almost 70,000, but to some this brings alarm, since the Manx-born are now a minority. This changed social and economic scene is given some attention in the first of two new chapters. A major part of the Island's economy is represented by its function as an "offshore" finance base, and this is as self-evident as the diminished role of traditional mass tourism. It is still a beautiful place, and can offer the visitor tranquil havens unchanged for a century or more. As "conservation" gains an increasing public acceptance the Island landscape and its tramways should surely achieve enhanced recognition.

F K Pearson, Arnside, Cumbria, August 1992

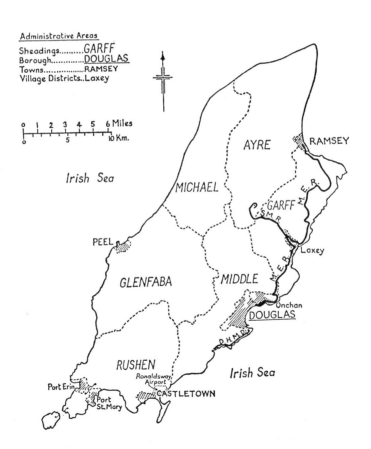

By 1991 the Island population had reached 69,788 with Douglas at 22,214, Onchan (technically still a village) 8,483, Ramsey 6,496, Peel 3,829 and Castletown 3,152. Port Erin had 3,024 inhabitants. No other "village district" reached the 2,000 level, apart from Braddan and Malew. (JCC)

Chapter 1

The Coast Electric Tramway

...the Isle of Man has been seized by the epidemic of progress, and its people have gotten an electric railway...
Street Railway Journal, May 1894

AN OBITUARY OF FREDERICK SAUNDERSON, published in 1911, included the words: "Then came the great boom year of 1887, on the strength of which Mr Alexander Bruce, manager of Dumbell's Bank, and other men of more or less standing, including several Keys, launched several big ventures. Mr Saunderson was swept into the vortex, and again came out as a Civil Engineer."

Saunderson was born in 1841 in the city of Armagh, and his early life was spent in railway construction engineering in Ireland. About 1865 he arrived in the Isle of Man, where he had family ties with the Rowe family, closely connected with the Castletown lead mines. Later he worked as assistant to Alured Dumbell, then High Bailiff of Ramsey and by the late 1880s was engaged in real estate promotion, typically the South Ramsey Estate of circa 1886. He also designed some waterworks schemes, but his enduring monument is the electric tramway running north from Douglas.

The contorted geology of the clay slates of the northern part of the Island has led to the formation of a jagged coastline from which deep ravine-like valleys run inland, chiefly orientated east-west. This difficult terrain had deterred earlier promoters, but by the early 1890s fairly practical surveys had been made, though they still involved gradients which would be heavy for a steam line (see Appendix 1). Now, however, Alexander Bruce evolved his own similar project and, unlike the others, had access to both the technical expertise — with electric traction — and the finance to make it a reality.

In Onchan parish, just north of Douglas, lay the considerable estate of Howstrake, mostly rough grazing, with a summit level on Banks Howe of 427ft. Bruce and his associates saw in this rolling landscape a field for estate development on the grand scale, and resolved to lay out part as pleasure grounds and other parts for housing. In September 1889, Bruce and Saunderson made a provisional agreement to buy part of the Howstrake estate from the trustee, John Travis, and the three members of the Callow family concerned. This was found initially to infringe the trust deed, and an Act of Tynwald had to be obtained (in 1892) to authorise it.

The plan filed with the 1889 agreement shows that the intention was to give access to the new property by building a road along the coast. The first scheme included a severe gradient cut through the steep brow beyond Port e Vada, but a later section shows an incline with successive gradients of 1 in 50, 1 in 30 and 1 in 25, beginning 655ft from the end of the Strathallan Crescent promenade. This was to be achieved by building a level sea wall across Port e Vada creek and superimposing an embankment with stone-faced slopes, thus forming a reclaimed site of which part was used in 1895 by the Derby Castle company for a variety theatre. The road next passed over the edge of the Hague estate before passing on to Howstrake lands. The first part of the road took in a strip of land which the town commissioners had given to the Derby Castle company in 1888.

The scheme for the area beyond Port Jack is shown on a plan of August 1891 for a "Proposed New Road From Derby Castle Gate to Onchan Harbour". It bears the name of Alfred Jones Lusty, a London merchant of immense wealth who was financial backer for Saunderson and others, and who resided for a time at the XVI century Howstrake mansion. A significant later amendment to the scheme altered the gradient to a continuous 1 in 24.

The powers required were granted in the Howstrake Estate Act of March 22, 1892. This not only legalised all the above features of the Howstrake project, but also included tramway provisions. On the entire Howstrake estate, along any roads (new or existing) more than 36ft wide, the grantee (Saunderson) could construct a single or double line tramway and work it by means of animal, steam, electric or other power. The free conditional use of parts of the Hague estate was permitted, and one such plot was made over to Saunderson "... for the erection of electric plant and machinery, such electric plant and machinery to be worked with approved smoke consumers". The original depot and power station also occupied some former sea bed; later, car sheds were built partly on land leased from the Hague estate, which added to the complications of Derby Castle depot's land titles. In view of a November 1889 agreement between Isle of Man Tramways Ltd (the then operators of the Douglas horse tramway) and the Derby Castle Company, the new act provided for the pre-existing optional right of the horse tramway to extend its line as far as the new Derby Castle "pavilion". As will shortly be evident, this extension was not carried out. All the

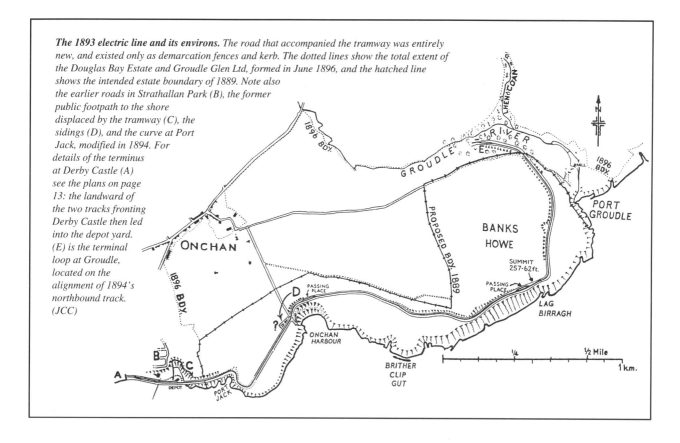

The 1893 electric line and its environs. The road that accompanied the tramway was entirely new, and existed only as demarcation fences and kerb. The dotted lines show the total extent of the Douglas Bay Estate and Groudle Glen Ltd, formed in June 1896, and the hatched line shows the intended estate boundary of 1889. Note also the earlier roads in Strathallan Park (B), the former public footpath to the shore displaced by the tramway (C), the sidings (D), and the curve at Port Jack, modified in 1894. For details of the terminus at Derby Castle (A) see the plans on page 13: the landward of the two tracks fronting Derby Castle then led into the depot yard. (E) is the terminal loop at Groudle, located on the alignment of 1894's northbound track. (JCC)

work was to be completed within three years of the Act's promulgation on July 5, 1892.

The gauge of the tramways was specified as three feet. An overhang of 21 inches outside the wheel faces was permitted and, perhaps with street tramway construction in mind, the track was to be laid so that the upper surface was level with the road. A public road crossing was permitted at Onchan harbour. Clauses like those of the 1876 bay tramway Act granted exclusive use of the track and perpetuated the anomaly of red leading lights and green rear ones. From September 30 to the Saturday before Whit week, the grantee was to run not fewer than six cars daily, and from the Saturday before Whit week to September 30, the grantee was to run not fewer than one car every hour. This clause was inserted at the insistence of the Derby Castle company (one wonders at the real benefits for the Derby Castle company in having casual visitors whisked away to Groudle!).

Reading the Act suggests that Saunderson alone was concerned, but the real entrepreneurs were Bruce and Lusty and their associates. Alexander Bruce, born in Banff, Scotland, on March 21, 1843, had served an apprenticeship with the City of Glasgow bank, and then came to a Douglas subsidiary, the Bank of Mona. When the Glasgow bank failed in 1878, he became general manager of Dumbell's Banking Company, an insular concern already secretly on the brink of insolvency. Bruce, a man of powerful character with a particularly captivating magic of personality all his own, took all this in his stride; he kept Dumbell's under full sail,

hopefully seeing in expansion a cure for its ills, and almost succeeded. The schemes we are describing were only a part of its endeavours, and by 1892-3 he was also town treasurer of Douglas and a Justice of the Peace.

Bruce had already sought advice on electric tramways, and had been referred to Dr Edward Hopkinson. Born in May 1859, Hopkinson in 1882 became assistant to Sir William Siemens. Sir William began life as Wilhelm, brother to Ernst Werner Siemens of Siemens and Halske, whose pioneer electric railway of 1879 is mentioned in Chapter 8. When he came to Britain in 1850 it was as an agent for Siemens and Halske, who began business (marketing electric telegraph systems) in 1847. His major role in the installation of the Giant's Causeway line in 1883 saw Dr Edward as his assistant. His open-hearth steel-making process represented another facet of his many abilities, and he was knighted as "Sir William" in 1883, regrettably dying the same year. In 1884 Dr Edward joined Mather and Platt, of the Salford Ironworks, became a partner in 1887, then managing director and by 1899 was vice-chairman. He was also vice-chairman of the Chloride Electrical Storage Syndicate. Sir William Mather had obtained in 1883 the British rights for the Edison dynamo, and Edward's brother, Dr John Hopkinson, had evolved from this the Edison-Hopkinson dynamo, predecessor of the "Manchester" dynamo which Mather & Platt began to manufacture. Meanwhile, Edward gained traction experience, first with Siemens at Portrush, then (after joining Mather & Platt) at Bessbrook and on the City and South London Railway.

With the Act passed, the promoters formed themselves into the Douglas Bay Estate Limited, registered on September 10, 1892 with a capital of £50,000. The stated objects included the acquisition of Saunderson's rights as "grantee", and the intended execution of his tramway and road schemes. Construction began at once of the stone embankment across Port e Vada creek, and beyond this a roadway was built corresponding to the section reproduced, but with only a single tram track.

Beyond Onchan harbour, the new road ran roughly parallel to the coast as far as the northern boundary of the estate at Groudle Lane. Beyond here was another potential attraction, the Groudle river's glen, and with the co-operation of the lessee, R M Broadbent, further land was added to the Douglas Bay estate to extend the road and tramway to a point opposite Broadbent's intended new Groudle hotel. Broadbent also owned Bibaloe farm to the north of this, and during the next four years other land purchases widened the boundaries of the property owned by the 1896 Douglas Bay Estate & Groudle Glen Limited to those shown on our map.

By 1982, Bruce had privately resolved that the Howstrake tramway should be the testing ground for a more ambitious project — an electric tramway northward to Laxey. By early 1893 Saunderson had prepared a survey carrying a single line and loop tramway beyond Groudle to a point at Baldromma-Beg, the intended new limit of the Howstrake lands, and this location east of the Liverpool Arms hotel on the main Lonan-Laxey road was the start of the intended future continuation to Laxey. The plan was than made public by the creation of another new company, the Douglas & Laxey Coast Electric Tramway Company, registered on March 7 1893 with an authorised capital of £50,000, to acquire and construct tramways between Douglas and Laxey and subsequently to operate them.

The capital for the tramway to Laxey actually came from the Howstrake company, and the subscribers were thus largely the same. The signatories were Alfred Jones Lusty, Alexander Bruce, Frederick Saunderson, F G Callow (advocate, of Douglas), Richard Evans, of Barry, Glamorgan (general manager of the Barry Railway), Frederick Vaughan (a solicitor, of Cardiff) and Edward Franklin, a colliery proprietor of Radyr, Glamorgan. The three Welshmen were evidently brought in by Lusty, who himself hailed from South Wales. To build beyond Baldromma-Beg required a further Act of Tynwald with powers of compulsory purchase, and as a first step Saunderson prepared a plan and section for the complete Douglas-Laxey tramway, now intended as a double line on reserved track throughout. This plan survives in the Manx museum.

At this time, March 1893, the interim single-line tramway to Groudle Glen was already being built. On May 15 the Press reported the arrival of rails,

concurrent with the erection of the power station and car sheds and the formation of the new roadway. The single line was laid on the alignment of the outer (seaward) of the future twin tracks, with most of the poles in their intended central position but with single bracket arms. The roadway was not given much attention at this stage, apart from a line of stones dividing it from the reserved track of the tramway. The layout is shown on the accompanying plan, based on a minutely exact section survey by Saunderson dated August 16, 1893. The sidings at Onchan are known only in terms of site area and position (now obscured by housing development). The 1892 scheme had also intended a rather extraordinary layout for Derby Castle's depot, complete with a row of terraced houses, but the only actual deviation from 1894's future alignment was around the site of the Douglas Bay hotel at Port Jack.

Mr G A Ring, the new Bill's petitioner, appeared before Tynwald Court on April 14 1893. Some members of the court thought that the Howstrake line was only being built to Groudle, and wished to stipulate that the line must be a continuous one from Douglas to Laxey. After personal assurances by Saunderson, the court carried the necessary motion and the Bill was then taken up in the Keys, after £600 had been deposited with Dumbell's Banking

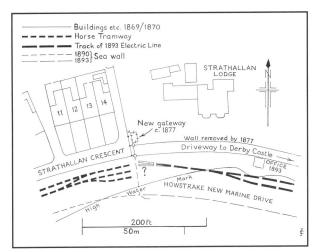

The 1893 terminus at Derby Castle. (JCC)

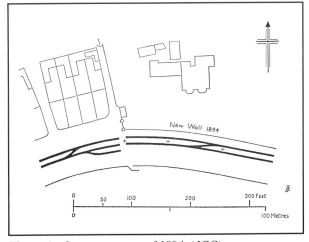

The revised arrangements of 1894. (JCC)

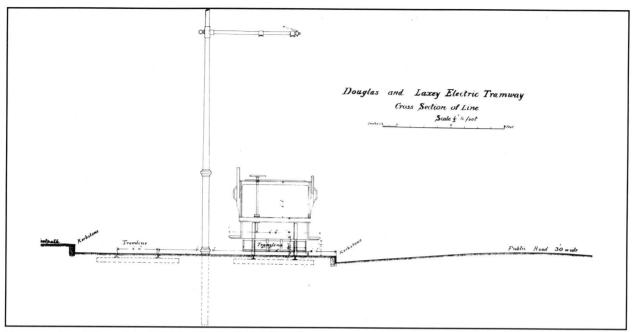

Cross-sectional view of the 1893 line by Frederick Saunderson.

Company. Saunderson's evidence in the Keys revealed that he originally wanted permission for gradients as steep as 1 in 12. James Walker, engineer to the Harbour Commissioners, had walked over the ground and agreed professionally with the line as proposed. The company sought exemption from any obligation to carry goods, but members saw that the new line would mean the end of any steam railway proposals, and after necessary concessions by the company the Bill was passed by the Keys on Friday, April 21.

In the Legislative Council, the Bill passed its first reading, and a petition by the rival Manx East Coast Railway Company was not granted a hearing. The Council wanted compulsory obligation to carry goods, a lower maximum fare, a minimum year-round service, and official inspection. Saunderson now offered fares over the whole distance of 1s (5p) single and 1s 6d (7.5p) return, with one daily journey in each direction and up to ten tons of goods per day. While being questioned about fares, Saunderson stated: "We have no third-class carriages. All our carriages will be first class" (laughter). "They will be exceedingly well got up". A further question elicited the fact that the Douglas Bay estate was to build the line and hand it over to the Douglas and Laxey Coast company in exchange for £50,000 in shares and debentures.

The council met again on April 28 and passed the Bill, having first ensured that the fare was lowered to 2d a mile (with a 3d minimum), that luggage was to be charged at a lower rate than first proposed and that reasonable provision should be made for goods. Two weekday journeys had to be operated throughout the year. The wish for steeper gradients had arisen from plans for a branch to Onchan, where 1 in 15 might be encountered. The Governor thought this risky — "... I do not want to kill my neighbours" — but had agreed to a form

allowing for future consultation. Post Office clauses were inserted in May after the Bill had left the council, and the Keys' acceptance on May 10 was followed by its being sent off for the Royal Assent. On May 15, the *Isle of Man Times* described the work as "the greatest local improvement".

The resulting Douglas & Laxey Electric Tramway Act 1893 was promulgated on November 17. Where necessary, it supplanted the Howstrake Act, and once the Howstrake tramway was completed and acquired, the new company could purchase land compulsorily from Baldromma-Beg northwards to Laxey; two years were allowed for completion. The maximum gradient was fixed at 1 in 20, and curvature at a minimum radius of 90ft. Speed on sections adjoining highroads was to be limited to 8 mph, and roadside sections did not need to be fenced unless they were lower than the adjoining road, though a stone kerb could be laid if desired. Crossings of public roads were to be laid level with their surface, and were subject to a speed restriction of 6mph. Motive power was to be animal or electric only, though steam or other forms could be used if the Highway Board gave permission in writing. The Act specified a compulsory government inspection of the tramway prior to its public use. The company could charge up to 2d a mile, with a first minimum of 3d, the tolls to be shown in the car, and each passenger was allowed 28lbs of luggage free. Goods and mails were to be carried, the freight charges were 3d a mile for each 28lbs or part thereof.

By the end of May 1893, work was well advanced on the new generating station and car shed. The site selected by Saunderson was the erstwhile floor of Port e Vada creek. As local raconteur Dr Richard Farrell* later put it, "There is no such creek. There was two years ago. In yonder cave, boys undressed to bathe in this charming little creek; there is no trace of it now. The creek was in the way of modern progress, and modern progress, like necessity, knew no law..."

The floor of the creek was filled to form a level site behind the new seaward embankment, on which three buildings were erected in a common block. To house the cars, a three-track, corrugated iron depot was erected, 112ft long, 30ft 3ins wide and 17ft 6ins high, with space for nine cars and pits for six. Next to this was an overhaul workshop, 62ft x 13ft. Adjacent lay a stone built engine room 60ft x 37ft, having an iron roof (height 23ft), and next to it there was a boiler house of similar construction, 49ft by 42ft, with a height of 19ft 6ins; one wall was of wood to allow for extensions. Water for the boilers came from two streams which fed an underground storage tank. A 60ft tall chimney, 5ft in diameter, completed the complex.

Steam was supplied by a pair of Galloway boilers (a variant of the Lancashire type), each 20ft long and 6ft in diameter, with a pressure of 120lbs per square inch, and with a dual installation of feed pump and injectors. All steam piping was of cast iron and in duplicate. The boilers supplied two 90hp Galloway vertical compound engines of marine design, with 10-inch high pressure and 20-inch low pressure cylinders, 18-inch stroke, running at 150 rpm. From the 9ft diameter engine flywheels, link leather belts drove two Mather & Platt "Manches-

The embankment at Port e Vada seen early in 1893 — the contractor's railway and wagons in centre foreground. (Collection A Tranter)

ter"-type dynamos at 700rpm, giving an output of 100 amps at 500 volts. Each dynamo had a Kelvin electrostatic voltmeter and amperemeter, and wiring was such that either the switchboard or the actual overhead line could be connected. A subsidiary switchboard was interposed between the rails and the earth plates to measure the "earth currents". The switchgear was also by Mather & Platt, and was of an archaic type with lead fuses instead of circuit breakers; this was destined to be replaced in 1898 by a new installation. For the two miles between Douglas and Groudle, the overhead itself was sufficient to distribute the traction current.

Track consisted of 56lbs per yard rails, spiked by 4½-inch dog spikes to uncreosoted Scots fir and larch sleepers measuring only 6 ft long by 7ins and 3½ins thick, with earth ballast. Fang bolts were inserted at the joints and at the middle of each rail, but these were later replaced by hardwood chairs screwed down to the sleepers; on the curves these were on the outside of the rails. The tapered poles had ornamental collars (long since removed) and were 20ft high from ground level, the depth below the ground being 5ft. Normal poles were 6ins in diameter at ground level and 3ins at the finial, but a heavier type was used where necessary, 7ins at ground level and 4ins at the finial.

On July 4 1893, the new hotel at Groudle re-

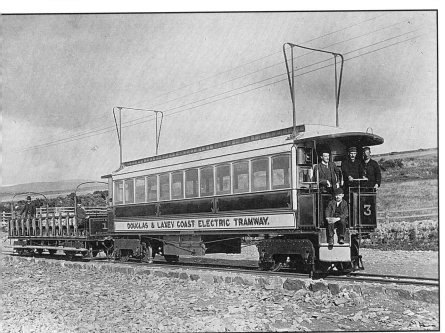

No 3 on trials at Braeside, August 1893. Saunderson occupies the front seat of the trailer, whilst Joshua Shaw stands on the front platform, elbow on handwheel. For a discussion of visible control gear elements see Chapter 9. (M&P)

---

* Dr Farrell (1840-1925) was an Irishman who came to Douglas about 1881 and opened a successful private school, Victoria College. He became a horse tramway director in 1890 and was a prolific public speaker — once involved with the fortunes of the electric line, he became one of its most prominent propagandists.

Left: By September of 1893, the line was in business — here No 3 stands at the terminus, with the sinuous (pre-1893) sea wall as background. (Manx National Heritage)

Below: No 3 in the depot, 1894. It now sports the first of three sprung variants of the Hopkinson bow collector. Note the controller drum, with adjacent hand aperture in the side screen. (M&P)

ceived its licence, and was opened the following day, although the metalling of the new roadway was incomplete. Groudle Glen and the Lhen Coan, with Broadbent's addition of rustic paths and bridges, became the kind of primeval public park in which the contemporary visitor delighted. The August 5 advertisement of the Groudle's opening hopefully stated "approached by and at the terminus of the New Electric Tramway", though the trams were not yet running. On August 8 the Press reported that the cars had now arrived and that the two and a half miles of track were in every way complete, but by August 15 current collection troubles were still holding back the opening.

The difficulty lay in the method of current collection. The wiring was direct suspended at the cross arms, and drooped between them. At each end of the car was one of Dr John Hopkinson's fixed collector bows, intended to leave the wire at each supporting pole while that at the opposite end of the car was in contact with the sagging conductor wire. Difficulties continued until as late as Saturday, August 26; how engineers' efforts were viewed by the hundreds of visitors now promenading the new road is not recorded. On that date, a car got through to Groudle with Dr Edward Hopkinson, Frederick Saunderson and others aboard, and more test cars were run on the following Monday, apparently carrying members of the public*.

Regular public service commenced on Thursday

Left: Although the erection of the Derby Castle theatre (seen in the background, extreme right), dates this picture as of 1895, the castellated wall running along from the entrance gates had been erected early in the previous year and now more or less paralleled the tramway tracks. This, therefore, is the layout as from spring 1894 with the horse tramway meeting the "Douglas and Laxey" virtually end-on (see earlier plan). (Manx National Heritage)

No 2 at the new Laxey terminus of 1894 — today's depot site to the left. Beyond the tower wagons lay the Rencell Road, then in a cutting. This car now carries the second of Dr Edward's modifications of the Hopkinson bow collector, as did all the new (1894) cars. (M&P)

September 7, and lasted for 19 days. Since Sunday running was unlikely, this saw closure as of Thursday September 28, and a reference to the line having closed for the winter appeared in the Press on September 30, with editorial regrets that no service was to be provided even on Tuesday half-days. More than 20,000 passengers had been carried, at the 3d minimum fare, with 1,689 car (train)-miles and earnings of 35.36d per car mile.

Among Mather & Platt's men on site during the trials was a young man of great promise, Joshua Shaw. He was appointed to IOMT & EP staff in 1894, when only 22, became manager in 1899, and stayed in the island until early 1902, when he became resident electrical engineer to the Mersey Railway and its general manager and engineer in 1908. Although he retired in 1938, he continued on the Mersey Railway board until nationalisation in 1948. He died, in his ninetieth year, early in 1962.

Construction was resumed in February 1894. First, the line to Groudle was doubled, using the single track as a construction line and adding a further track on the side remote from the road, while contractor Mark Carine built the impressive Groudle viaduct of three 20ft spans and a culvert over the Lhen Coan. A large rustic station, 47ft 6ins by 12ft,

was added at Groudle a year or two later. By April, it was expected that the double line as far as Groudle would be completed a week before Whitsun. From Groudle to Baldromma-Beg, the contract specification required a single line on a 19ft formation adjoining a 21ft roadway to be completed by May 1, 1894. This was a construction line, to be used by Douglas Bay Estate from May 12 in carrying the line northward.

On completion, the Howstrake tramway and its plant were to become the property of the Douglas & Laxey Coast Electric Tramway Company, and the tramway was transferred by a £38,000 agreement between the two parties, dated March 30, 1894. The land remained with the estate company and was regarded as an easement, recorded in a deed of July 9, 1895. Beyond Baldromma-Beg, Douglas Bay Estate Ltd was to hand over the lands acquired, the completed tramway thereon, all the plant, and a station at Laxey on which not less then £1,000 was to have been spent; this transfer was made by a deed of June 1896. The Howstrake company was also to lay out the 50-acre Howstrake Park and hand it over to the tramway, but this was bought back by the Douglas Bay Estate & Groudle Glen Ltd in June 1896. It became the site of the Howstrake Holiday Camp.

* Dr Edward's diaries reveal him as "much travelled" at this time: he was on the Island many times between January 30 and August 30 — five times in August alone. On August 26 he recorded: "Started running a single car."

In 1894 the pattern was similar — on September 25 he apparently had supper at Ramsey with Bruce. Snaefell too brought him to the Island a total of nine times in 1895. (Acknowledgements to Brian and Ron Hopkinson.)

The Groudle line reopened on Whit Saturday, May 12, 1894, after successful trials on the Thursday, and by July was carrying 78,000 passengers a week. Three cars were used (assumedly those of 1893). These were by now variously fitted with two successive patented variations by Dr Edward of Dr John's bow collector, in which the contact bar was now pivoted under spring tension. The view of No 3 on page 16 shows the first variant. The end-on photograph of No 2 at Laxey shows the second, which was fitted to the 1894 cars at the outset. By the following year, a third and final variant appeared on the Snaefell cars and the coast line's 10-13, and with a little further variation continues in use on today's Snaefell line.

at the Board of Trade, implied satisfaction, though at facing points at the termini he sought to have pointsmen equipped with flags and (at night) lamps. He also wanted protective guards at either side of the road crossings, together with notices warning against the danger of touching the overhead wires. Bruce and Saunderson undertook to fulfil all these requirements.

Major Cardew reported at much greater length. He acknowledged Dr Hopkinson's (and Mather & Platt's) foremost position in this field and dwelt on the arduous duty placed on the electrical equipment. The battery house at Groudle was fully described, as were the storage cells themselves — unfortunately his description of the cars' control gear was more ambiguous — and he thought highly of the modified Hopkinson bows. His chief qualms were at the use of 500 volts supply, although he knew of its common use in the USA. The line was divided electrically into six parts and Board of Trade regulations for the return circuit had been complied with. In all he was well satisfied, provided adequate record of the earth return circuit's performance were kept and the safety measures sought by Rich executed.

With success achieved in the government inspections, the formal opening took place on the afternoon of Saturday, the 28th, a special car of the new (1894) type carrying the directorate through to Laxey.

The following Saturday's Isle of Man Times gave the event a full page, Bruce and Saunderson being specially praised, together with Dr Hopkinson and his assistants, Ramage and Wood, also Joshua Shaw (overhead specialist) and Barnard of cable-makers Callender's. The official party's arrival at Laxey station (a 65ft 6ins by 15ft building opposite the present Laxey Car Shed) was a memorable occasion, with the combined Laxey and Laxey Temperance bands

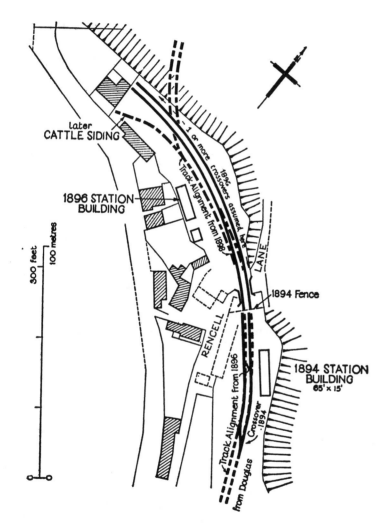

Laxey Station and trackwork south of Glen Roy, 1894-87. (DGC)

Construction continued apace beyond Baldromma-Beg, still by the Douglas Bay Estate Company, and the governor for the first time sought the assistance of the mainland Board of Trade in appointing an inspector. In practice, two inspectors were necessary, one for the civil engineering aspects and one for the electrical side, and so Colonel Rich and Major Cardew visited the new line on July 27 and reported the next day.

Colonel Rich, latterly senior inspector of railways

playing *See the conquering hero comes,* and a triumphal arch bearing the words "E.T.C. Welcome to Laxey Glen", on one side and "Shee dy veagys, glion Laxey" (Peace and plenty to Laxey Glen) on the other.

Bruce, speaking from a lineside platform, was received with cheers, and made witty references to the line's absent contractor, Brebner, the local Members of the House of Keys, landowners, Dr Hopkinson, Saunderson and others, hearty laughter greeting his sallies. He had previously been read a welcoming address by the Rev J M Spicer of Christ Church, the proceedings being conducted by Thomas Corlett, MHK. Other speakers were Dr Hopkinson, C B Nelson, and Saunderson, and then Dr Farrell, who gave his customary classical oration.

The technical press, in both Britain and the United States, carried considerable references to the new line, the Electrical Review stating that no electric traction scheme carried out in Great Britain had involved heavier engineering works. The additional generating equipment requires further reference, for the extension to Laxey saw considerable enlargement of the generating facilities and the creation of a proper feeder system. In these early years, the line was a veritable proving ground for the British electrical industry.

At Douglas, a third boiler, engine and generator and new switchgear augmented those of 1893. The extra generator, of the newly evolved Hopkinson type, differed materially from its predecessors. The field coils were now positioned above the armature instead of on either side, forming a magnetic circuit in the form of an inverted 'U'. The relative losses (in magnetic terms) proved to be about 24 per cent against 33 per cent for the less efficient Manchester type, in spite of leakage through the base. A further shed for eight cars was also added, being 166ft long, 22ft 6ins wide and 18ft high, and the staffing of the power station and sheds was increased to a smith, two station foremen, a fitter, two carpenters, three general hands, an engine driver and fireman, and several switchgear men. There were also eight apprentices, drawn from families prominent in Douglas life.

At Laxey, a further power plant was erected, on a site some little distance below the line, on the south bank of the combined Laxey and Glen Roy rivers and close to the steep south side of the valley. The boiler house and engine room were built of local stone, with a corrugated-iron roof, and an iron chimney 60ft high and 5ft in diameter. The two engines and dynamos were also of the same type as the 1894 set at Port e Vada, the switchgear likewise. Water for the boilers came from a concrete tank. The boiler room measured 65ft by 27ft and was 19ft high, while the engine room was 58ft 3ins by 24ft and 24ft 6ins high, again built so as to allow room for expansion. A short feeder

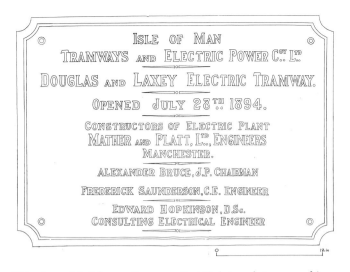

"Black marble" (actually enamelled Belgian slate as used in contemporary clocks) plaque installed on the north wall of the Derby Castle engine house. The maker was one J Hilton of Manchester. It was moved to the west wall in 1898 when an elevated switchboard was built. (SB/FKP)

led to a point about one third of the way up the gradient from the Laxey terminus, and a single feeder ran southwards to Fairy Cottage and possibly beyond; elsewhere, the double overhead evidently sufficed for the rest of the northern section. From Douglas, an underground feeder with intermediate section boxes led to Half-Way House, using a lead-covered steeltape-armoured 37/14 cable by Callender's, which was still in peak load use in 1969. In all, there were six electrical sections between Douglas and Laxey.

The wooden Groudle battery house represented an early attempt to deal with the fact that, while the average load to keep two cars in service was negligible, a coincidence of two uphill starts would overload any one of the three Douglas generators. To quote the *Electrical Review* of 24 August 1894:

> … there are 240 cells of the Patent Chloride type made by the Chloride Electrical Storage Syndicate… 120 unprotected cells and 120 protected cells with teak and asbestos separators… capable of being discharged at the rate of 500V at 140A for three hours, at 90A for six hours, at 70A for nine hours… The working of these accumulators will be watched with the closest interest, both by reason of the comparative newness of the chloride cells, and the fact that fixed accumulators have been rarely used to supply power for traction purposes…

The Groudle storage battery was charged once or twice a week, and for the remaining days cars drew on the stored current; the capacity was ample for any possible demand. A 12kW booster by Mather & Platt was installed for charging, converting 450V 35 amps to 150V 90 amps, and this could be used at other times to raise the line voltage, functioning as a series generator. By 1899, the original cells had been replaced by Chloride 'R' type, with a 50 per cent higher discharge rate. This storage system was copied in several early mainland installations, to cope with fluctuating day loads, but later became obsolescent. On the Manx Electric it survived until 1944, and was thus, with the Mersey Railway, one of the last surviving examples in the British Isles.

Although the six new electric cars bore the title Douglas and Laxey Electric Tramway, a further change of owning company had already taken place in the months between the end of 1893's

19

experimental service and the resumption of traffic in May, 1894. The Douglas & Laxey Coast Electric Tramway Company Limited had made a successful bid of £38,000 for the Douglas horse tramway, and on April 30, 1894, changed its name to Isle of Man Tramways & Electric Power Company Ltd, with a capital stepped up from £50,000 to £150,000. The prospectus appeared early in April, and invited subscriptions to a total of £125,000, with £50,000 in debentures. The lists were to close on April 14, and within a week it was reported that the capital had been "more than realised". The actual total realised was £140,000, plus £50,000 in Series A debentures. The memorandum and articles were those of the D & LCET company, and the office was at 7 Athol Street, Douglas.

The directors of the new company were Alexander Bruce, A J Lusty (by now a director of the Madras Electric Tramway Co Ltd), F G Callow, Dr Edward Hopkinson, J A Mylrea, JP (of the Isle of Man Steam Packet Company), W P J Pittar, and Dr R Farrell. W E Young was secretary, Saunderson was engineer, and standing counsel was the Attorney-General. The horse tramway was handed over on May 1, 1894, and the two lines thereafter ran as a combined undertaking, with J Aldworth as manager.

The words "Electric Power" in the title revealed that the company intended to furnish a public supply. The brand new Douglas Bay hotel became its first customer in 1894, with some 250 lamps. The new company installed at Derby Castle a 1,000V Mather & Platt 30 amp alternator, on hire, powered by a 500V motor. In 1896 a Bellis/Mather & Platt 75hp direct-coupled steam-driven set (No 458) giving 50 amps output was added, both machines feeding a combined switchboard which permitted them to work independently or in parallel. By 1900 the public supply side of the undertaking comprised six high-tension and four low-tension mains, with seven transformers totalling 71kW. Besides the Douglas Bay hotel, the consumers included the Derby Castle Opera House, private houses and a number of Brockie Pell 15 amp arc-lamps which lit parts of Onchan village and much more of Douglas end of the tramway. In 1900 this interesting example of an early public AC supply totalled some 3,190 lamps of an average eight-candlepower, the company charging 6d (2.5p) per Board of Trade unit. Some pavement mains inspection covers, bearing the inscription IOMT & EP, still survive in Onchan today (1970).

The price paid for the horse tramway no doubt reflected the provisions of its Act of 1876, which provided for compulsory purchase by the local authority in 1897. The horse tramway's essential function as the feeder to the Douglas and Laxey line is self-evident. From the end of 1893, Bruce had two aims — to at once secure ownership of the horse tramway (in the face of emerging rival bids) and then to eliminate the risk of compulsory purchase in 1897. The position was to be made more complex by the 1896 change by which the Douglas Town Commissioners became the Corporation of Douglas. In his first overtures in December 1893, Bruce asked that the D & LC be allowed to double and electrify the horse tramway in return for an annual payment to the town. He additionally sought permission to build tramways "to other parts of the town" and wanted assurance as to the renewal of the "lease" of the bay line for another 21 years. Intensive discussion with the town commissioners ensued — Bruce's "payment" was to be a generous one, and the proposed new tramways (as will be seen later) were much desired. However, a rival bidder came on the scene in February 1894 with a promise of penny fares and (temporarily) ownership of a concession to construct a promenade cable tramway using Dick Kerr's relatively successful patents. The chief candidate for a totally new tramway was the by now impoverished area of Upper Douglas, the first part of the town to be developed but now left far behind in the visitor popularity stakes by the rapidly evolving development of the promenades. This complex scenario was to occupy Bruce and his new Isle of Man Tramways and Electric Power Company for some three more years.

By July 1894 the previously mentioned rival purchaser had been out of the running for six months, and Bruce was able to come to the Commissioners with quite concrete proposals for an Upper Douglas line. There had been, meanwhile, a Town Surveyor's investigation into the installation of either an electric tramway using conduit collection, or cable line. But now the whole Upper Douglas question was to be pigeon-holed yet again. The hapless residents of Upper Douglas were still in a transport limbo in December.

However, Bruce seems to have had some encouragement in respect of the bay tramway, whose purchase was successfully concluded in May. By 1899, he was to see its annual passenger figure climb to nearly 1.75 million (1,725,155).

From 1894 its earnings were of course incorporated in the I O M T & E P accounts. A summary of these operational results appears at the beginning of Chapter 3.

Still determined, on March 27, 1895, Bruce made a new offer. IOMT & EP would build and operate an Upper Douglas (cable) tramway and provide electric lighting for the promenades and Victoria Street, in return for authority to double the remainder of the horse line and electrify it, a 21-year lease of the line from 1897, and the right to sell electric power within the town. Also sought was a tramway extension to the IMR railway station. Ten per cent of bay tramway receipts were to be payable to the Town (at about the same time, the town of Douglas was proposing to build a tramway and lease it to an operator). Well over 50 per cent of

The "spit and polish" of the Derby Castle engines and dynamos is splendidly shown by this Warburton photograph taken sometime after the 1894 opening to Laxey. The differences between the 1893 and 1894 dynamos are most apparent. The Snaefell machines of 1895 were almost identical to that of 1894 (right) but were larger (60 rather than 50kw). Items like handrails were emery polished lengthwise then (in bands) across so the fine markings formed a continuous pattern. (Manx National Heritage)

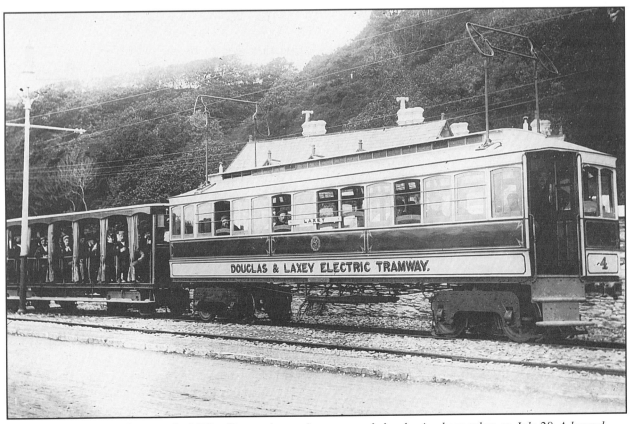

This view of No 4 long hung in the MER office, and was always regarded as having been taken on July 28. A legend persists that No 4 never did make the journey for which it appears ready to depart, due to a technical failure. (MER)

Right: Immediately behind the chimney is the boiler house with the taller engine house to the rear. This view in the Derby Castle yard is in late summer 1894. The relatively utilitarian buildings give little hint of the mechanical excellence of their contents. (M&P)

A short working at Groudle, summer 1894. (M&P)

Upper Douglas residents were by now in favour of such a line, and with this background of public support, Bruce met the town commissioners on May 30 and enlarged upon his March proposals, for the moment deleting any reference to the bay tramway's electrification. The new offer was to build and operate the Upper Douglas line, meanwhile providing a horse bus service, to pay the Commissioners 15 per cent of bay tramway receipts and to remove some bay tramway depot accommodation which at this date spanned the promenade at the bottom of Burnt Mill Hill (Summer Hill). From this came the present Derby Castle horse car sheds. In return, he sought the 1897 lease renewal and the previously-mentioned track doubling.

There was an uncomfortable wait until, at the end of June, the Commissioners came to accept the offer of May 30. With almost incredible speed an Upper Douglas Tramway Act came to be passed on November 8. The IOMT & EP horse buses had commenced service from July 20 (the commissioners in some way saw this as a reciprocal "deal" related to the horse tramway track-doubling). The creation of the cable tramway was not without its problems, requiring an amending Act mid-way through construction (May 13, 1896) but the line still managed to open for traffic on August 15 that year. Negotiations for the bay tramway electrification were to be resumed for the last time early in 1897; Douglas town council had written on February 17 asking for terms on which the company would light the promenade from July 1, and the IOMT & EP replied on March 6 with a composite offer to light, free of charge, all the promenades and much of the Upper Douglas route — in return for permission to sell current in Douglas to private consumers, to electrify the bay line using overhead wires, and to extend it to the IMR station. Bruce also offered to take a six-man corporation party to Bristol, Rouen and Hamburg, and stated that the tramway conversion would cost the company £20,000.

Subsequent events are described in a 250-page report produced by T H Nesbitt, town clerk, on December 1, 1897. By March 19, 1897, a special committee had been set up, and on March 23 the company agreed to pay for six of the corporation party of ten (eight committee men, surveyor Taylor and town clerk Nesbitt) on the proposed mainland and continental tour. The council accepted this on March 30, and planned a tour of London, Paris, Frankfurt, Dresden, Berlin, Hamburg, Cologne, Brussels and Rouen, returning by way of Brighton, Bristol, Dover, Prescot and Liverpool.

Departure was by the SS Snaefell on Thursday, April 1, and from London by the South Eastern & Chatham Railway next day. Visits to Paris, Versailles, Frankfurt, Leipzig, Dresden, Berlin, Hamburg, Cologne, Brussels and back to London were achieved by Monday, April 12, a sequence involving much overnight travel and such odd nocturnal spectacles as Aldworth, Nesbitt and Taylor staring at gas lamps in the Champs Elysées in Paris during an evening downpour. Rouen, Brighton and Dover had to be left unvisited, but the sights seen included a Simplex conduit line at Prescot and practically every variety of traction in Paris; the list is interminable. Three thousand miles had been covered, and all participants had severe colds. In London, they had an interview with a leading authority, Professor Kennedy, and his later written replies to questions drafted on April 12 were wholly in favour of electric traction on the overhead system. The committee endorsed this choice with enthusiasm; conduit tramways had a strong hold on their affections, but their expense was feared.

In answer to council requests during July and August 1897, Aldworth sent details of proposed overhead construction, and mentioned the intended use of single-deck motors about 25ft long and 6ft 6ins wide, hauling trailers chosen initially from the best of the horse cars. A cross-section of a car passing another at a centre refuge, and more detailed data, followed. On August 31 the committee voted 6:1 in favour of recommendations which would permit electrification of the bay line.

On Thursday, September 7, the council was faced with a protesting "memorial" signed by 32 house occupiers on Loch Promenade, and adjournment to October 7 was followed by two more memorials, one consisting of 71 signatures from car proprietors. A further adjournment followed until after the November elections, and when the new council met on November 22 it was read a letter from company secretary Young announcing that the offer of March 6 was withdrawn. Once more, prejudice had triumphed over reason.

Milnes' 1893 enamel builder's plate, (3.75ins overall). (JCC)

Right: This view of a Snaefell car at the original depot terminus shows the substantial station building and the sector table used instead of points. The car is in "intermediate condition" — that is, has so far only acquired sliding windows. (1896) (Author's collection)

Below: The 1895 summit station was the starting point of a wooden catwalk leading to the hotel illustrated on page 31. This somewhat elementary structure remained little altered until the demise of the separate hotel and the erection of a new combined facility in 1906. (Manx National Heritage)

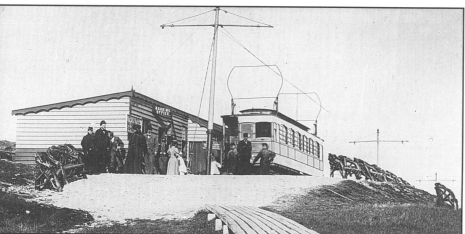

Opposite: Brand new Snaefell trackage at Lhergy Veg, 1895. The wall was substantially buttressed in 1906. (M&P)

Below: The newly completed second station of 1897. Dumbell's Row is immediately behind the car, with the mines spoil heap to the right. The access ramp to the Vicarage (right) must have been one of the shortest lived constructions ever. The car now boasts its newly installed clerestory with infinitely varying window sizes. (Manx National Heritage)

Chapter 2

The Snaefell Mountain Railway

The mountain ... commands a prospect from its summit which for extent and beauty it would be difficult to match in the United Kingdom...
The Barrow Route to the Isle of Man, 1883

WITH THEIR VISITOR TOTALS AND prospects completely transformed by the new electric tramway, the people of Laxey village honoured its promoters by inviting a director to open the church bazaar, late in 1894. Dr Farrell came, and in his speech revealed a new ambition, declaring: "My friends, I will let you into a secret. We are going to put an electric tramway to the top of Snaefell."

The Snaefell mountain, 2,034 feet high, stands at the heart of the mountainous northern half of the Isle of Man and is the Island's highest point. On a clear day, the visitor can look out from the summit and see not only the entire Island, but also across the Irish Sea to four kingdoms, to pick out the mountains of the English Lake District, the Mull of Galloway in Scotland, the hills of Anglesey and North Wales, and the Mountains of Mourne to the west, in Ireland. This was to be the objective of the first mountain railway in the British Isles.

A survey for a steam-worked mountain railway had been made in 1887-8 by G N Fell, as part of the Douglas, Laxey & Snaefell Railway, described in Appendix 1. George Noble Fell (1849-1924) was the son of John Barraclough Fell (1815-1902), originator of the Fell centre-rail system for mountain railways, which had been adopted on the Mont Cenis railway, and in Brazil and New Zealand.*

The family had Manx connections, and with his father's retirement from practice, George Noble Fell became active on his own account in pressing the merits of the Fell system for mountain lines. He was also a light railway engineer, and from 1896 was an associate member of the Institute of Civil Engineers.

In 1893-4 a Snaefell Railway Company still existed, with offices at Athol Street, Douglas. Fell's Douglas Laxey survey was used in part by Saunderson in 1893-4, as parts of his route appear on Saunderson's initial survey plans. By 1894, Fell must have been in direct contact with Bruce, who

---

* These lines are described by L T C Rolt in *A Hunslet Hundred* (David & Charles, 1964).

was at once attracted by the possibilities of a line up Snaefell, using the Fell system with electric propulsion. Fell's ready-made survey of 1888 was evidently employed, and the whole line came into being in the incredibly short time of about seven months. The line was solidly built and soundly engineered, and is still in full use today.

The line avoided the usual legislative delays — by being built on lands purchased or leased by voluntary agreements, without any need for the authority of Tynwald or any other statutory power, as no property had to be taken compulsorily. The land occupied by the lower end of the line at its depot was mainly purchased by Bruce, between January 26 and March 2, 1895, and that higher up the mountain was bought by the Snaefell Mountain Railway Association from the Trustees of the Commons. This purchase, sanctioned by Tynwald on July 9, 1895, comprised the trackbed, the sites of the summit station and hotel, the power station, Sulby pumping station, and the rights of way thereto, and a 50-year lease was taken on the remaining land within 440 yards of the summit. The trustees were to receive one penny per passenger (minimum £260 per year) and certain levies arising from profits on the hotels.

The Snaefell Mountain Railway Association was a private grouping of Bruce and his colleagues, formed on January 4, 1895. The only signatories of its constitutional documents were Alexander Bruce, J D Rogers, C B Nelson, William Todhunter, Francis Reddicliffe and J R Cowell, the other 14 remaining anonymous. Cowell and Bruce were now chairman and vice-chairman respectively of the Board of Advertising, a new tourist publicity body. No public

Looking downhill at the mountain power station, 1895. (M & P)

record is known to exist of the Snaefell Association's proceedings.

Meanwhile, on Wednesday, February 20, 1895, the first annual general meeting of the Isle of Man Tramways & Electric Power Co was held at the Strathallan Crescent offices, with Bruce presiding. Net profits were stated as £10,507 8s 10d, and the October dividend of six per cent on preference, and $7^{1}/_{2}$ per cent on ordinary, shares was repeated for the second half-year. Four new cars (Nos 10-13) were on order from G F Milnes & Co for the coastal line, the electrical equipment to be installed by IOMT & EP at Derby Castle.

Three weeks previously, the line had been snowed up, but had reopened on February 2 and carried the mails free of charge for both Laxey and Ramsey. The Howstrake Park was to open in 1895, and part of the estate was being laid out by Douglas Bay Estate as an 18-hole golf course; through return tickets for golfers were to be issued for 6d from the Jubilee Clock. The directors' report referred to

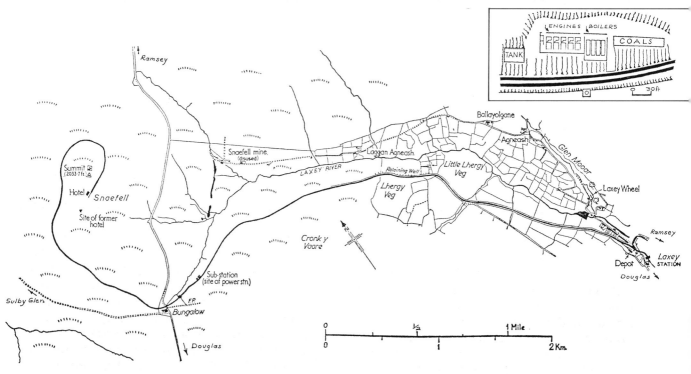

The Snaefell line with plan of the power station inset. A trailing siding now exists on the downhill track opposite the site of the Bungalow hotel. For a gradient profile, see Appendix 4. (JCC)

plans for improved station facilities at Derby Castle and Laxey.

Dr Farrell, allotted two minutes, nonetheless made a lengthy speech with some Manx anecdotes. His book, *Beyond the Silver Streak in Manxland — The Great Electric Railway*, was about to be published by John Heywood of Manchester, and is commended as a surely unique piece of tramway promotional literature. He recited a "remarkably high encomium" (expression of praise) allegedly exchanged by two rural Manxmen boarding a car at Ballabeg one wet winter's night:

'By gosh, Quilliam, it looks lek stepping into a fust class pub,' said one.

'My word,' replied his companion, 'bud the derachthors are plucky buoys.'

'Garn Man; they say that every sowl on the board is from a different nation.'

'Lor' a massey, is that thrue?'

'Thrue as Gospel.'

'Well, that beats Owld Nick; there's not the lek of it in the unyvarse.' (Loud laughter).

The choice of the 3ft 6ins gauge for Snaefell seems to have been directly influenced by Fell's Mont Cenis experience, since the three New Zealand lines and that up Snaefell were built to virtually the same gauge as the Alpine railway. A double-headed bull-head brake rail was used to provide the working surfaces for a powerful calliper brake, while the flanges of horizontal guide wheels fit below the heads of the rails. On the steam Fell lines, the horizontal wheels were driven by separate cylinders and could be forced against the rail by spring pressure to obtain adhesion far greater than in proportion to the locomotive's weight. A further refinement, patented by engineer Hanscotte of the Fives-Lille locomotive works, was to apply pressure to the horizontal wheels using compressed air, the pressure varying with the gradient, and this variant was used for the only true mountain railway built as a steam-operated Fell line, the Chemin de Fer du Puy de Dome at Clermont-Ferrand (1907-26). The elder Fell had advocated the use of the system in the Channel Tunnel, and G N Fell later adapted these plans for electric traction; in 1913, when working on a scheme for a line from Lons—le—Saunier to Geneva, he sought permission to carry out some trials on the Snaefell line. At the time of his death in 1924 he was still actively working on a scheme for a Franco-Italian link over the Monginevro pass.

At Snaefell, the inherent limitations of DC supply meant that a new generating station had to be built near the mid-point of the line, and a stone-built power house was erected high up the river valley in on a dramatic mountainside perch, 2.8 miles from Laxey. All the equipment had to be taken out by the mountain road, which was crossed on the level, and then lowered down the mountainside by ropes and

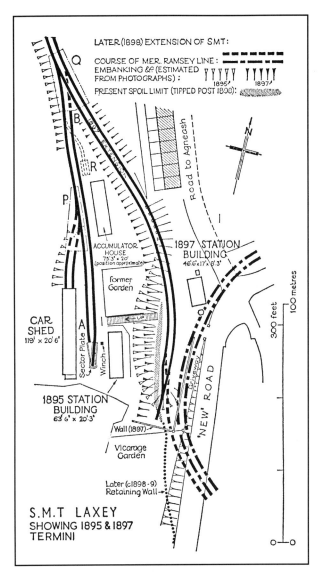

Snaefell line stations at Laxey. The depot pointwork (at P) is that existing today. The original arrangement, to about 1931, seems to have used a further sector plate, whose operating winch survived until recently. Track at A and the sector plate beyond this point were removed at some date after 1896, track from B to sector plate and track shown dotted in outline Q removed in 1897. R indicates the Civil Aviation Authority railcar shed and access track — see page 85. (DGC)

tackle; this took 14 days, during which Mr Willis also erected the ten miles of single overhead line in a mere eight days. Coal for the power station had to be brought up by the tramway from Laxey, and water was pumped up through a two-inch pipe from a pumping station on Sulby river, equipped with a Galloway's boiler and 4hp Tangye engine and pump.

The Snaefell power station was the most powerful generating plant yet built on the Island. The boiler room, 36ft by 43ft and 16ft 3ins high, housed four Galloway 120lbs per square inch boilers, each 26ft long and 6ft in diameter, with feed pumps and injectors. The 60ft iron chimney of 5ft diameter was on the other side of the line, and the flues passed beneath the track. The boilers supplied steam to five

120hp Mather & Platt horizontal compound engines, each with a 7ft flywheel and a speed of 150 rpm; the cylinders were of 16-inch stroke, cylinder diameters being 12ins for the high-pressure one and 20ins for the the low-pressure. Each engine was coupled to a 60kW Hopkinson dynamo, the whole installation being housed in an engine room measuring 72ft by 30ft, and 12ft 3ins high. The switchgear was mounted on a frame of polished ash.

From the power house, an underground feeder of the type supplied by Callenders in 1894 for coastal line, ran downhill again and supplied the overhead line at intervals of one mile. At Laxey depot, it entered a wooden battery house with 250 chloride cells and a capacity of 560 ampère-hours; this building measured 75ft 3ins by 20ft and was 8ft 3ins high. The plant was over-generous, and later much of the power produced from coal and laboriously transported up 1,130 ft of mountain, was returned to feed the coast tramway, through a further feeder connecting the battery house to Laxey power station.

The contractor for the Snaefell track was Mr Herd of Douglas, and a later description of it is taken from the inspector's report. Fell and Hopkinson personally supervised their respective branches of the work. By an agreement of April 23, 1895 the Manx Northern locomotive Caledonia was hired for £20 per week, and was shipped from Ramsey to Laxey in the Porpoise and used with aid of a temporary third rail to reduce the gauge to the necessary 3ft. MNR timber trucks Nos 20 and 21 were also hired, at 3s each per day, and the agreement specified that the engine was to be properly housed at night and that the Snaefell Association had to pay the driver 6s 6d and the fireman 4s 2d for a ten-hour day. In mid-August, Caledonia took up a trainload of dignitaries of the LNWR and L & Y. Orders had been placed for six electric passenger cars, and to house these, a six-car brick shed with a curved iron roof and pits for all six cars, was built at the lower terminus. This was 119ft long, 20ft 6ins wide and 18ft high.

This depot, which is still in use, was adjoined by the original and short-lived station, a 63ft 6ins by

20ft 3ins building approached from the public road by a long flight of steps which intending passengers had to climb. In place of normal points, the line used sector tables, that at the Laxey terminal stub being worked by a two-way winch which appears in opening-day photographs. In 1897, the sector table at the summit was removed, its pit filled in, and a special type of point installed in which a pivoted section of rail was swung across from one side to the other where the two tracks came together. The summit was provided with a wooden station building, 50ft by 13ft 6ins, and a single-storey wooden hotel. The hotel was some 180 yards from the station building, from which it was approached by a wooden catwalk. As first photographed (in 1895) it is seen to comprise a T-shape in plan, but by the following year it had been doubled to become an 'H', 65ft by 70ft, with a further addition to the west added by 1900.

By August 16, 1895, the work was sufficiently complete for formal inspection, again by Colonel J H Rich and Major P Cardew, who reported next day. It was not the legal requirement, but the government regarded the Snaefell line for this purpose as an extension of the coastal tramway. A former Mather & Platt engineer recalled that, at 6am on the day of Major Cardew's inspection, a linesman shorted the switch panel across the already charged traction battery, converting the switchboard into a major electrical bonfire. In four hours, the charred wood was cleaned off, painted with Brunswick black, and the refurbished switchgear mounted with the paint still wet, the inspector himself saying, "I haven't seen a better job!"

Colonel Rich described the line as four miles, 53 chains in length, with a 21ft formation, two thirds cut into hard ground or rock and one third built on soft material "thrown out". The spacing between the tracks (as on other IOMT & EP lines) was 7ft. The "50lbs" (actually 56lbs) rails were fang-bolted to 9ins x 4½ins creosoted sleepers 7ft long, and were in 24ft lengths. The Fell rail weighed 65lbs per yard. The line climbed 1,820ft, for 85 per cent of the distance at a gradient of 1:12. As shown in the profile diagram, level stretches existed at the termini and the Bungalow. Most curves were of ten-chain radius but near the summit there were some of seven and five.

Apart from a wish to see more drainage and a watch kept on the formation for settlement, plus provision of lamps at the stations and the fencing of "turntable pits", Rich was satisfied. He, incidentally, explained the adoption of right-hand running as intended to keep the ascending cars on the soft part of the formation.

Cardew saw the electrical equipment as basically

Left: Mather and Platt view of a Snaefell bogie as delivered. The (loose) cover may have been placed over the commutator and brush gear. (M&P)

similar to that of 1893-4, used on the coastal line but, of course, the cars were higher powered. The four-motor tractive effort of 3,500lbs, set against the 1 in 12 opposing forces of 2,850lbs, meant that a single motor failure would incapacitate a car. At this time, proposals for regenerative braking (in which the car motors were used as dynamos, returning current to the system) involved running downhill at 12 mph, if the cars were unaltered electrically and he wanted extensive proving trials before approval would be given. He was alarmed at the proposed 550-volt supply and suggested 520 as the station maximum, considering the power station to be "uneconomically" sited.

The voltage was evidently adjusted, for the Governor gave permission for the line to open, and a special car carrying government worthies followed on Tuesday August 20. Opening the following day, the line carried an average of 900 passengers a day for the remainder of the season, at a return fare of 2s. A Mr Carter was appointed engineer by the parent Snaefell Association.

It is convenient here to deal with the six cars of the Snaefell line, which have remained in sole charge for almost 100 years and are still largely in their original form. As built, the bodywork and bogies were by G F Milnes, the electrical equipment by Mather & Platt, to the designs of Dr Edward Hopkinson, including his third sprung adaption of

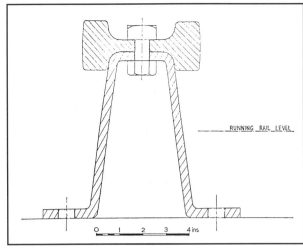

The Fell rail: a section. (SB)

his brother's rigid bow collector. The form of Snaefell Nos 1-6 was basically derived from the 1894 cars on the coastal line, but they were less expensively finished, the interior being entirely of pitch pine, including the elaborately panelled bulkhead. Their dimensions were: length over couplers 35ft 7$\frac{1}{2}$ins, height over roof 10ft 4$\frac{1}{2}$ins, and width overall 7ft 3ins. They were ash-framed and teak-panelled, with double transverse seats for 40 and bulkhead seats for six, later increased to 48 all told, by adding a single corner seat at each end. As built, they had shallow arched roofs and were glazed only in the

Snaefell Opening Day, August 21, 1895. Dr Edward Hopkinson is seated on the terminus sector plate winch, George Noble Fell stands against the car, with foot on rail, and Bruce is immediately behind Dr Hopkinson. (MER)

No 2 approaching the summit, 1895. The garter surrounding the car's number carries no inscription, but a brass plate on the underframe has the same wording as on 1893-4 cars, eg "Mather & Platt Limited, Engineers, Manchesster". (R Hargreaves)

vestibules, the six main side windows being unglazed and fitted with adjustable striped roller blinds. By April 1896, they had been fitted with sliding windows in place of canvas blinds, in the winter of 1896-7 they gained their present roof clerestories, and in 1900 were graced with enormous advertisement boards. For notes on the cars' livery see Chapter 9.

The two-motor bogies were of a special long wheelbase type (6ft 10ins) to incorporate the Fell brake equipment and their two Mather & Platt 5A 25hp motors. These motors, which were still in use in 1968, were of an archaic form, with extended pole pieces and an enormous single field coil. The armatures were of the ancient series-wound type, and the techniques perfected at this time for rewinding them, using modern glass fibre insulation, were a typical revelation of Manx Electric technical skill. Regrettably, events since 1970 showed the new method to have only delayed the onset of "exponential" failures, and re-equipment took place 1975-9.

The original control system provided for series-parallel working from the upper end, and series only (with five notches) from the lower end, where most propulsion was by gravity — the simpler control was sufficient for local manoeuvres. Trials were carried out in 1895 with a car wired for regenerative braking, which returned up to 50 electrical horsepower to the line and saved a good deal on brake blocks,

but Joshua Shaw thought it demanded too much driving skill and altered the motor circuits back from shunt to series. The idea was discussed again with Sir Philip Dawson in 1904, but not adopted. About this period, K11 controllers were fitted at the upper end.

About 1906, two stiffening channels were bolted to the lower faces of the original underframes, and the guiding wheels were relocated to a position outside the inner bogie cross-member. A rigid bogie brake screw column replaced the original type, which was flexibly jointed to a staff mounted on the platform. About 1954 the uphill end controllers were modified to Form K12 and new GEC main switches were fitted, replacing the original ones and their 0-500 ammeters.

The other three items of rolling stock comprised an unnumbered tower wagon trailer, a small unnumbered goods wagon, built in 1895 by Hurst Nelson to carry supplies for the hotel, and a coal car numbered 7 and nicknamed Maria. This last is a double-cab six-ton wagon-bodied underframe, of unknown name and parentage. However, its underframe carries the same rolling mill marks as those of the 1896 Douglas cable cars, and its truss rods are likewise of standard Milnes design. This compact vehicle acquired trucks, equipment and bow collectors from a passenger car each winter and took the next season's stock of coal up to the generating station. It was certainly in use in 1900, and may well be original (1895). After generation ceased at Snaefell power station in 1924 it was used only for construction work, the last occasion being some Air Ministry work at the summit in the winter of 1954-5. In 1898-9, attempts were made to secure winter mineral traffic from the Snaefell lead mine, and sections of a light railway plan by John Todd survive, bearing the date October 5, 1899. This would have included major inclined planes.

The Snaefell Association now proceeded to sell its line to the Isle of Man Tramways & Electric Power Co, as intended from the start. At the IOMT & EP annual general meeting on February 28, 1896, the directors' report explained that a debenture issue was needed to finance the cable tramway and Snaefell purchase, and a private meeting followed at which the Snaefell line's purchase for £72,500 was agreed, on a motion by R M Broadbent. The agreement called for £32,500 in cash, the rest in equal amounts of six per cent preference and ordinary shares of the tramway company. The amount clearly included a profit to the association's members but it later transpired that the real cost of building the line had only been about £40,000, and that the £2,000 put into the SMRA by IOMT & EP had brought a return of 100 per cent. The Snaefell Association was wound up later in 1896, after presenting Bruce with an engraved service of silver plate and a gold watch bearing his family crest, together with presents of jewellery for his wife and three daughters. These were presented by J A Mylrea at a ceremony at Dumbell's Bank on August 21.

The two termini in Laxey were a good distance apart, and the long climb up to the Snaefell line's station was a deterrent to visitors. In the director's report, presented on February 20, 1896 it emerges that the coast tramway, which in 1894 had ended opposite the present Laxey car shed, had been extended in the winter of 1895-6 by a bridge across the Rencell road, to a station just short of the future viaduct. This was a new single-storey building, 43ft 3ins by 19ft 6ins. From here, through passengers could walk across the road viaduct towards the Snaefell line's steps.

However, by February 1897 land had been purchased alongside Dumbell's Row to bring the line to a new low-level terminus. The earthworks involved cut right through the original flight of steps, which survive today as a fossilised slope between two heavily overgrown walls. On reaching level ground, the up and down tracks came together in a pivoted switch of the type now installed at the summit, and a rustic station building was erected, measuring 46ft 6ins by 17ft. This replaced the somewhat larger station on the hillside, which now stood disused — see drawing on page 32.

The line to the depot now diverged from the downhill running line on the gradient, and a special turnout of unique design was installed, with four moving sections which provided a five-stage "curve" on the turnout, complete with Fell rail. This survived until 1981, but the centre rail was not used for normal braking as the crew slackened off the rear brake on approaching the point, and applied the front one immediately after passing it. Access to the

Below: The original summit hotel in 1895 — its plan was was then T shaped. (R Hargreaves) **Inset:** *The summit hotel as fully developed by 1900 — the original T has become an H plan, then an annexe was added (right). This view is from the north side. (DGC)*

The Laxey coast line terminus of 1895 with a wall notice announcing the Snaefell line whose patrons had a fairly lengthy walk — and a flight of steps to ascend— before reaching the Snaefell station. (DGC)

depot building was still by a sector table, which survived until about 1932; Mr Gale of the MER recalled a car falling into its pit!

It is not clear why the sector tables ("turntables") and the replacing pivotal switches were adopted, for the Fell gear was above the level of running rails and in later years conventional turnouts were installed at several places. Apart from these, the 1895 operating rules are still applicable today, though the line also has a level crossing with the road through Laxey Village, and there are red and green light signals controlled from Laxey station to govern entry to the single line. The present rule book also contains an injunction to "post a flagman in rear" if an involuntary stop is made on the descent; this results from a 1905 collision, described later.

The creation of the present station in 1898 belongs to the Ramsey line story in the next chapter, but meanwhile the Summit hotel had been extended,

and another large "hotel", known as The Bungalow and measuring 90ft by 80ft, was built at the crossing of the mountain road at the Half-Way Hut. The construction of a branch from here to Tholt-y-Will was seriously contemplated, and appears in company literature of 1896-7. From 1907 the trip could be made by motor charabanc, as described in Chapter 3. Dr Farrell had by this time taken to acting as impromptu guide to those travelling up Snaefell, and the summit would declaim:

> Here you see seven kingdoms — England, Ireland, Scotland, Wales, the Isle of Man, (the kingdom of) Man and, where is the seventh? Ah, the Kingdom of Heaven!

The line was solidly built, and after a landslide on to the track in the first winter the only major repairs needed were at Lhergy Veg in 1905-6, when the retaining wall slipped and had to be reinforced with substantial buttresses, which bear the dates of erection on their tops. The cost was £844. Apart from periodic erosion slips near Bellevue on the Ramsey line, caused by poor shore defences, this was the only physical instability recorded on the entire group of lines until the Bulgham slip of 1967. A new battlemented Snaefell Summit hotel, with a 100ft frontage, a depth of 60ft and a round tower 25ft high, was opened on August 10, 1906, having been built in only four months. The original wooden hotel was then demolished.

On September 14, 1905, the Snaefell line saw its

Right: The new Snaefell station building was perhaps the first exponent of the curious rustic style employed by the tramway over the next few years. It yet survives in Laxey station, though much altered. Note the remains of the access steps to the original station just above the roof line. (DGC)
Above: The Bungalow hotel of 1896 was a more orthodox structure whose style had echoes all over the British Empire — such wood and corrugated iron structures being obtainable "off the peg" though this example was probably purpose-built. (DGC)

SNAEFELL MOUNTAIN ELECTRIC TRAMWAY Co.

INSTRUCTIONS TO DRIVERS & CONDUCTORS

1.—Drivers and Conductors must not allow any person (excepting an Official of the Company) to travel in their compartments, or to occupy the platform or steps, neither shall they enter into conversation with any person while the Car is in motion.

2.—No Driver shall start his Car without the proper bell-signal from his Conductor.

3.—When the Car is in motion, the Driver shall always be on the Front Platform, and at no time, either when shunting or otherwise, shall a Car be driven or controlled from the back end.

One Ring from the Conductor means STOP.
Two Rings from the Conductor means START.

—Both Driver and Conductor are responsible for the proper working of the Brakes of the Car, and great care must be taken to have them properly adjusted to the wheels and to frequently use and test the Centre Rail Brakes, and any defect, however slight, must be immediately reported to the Car Inspector, in addition to entering the same in the Report Book.

5.—Care must be taken that the Centre Rail Brake-blocks are sufficiently apart to clear the Centre Rail before every start, and the front Centre Rail Brake must not be used for stopping, except in special cases of emergency.

6.—In case a Driver requires the rear Centre Rail Brake applied to the Car he must give One Ring, and if not applied sufficiently tight, he must continue to give Single Rings at distinct intervals.

7.—When the Driver wishes it released he gives Two Rings.

8.—No Car shall be driven quicker than 8 miles per hour, and under no circumstances must the Journey from Snaefell be done in less than 40 minutes.

9.—Every Car on the Down Journey must stop at the Signal Board before reaching the Hut.

10.—Drivers must use special caution in approaching the Turntables at Laxey and the Switch at Summit.

11.—Drivers must see that their Outfit of Tools or Fittings is on the Car before starting each Journey, and that their Sand-boxes are properly filled and Pipes in working order.

12.—Any Driver taking the Tools or Fittings from another Car will be instantly dismissed the Company service.

13.—In the event of an accident happening in connection with the Car, no matter how slight it may be, a full written report of the same must be given on the form provided for the purpose and be delivered to the Station-Master at Laxey immediately on arrival, and every care must be taken to obtain names and addresses of reliable witnesses of the occurrence. Drivers neglecting to do this will be held responsible.

14.—Under no circumstances shall a Driver enter a Public-house, or use intoxicating drink while on duty.

15.—Before going off duty, a written report of the state of the Car must be made in the Report Book provided for the purpose.

16.—The Conductor shall take his order to start the Car from the Station-master only, and shall then communicate the same to the Driver by the proper signal—namely, Two Rings.

17.—Conductors before leaving Snaefell must see that the Centre Rail Brake is sufficiently off to clear the centre rail, and on starting when the centre rail is entered they must apply the Brake so as to bear slightly upon the rail, and then await the orders of the Drivers as directed in Instruction No. 6.

18.—Always before re-starting they must make sure that the Brake is sufficiently off to clear the centre rail.

19.—Conductors must stand by the rear Brake all the Journey while the Car is in motion, ready to apply the Brake when signalled, and must only collect Tickets while the Car is stopped at the Hut.

Any Driver or Conductor infringing these Rules, or any of them, will be instantly dismissed.

The Directors earnestly request the Officials to see that these Rules are strictly complied with, and that any departure from or neglect of the same be at once reported to the Manager.

H Harrison. **MANAGER.**

Snaefell line working instructions. Note the erroneous company title. (MER)

only serious accident, a rear-end collision. During shuttle working to Bungalow (for a motor race) an ascending car stalled at Lhergy Veg from either a motor fault or loss of wire contact, and the third of a convoy of three cars later descending on the same track failed to stop in time. The compensation paid to injured passengers was considerable, and seriously affected the year's profits. The Fell rail has proved fully effective in preventing derailments or runaways, and no other incidents of this kind are on record. The re-equipment of 1975-9 is described in Chapter 8 from which the Fell rail provision became an emergency-only function.

Finally, a description of a ride up the mountain. Immediately on leaving the Laxey station, the car takes the right-hand track and begins the curving ascent to the rear of the Dumbell's Row, soon passing the downhill road's facing connection to the depot, formerly with its special point. Next comes a fine view across the valley to the 1854 Laxey Wheel, and the ridge on which stands the ancient village of Agneash, and behind them the hidden valley of the Mooar. The northwest limits of Baljean see the line climb over a rocky spur before a brief descent to the buttressed stone embankment at Lhergy Veg, the only point other than Bungalow at which the descending cars disengage their slipper brake. The field enclosures here are lost in wild vegetation.

Above Lhergy Veg, the line runs on the lands of the Commons Trustees, and is unfenced. The view across the Laxey valley is increasingly impressive, and includes the tree-enshrouded ruins of the Snaefell mine, and then Snaefell itself, skirted by the mountain road. Most of the formation consists of a cut-and-tipped shelf, and on this section the car passes the remains of the mountain power station. Soon the gradient slackens, and the car leaves Laxey valley to cross the mountain road and stop at Bungalow, the former hotel's site now hardly recognisable. Here the line passes into Lezayre parish. The remaining spiral climb round Snaefell is evident from the map and, given a fine day, this ascent, with its increasingly spectacular views, is certainly the most rewarding inland ride in the Island.

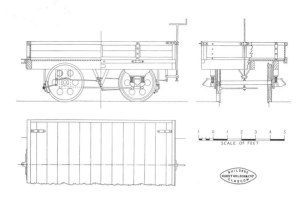

Top right: The SMT's Hurst Nelson wagon of 1895. As built it seems to have had removable handrails at one end. The builder's plate was almost 9in in length. (JCC)
Bottom right: The last appearance in service of No 7, "Maria", was fortunately captured by Mr O Clayton (1954). Its bogies were normally those of No 5 passenger car, whose wiring presumably made special allowance for the transfer.
Below: A Snaefell car in 1968 condition. The enormous roof mounted advertisement boards survived until 1970-71. (SB)

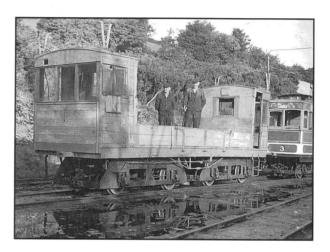

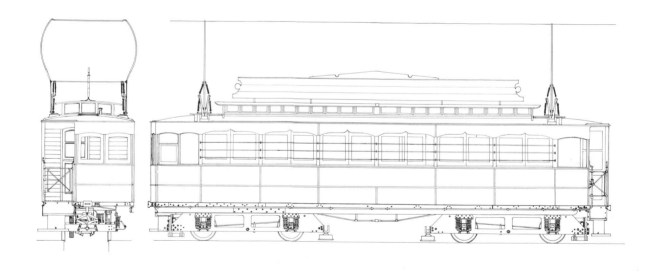

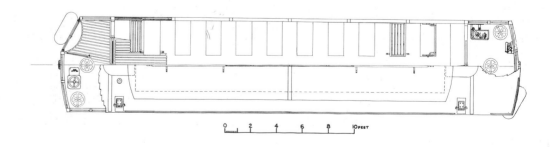

Chapter 3

A Tramway Colossus and its Cost

Your safe and commodious cars, which traverse a piece of coast and mountain scenery which suggests the great new road from Sorrento to Amalfi… are, in my view, great contributors to the education and happiness of the thousands who make the Isle of Man their annual resort.

Hall Caine, writing to manager Harold Brown, c 1904

THE EXPANSION OF THE UNDERTAKING between 1896 and 1899 was founded on the good results achieved by the coast tramway. The profit of £10,507 in 1894 increased to £14,467 in 1895, and the half-yearly dividend of six per cent on the preference shares and 7½ per cent on the ordinary was followed by six per cent on the preference and 8½ per cent for the second half of the year. At the annual general meeting on February 28, 1896, Bruce's entry was marked by loud cheers.

The year's total mileage on the horse and electric lines in 1895 (excluding Snaefell) was 302,121, and 1,923,316 people had been carried, the electric line's best one-day figure being 10,477. Laxey had received 7,148 cars that year. Winter receipts per car journey were between 9s 2d (46p) and 15s 1d (75.5p), contrasting with 47s 5d (£2.37) in August. The working expenses were given as only 34 per cent of receipts (11.64d (nearly 5p) per train mile), and 2,300 tons of goods had been carried. Mr John Mather questioned the aggregation of items and lack of allowance for depreciation, but Bruce explained that repairs and renewals had been charged

to revenue. To pay for the Snaefell and cable lines, the company's capital was increased to £315,000, of which increase £25,000 was in preference shares and £100,000 in series B 1896 debentures at four per cent.

The running time from Douglas to Laxey was about 40 minutes, and all cars were kept at Douglas, as shown by the winter 1896 timetable. Weekday departures from Douglas to Laxey were at 6.20, 8.15, 10.00, 12.0, 2.30, 3.30, 4.30, 5.30, 6.30, 7.30, 8.30 and (Sats) 9.00, returning from Laxey at 7.20, 9.00, 11.00, 1.00, 3.30, 4.30, 5.30, 6.30, 7.30, 8.30, and (Sats) 9.45. On Sundays, cars left Douglas at 10.0, 1.00, 2.00, 3.00, 4.00, 5.30, 7.30, and 8.30, returning from Laxey 45 minutes later.

The year's profits of £17,822 announced at the next IOMT & EP meeting on March 8, 1897 reflected the season's bad weather and the struggles of the cable line. Nevertheless, the same dividends were paid as in 1896 — already, unobserved financial malpractice was afoot. On the electric lines, passenger figures had reached 591,163 and car-miles 153,897, while the entire system of four lines had

The IoMT&EP erected this elaborate canopy (82ft by 35ft with an 18ft eaves height) over the Derby Castle tramway horse horse tramway terminal tracks in 1896. Note the elaborate detailing, including the company title. Only the bases of its columns survive today. (Manx National Heritage)

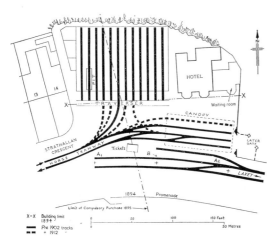

Derby Castle: the new joint termini and horse tramway depot arrangements completed in August 1896. Electric track A₁ to A₂ was to be removed by 1902-3, and the centre pole relocated to B. Later horse tramway alterations are not shown, nor is 1953's traffic island. (JCC)

carried 2,398,559. The Douglas car sheds had been twice extended, first by the addition of a new six-car shed in 1895 (125ft 6ins long, 21ft 6ins wide and 17ft 6ins high), and then in 1896 by a shed for 15 trailers, 166ft long and 27ft wide, but only 10ft 6ins high. A rustic ticket office, 12ft 6ins by 8ft, was built at the Douglas terminus early in 1897.

Bruce now sought a line to Ramsey, an aim equally shared by Ramsey shareholder J R Cowell, a director of the Manx Northern Railway. On April 9, 1896 a rival London consortium had sought leave to introduce a Bill in Tynwald for a Laxey-Ramsey railway, and had engaged G Noble Fell to survey it, but by October 28 the IOMT & EP had petitioned Tynwald for leave to present its own Bill. This proposed separate termini in Laxey for all three lines (Douglas, Snaefell and Ramsey). By December 10, the other group had withdrawn by consent, and the IOMT & EP's scheme was itself withdrawn "to allow of an improved plan, with communication between both tramways". This was by a so-called branch (actually an end-on connecting line) between the 1895-6 terminus and the point K shown on our Laxey area map on page 37.

In a new petition on March 25, 1897, Ring, Brown and Nelson appeared for the IOMT & EP. The connecting line was to cross Glen Roy from the second terminus of the Douglas line, pass through the Workmen's Institute, and then cross the four-road junction on the level to enter a roadside reservation leading to the second Snaefell station, which would become joint for both lines. Following opposition, this was withdrawn on April 13 in favour of an alternative plan by IOMT & EP's new engineer, William Knowles, CE (formerly of Liverpool tramways), for the line to cross Glen Roy, descending to 19ft 3ins below road level, and then tunnel under the road intersection with a girder roof, and climb at 1 in 24 into the Snaefell line terminus. The station

south of Glen Roy remained the main one, and the rest of the line to Ramsey was much as later built. The anticipated cost of the line and equipment was between £95,000 and £100,000, and the earnings, £11,000 to £12,000 per year, with working expenses estimated at 45 per cent.

The Douglas & Laxey Tramway (Extension to Ramsey) Act 1897 was passed on May 13, 1897 and promulgated on July 20. It provided for the new line to be a separate undertaking with its own capital, revenue and accounts. The IOMT & EP was allowed to contract for the line's construction (a meeting to approve this was held on February 7, 1898) and a capital charge of up to £30,000 on the general undertaking was permitted. Meetings between both concerns were to settle the division of revenue before the line opened. The tolls were fixed at 2d a mile, with a 3d minimum, and four cars per day were made obligatory, two in each direction. Goods traffic and mails were provided for, being now an established traffic though purely passenger cars were not expected to carry mails unless in the charge of a Post Office officer.

Compulsory land purchase by arbitration was included, and liabilities to adjoining landowners included fencing and providing new water troughs for cattle. The underpass in Laxey was to be able to carry road traffic equivalent to a 20-ton traction engine pulling two loaded trucks, and gradients were limited to 1 in 23, with 90ft radius curves. Speed was limited to 4mph across the Agneash road at Laxey, on the washing floors embankment, and on Ballure Glen bridge. At Bulgham, the line was to occupy the cliff-edge location of the old road, and any new road constructed to enable this re-alignment had to have the same width, length and gradient as its predecessor. The line was to be built within two years of promulgation.

Shaw and Aldworth went to the Continent in 1897, comparing notes with other undertakings, and the company also obtained advice from Granville Cunningham of the City of Birmingham Tramways. Possibly in consequence, before the 1898 season, trolley bases of the Boston Pivotal type, made by the Anderson Co, were fitted to the cars, and non-insulated trolley poles with non-swivelling heads replaced the Hopkinson bows. The round trolley wire (approximately 0.324in in diameter) was henceforth suspended by orthodox arched ears instead of the original Aetna type used by Mather and Platt. On the Snaefell line heavier wire of 0.372in diameter (a definite British Standard) was used, and here the Hopkinson bows were retained, probably because of the high winds. The Ramsey line was equipped for trolleys from the start, and used a new type of Blackwells stepped pole, again with both normal 6ins/4ins and heavy 7ins/5ins types.

On September 3, 1897 the IOMT & EP put out a letter to shareholders announcing the intention of

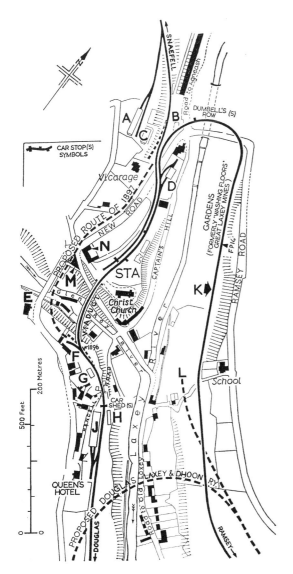

Above: Tramways at Laxey since 1897, showing Snaefell depot (A), site of 1897 Snaefell terminus (B), site of 1895 Snaefell terminus (C), goods shed (D), Commercial Hotel (E), cattle dock (F), 1896 station building (G), site of 1894 station (H), Laxey car shed (J), the Workmen's Institute (M) and the Laxey Industrial Co-operative Society's shop (N). K is the official starting point of the extension to Ramsey (F to K being regarded as a branch) and L is the trailing connection from the proposed Douglas, Laxey and Dhoon Railway to the former lead mines' washing floors, now occupied by gardens and dwellings. The MER's 1935 sub station is housed in the (untitled) lineside building immediately north of the Rencell Road (earlier "Lane") underbridge. A little further north, on the same side of the tracks, lies FP 15 followed by the 1896 station. Symbols are standard with those of the route maps in Appendix 4. (DGC)

Right: Profiles for the 1897 proposals at Laxey. The solid line shows the original proposal, crossing the road junction (B) on the level, and the broken line shows the later underpass scheme, with gradients in brackets. A is the divergence of main line and cattle dock sidings, C is the location of the section through the cutting (page 38), D is the vicarage garden entrance, E is the Agneash road crossing and F the mines' spoil heap. The first scheme would have involved a two-arch viaduct 77 years long and the second a similar but lower viaduct, plus an underpass 22ft wide. (DGC)

augmenting the capital of the general undertaking by £25,000 in £1 preference shares, and issuing £100,000 of 1897 preference and 1897 ordinary shares in the separate undertaking. By the date of the next AGM on March 10, 1898, 35,000 1897 preference shares and 15,000 1897 ordinary shares had been taken up, raising £18,781 towards the new undertaking, but £21,343 had already been spent on works. The capital of the general undertaking stood at £315,630. During 1897 the electric lines had carried 602,068 passengers, with 155,927 car-miles, earning 27.68d (about 11.5p) per mile, expenses being 43.34 per cent of receipts. The year's passengers on the whole undertaking reached 2,712,114, and the reduced profit, despite larger numbers carried, was put down to the fact that people had only made short journeys in the season's bad weather.

The date officially quoted for the start of the work on the Ramsey extension was November 1, 1897, though preliminary work began in August: the meeting which formally approved IOMT & EP's contract took place on February 7, 1898. It was engineered on a grand scale, spoil removed totalled 250,000 tons, and 60,000 tons of ballast were put down. A well-designed rail was used, weighing $62^{1}/_{2}$lbs per yard. A force of between 1,000 and 1,100 men, were paid 4d an hour; at one stage they demanded $4^{1}/_{2}$d and threatened to strike. Thirty horses were borrowed from the Douglas tramway, and the IOMT & EP bought a steam locomotive and 45 ballast wagons, plus other sundry vehicles. The engine was an Andrew Barclay 0-4-0 saddle-tank originally built in 1892 (works number 713) to the order of contractors Morrison & Mason of Glasgow; it was resold in October 1900 to Douglas Corporation (with the wagons) for use on the West Baldwin reservoir railway, and remained there until 1904. At West Baldwin it acquired the name Injebreck.

In 1899 and in 1901, respectively, former M & P "resident engineer" H N Thomas, and Joshua Shaw, prepared curricula vitae from which a glimpse of the workload of these two young men (then aged 33 and 30) can be gleaned. Apart from their routine duties, they had carried out the design and superintendence of the technical plant of the new line in its entirety — the Laxey turbine plant was a typical Joshua Shaw project. Shaw had been a Mather & Platt apprentice, Thomas at Beyer Peacock's (fellow Mancunians all).

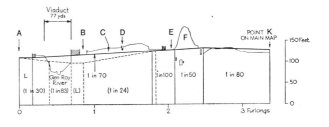

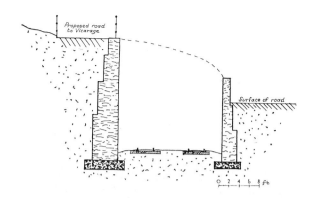

Section through intended roadside cutting at Laxey, from an original initialled by Knowles and Goldie-Taubman. (Stan Basnett)

Two more locomotives were hired, from the IMR came No 2, Derby, which worked from Laxey, after being shipped from Ramsey and brought up to the line on a wagon hauled by traction engines. Meanwhile, a separate gang built south from Ballure, employing MNR No 1, Ramsey, transferred by using baulks and rollers laid through the streets of Ramsey. The agreement of April 12, 1898 with the Manx Northern was £2 10s daily rent for the engine and 3s each for open wagons Nos 20 and 21, and low side ballast wagons Nos 24 and 29. The wages were 5s 6d (27.5p) and 4s (20p) a day for the driver and fireman, and 3s 2d (16p) a night for a cleaner, paid by the MNR and claimed back from the IOMT & EP.

Work at Bulgham began on November 15, 1897, after the Highway Board had agreed (a little over a month previously) to close the road for three months. In places, the road was diverted some 30ft inland and the tramway was built on its former dry stone walled embankment. But at one point it was built out on a partly cantilevered shelf. A proposed 45-yard viaduct was not built, the older road's retaining wall being used instead to support the new formation. By April 19 the road was still closed and even when reopened it was not properly metalled, nor was this completed to the satisfaction of the Highway Board until April 26, 1901. An angle-iron railing contrived to look like a solid bar was added to the parapet wall in 1899 to reassure the nervous passengers alarmed at their 600ft high vantage point.

Work at Laxey was meanwhile held up by a change of plan. By March 1898, the Highway Board had consented to a road crossing in Laxey, and the church authorities had agreed to the line passing through the churchyard to a station in mine-captain Reddicliffe's garden; his house survives in part as the station hotel. This eliminated the unpopular underpass, but meant that the Snaefell line would have to be altered yet again to bring the two lines into today's

common station. Work began on March 14, 1898, and contractor Mark Carine then built the curved four-arched viaduct in only four months. On the far side, after a girder underbridge end-on to the viaduct, a joint station was laid out for the coastal and Snaefell lines, bordered by a triangular grass plot with rustic seats and kiosks. The station building was moved across from the Snaefell terminus and re-erected, the board over the verandah now announcing "LAXEY JUNCTION — change for Snaefell". In 1899, a huge wooden refreshment room with restaurant and bar (140ft by 40ft) was built alongside. It was destroyed by fire on September 24, 1917.

Beyond Bulgham was Dhoon Glen, later provided with a rustic building that included a stationmaster's office. The glen was rented by IOMT & EP, which charged 4d for admission and paid 1³/₄d to the owners; a similar charge was made at the other four glens, Groudle, Garwick, Laxey and Ballaglass. Small waiting-rooms were provided at Glen Mona, Ballaglass and Port Lewaigue. North of Dhoon Glen lay the 53-acre Dhoon granite quarry, leased by Bruce in October 1895, the prospects of which were a factor in the Ramsey line promotion, and whose setts had paved the Upper Douglas cable line. The quarry sidings were (eventually) to include

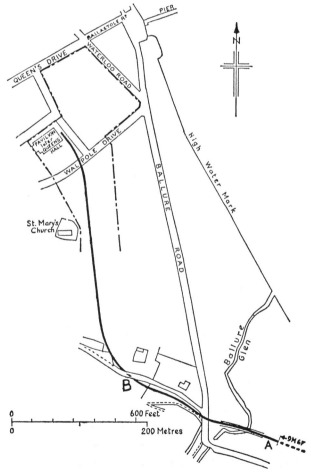

Ramsey entry as proposed in 1897, with underpass at B. Limits of deviation at the terminus are shown in chain dotted line. During 1898 the line ended at point A. (JCC)

a weighbridge, not a common tramway installation. Bruce had imported men form Dalbeattie, the Scottish granite centre, to develop the project, and his aim (soon realised) of exporting setts to the mainland gave added purpose to an 1897 plan for a line ending at Ramsey harbour. There was also a quarry and siding for building stone at Ballajora.

The original plan at Ramsey was to cross Ballure Glen and end at the Pavilion, but meanwhile the town commissioners had proposed a new line along the shore from Port Lewaigue, to a point near the Queen's pier. A ratepayers' meeting had approved the idea, even though it would have involved a 1d or 1¹/₂d rate. The IOMT & EP duly met a Tynwald committee, while some preliminary work was done at Port e Vullen.

Drawings by Knowles show that the promenade from Port Lewaigue was to be 50ft wide, with a 4ft footpath, 20ft tramway, 16ft roadway and 10ft seaward footpath, all to be built by the IOMT & EP with a £2,250 contribution from the Ramsey town commissioners, agreed on June 29, 1897. Tynwald approved the alteration on August 7, and revealed plans for a further extension along the existing south promenade to Ramsey harbour, with approving comments. Just when and why the company abandoned this scheme was never publicly stated, though it emerged later that Bruce had told the Ramsey town commissioners in the spring of 1898 that the scheme would have to be dropped, reportedly for geological reasons. The initial deviation is shown on our route map, commencing at Close 262.

Notwithstanding its enormous commitment, the IOMT & EP also became involved in behind-the-scenes moves for taking over the Manx Northern Railway, traffic on which would be affected by the new line. By January 24, 1898 IMR chairman Sir John Goldie-Taubman had got wind of this, and wrote to MNR chairman J C Lamothe deploring any such merger and suggesting that the MNR put its line up for sale on the open market. Lamothe admitted negotiations and said that the MNR's only object was to get the best price, and Bruce confirmed to IMR director Stevenson (chairman of Dumbell's Bank) that it was the MNR which had approached the IOMT & EP, and not the reverse. On February 3, offers from any party were invited, and on February 22, MNR acting chairman Todhunter offered to sell to the IMR for £72,500, with a February 28 deadline. Nothing came of this, but a typewritten IMR analysis of the whole affair survives, revealing that the IOMT & EP was prepared to electrify the MNR and build its own electric line from St John's to Douglas. It ends with the words: "The promoters of the Electric Company are very popular in the Island and have immense influence, both legislative and financial..."

By July 1898 the new line had been built as far as Ballure, just short of Ramsey, but with only a single line through the deep cutting at Ballagorry. Once again Colonel Rich and Major Cardew came to

IoMT&EP's locomotive, later Douglas Corporation Water Department's Injebreck. (FKP)

inspect the new line, reporting the same day, July 18.

Colonel Rich found the 3-chains 4-furlongs connecting branch tramway incomplete, as was the line into Ramsey beyond Ballure. Apart from in the Ballagorry cutting, double track was complete throughout. The rails of 62¹/₂lbs per yard section were in 31ft 6ins lengths, on 9ins x 4¹/₂ins sleepers, 6ft long. Fang-bolts were used in addition to spikes. Laxey's brick-arched masonry viaduct had four 30ft spans and there were also listed the similar span at Minorca, two girder underbridges, the 18ft culvert at Ballaglass and other smaller structures. The maximum gradient was 1 in 24, and the minimum curvature 2¹/₂ chains.

Rich, taking exception to the lack of numerous finishing touches and, more seriously, of protective devices at Ballagorry's single-line section, refused his approval. Cardew was much more satisfied with the electrical side of the undertaking and merely sought a later check on the performance of the new cars and the return circuits.

Following extensive work on the points at issue, the line to the Ballure railhead opened on Tuesday, August 2, and for the first time the IOMT & EP received full government recognition of its efforts. The opening was attended by the Lieutenant-Governor, Lord Henniker, accompanied by the Lord Bishop, Ramsey's High Bailiff, J M Cruikshank, the Chair-

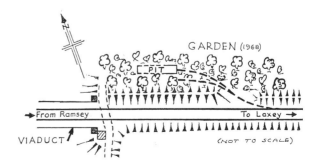

The site of the Ballure depot, 1898-9. The junction was about 145ft from the bridge. (JCC)

Ballaglass power station, 1898. (DGC)

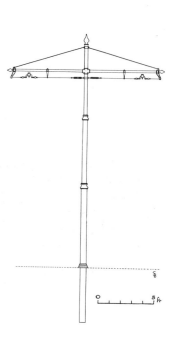

Ramsey extension pole by R W Blackwell, 1898. (SB)

man of the Ramsey Town Commissioners and other gentlemen, not forgetting Messrs Bruce, Knowles, Saunderson, Mylrea, Aldworth and Dr Farrell. The Governor and the Lord Bishop travelled from Douglas by the shareholders' "special", made of two new motor cars, and all stations en route were flag-bedecked. Brief speeches at Ballure were followed by a drive to the Pavilion, for a splendid repast and further speeches. Cruikshank referred to probable losses by the Manx Northern due to the new line, but the Governor, in a further speech, made the point that both lines might become part of a route all round the Island. He saw the MNR route as advantageous for the tourists' return journey. Bruce replied to a toast to the IOMT & EP by summarising the work from its inception, and the special then returned to Douglas in 80 minutes.

Public traffic to Ballure began on the same day and continued until Monday, October 24, when the extension was closed again for completion. Fares during the 1898 season, from Douglas, were 3d to Groudle, 6d to Garwick, 9d to Ballabeg and 1s to Laxey, with return fares of 3s 6d to Snaefell and 3s 6d to Ballure (for Ramsey). No depot yet existed at Laxey for the coastal line, but a shed for six cars, with pits for three, was built at Ballure, 126ft 8ins long and 21ft wide. In 1899 it was dismantled and re-erected at Parsonage Road.

The new generating equipment again used steam power and accumulators. In the new distribution system, the 1894-5 switchgear at Douglas was replaced by a larger installation with five slate panels, and a new seven-panel board was installed at Laxey, together with an additional Robb Armstrong engine with direct-coupled generator and an additional Galloway's boiler. A new feeder cable of the 1894 pattern was put in from Half-Way House to Ramsey, with feeder pillars at half-mile spacing, and a combined pilot and telephone cable was added between Laxey and Ramsey, all at the expense of the separate undertaking.

At the new steam power station at Ballaglass,

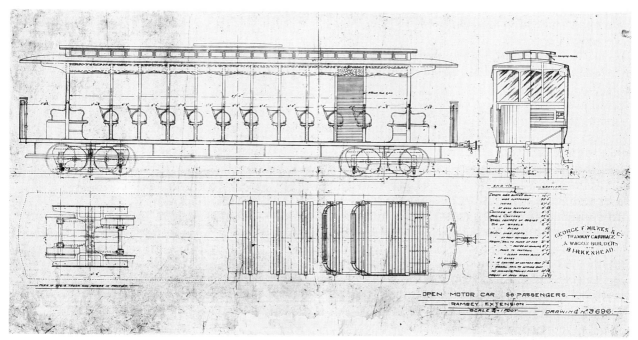

Milnes 1887-8 drawing of an ECC as ordered. The bulkhead lantern box is absent, but the car is shown as fitted with roller shutters as built. (MER)

12¹/₂ miles from Douglas, a fast flowing stream, the Corony, brought water to the very door, and the tramway passed high on an embankment down which coal brought from Ramsey readily fell to the bunkers at its foot. The station was most ornate, with walls panelled waist-high with varnished pitch pine cut "on the quarter", and the tiled floor patterned round each piece of the plant.

The building is of stone with a slate roof, and consists of two large halls with a boiler house and coal store

Above: The temporary terminus at Ballure on opening day, Tuesday August 2, 1898. Those on the "platform" include a white-shirted personage who may well be Bruce. The cars are in the IoMT&EP's "1898" livery, with a white "eaves board" and bulkhead crown piece (including the lamp box) but with varnished posts and bulkhead window framing. (R Powell Hendry)

placed end-on. *(See plan accompanying section map.)* One hall was the engine room, measuring 73ft by 32ft 6ins, the other was a battery room 65 ft by 32ft 6ins; the boiler room and adjoining coal store were each 56ft by 31ft. Two boilers (again by Galloways) were installed. They were each 26ft long and 6ft 6ins in diameter, the same as the new boiler at Laxey. The boilers had feed pump and injector equipment, and also Ledward's No 8 ejector condensers and centrifugal circulation pumps, driven by a 10hp motor supplied by the Electrical Construction Company. Until 1990, the exterior view differed little from that in 1898, lacking only the iron chimney; this was 60ft high and 5ft in diameter.

Contractors for the generating equipment were now Dick, Kerr & Co, who installed two Robb Armstrong tandem compound engines direct coupled to ECC six-pole multipolar generators. The engines, fed with steam at 120lbs per square inch, were of 180 indicated horsepower at 175rpm, and each generator produced 240 amps at 500 volts. The makers' numbers for these two generators and the similar new set at Laxey were 4332-4, and the armatures measured 51ins by 16¹/₂ins. Other equipment in the engine room included a booster set, comprising a 500V/150V shunt-wound motor generator (ECC No 4476) for charging the batteries, and a 150V series generator (ECC No 4477) used for raising pressure on the new feeder system. An additional feeder ran two and a half miles northwards from Ballaglass to assist in maintaining voltage on the steep grades. Switchgear totalled seven slate panels (two for the generators, two for battery circuits, two for testing and one for booster), and the battery room contained a chloride battery of 260 type 'R' cells rated to give 140 amps for six hours.

The financial results for 1898 were announced at the company's meeting held at Strathallan Crescent on March 31, 1899. Car mileage for Douglas-Laxey was 132,169, with costs of 10.66d/mile against receipts of 28.13d. Snaefell earned 33.37d/mile

An ECC (No 14) ascending from Laxey circa 1903, its 1898 paintwork already modified to the MER's new style (see Chapter 9). (Stan Basnett)

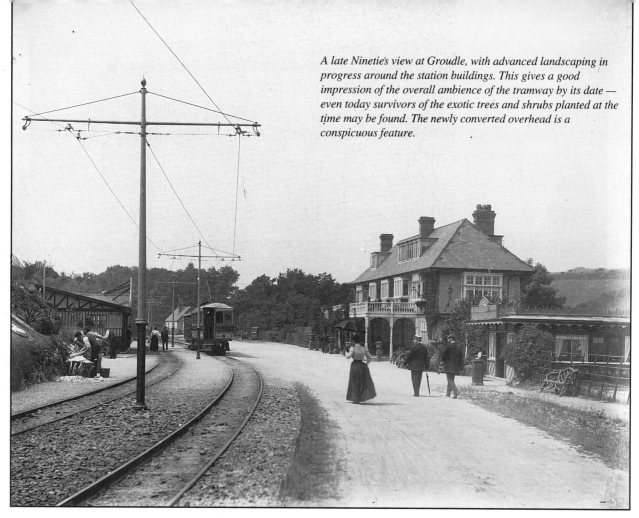

A late Nineties view at Groudle, with advanced landscaping in progress around the station buildings. This gives a good impression of the overall ambience of the tramway by its date — even today survivors of the exotic trees and shrubs planted at the time may be found. The newly converted overhead is a conspicuous feature.

against costs of 20.24d, and car mileage for the whole system was 443,409, with a passenger total of 2,711,696. The "separate undertaking" had raised £28,703 in shares and had an "advance re debenture stocks" of £65,000; its capital now amounted to £106,535. Income from the revenue account had been £71. The general undertaking had a healthier aspect and a dividend of six per cent was paid on both classes of share, but this was later found to have been achieved by "shop window" accountancy. Bruce looked towards the coming season as that in which the new line would begin to earn, and gave its cost as £6,000 per single-track mile, as against the £11,000 of the Blackpool—Fleetwood line of which he was also a director. All had previously ridden to Ballure, and a group photograph had been taken at Ballaglass.

At Ramsey, the stated aim was now to end at the Pavilion, but in June 1898 provisional agreement had been reached to extend beyond, and the company had bought the Palace concert hall (a miniature of the one in Douglas) to use its grounds for a new terminus, the building itself being let. By May 16, 1899, Ramsey town commissioners dictated their revised terms for this extension — that the IOMT & EP should pay them five per cent of the gross earnings of the tramway within the town for 20 years, starting in 1904. The length of town tramway for this calculation was put at half a mile, out of a ten-mile total. Bruce refused, bought further land at the Pavilion, and ordered four Bonner road-rail wagons with which he could haul goods from any

part of the town "without the assistance of tramlines". A line would still run on to Mr Cruikshank's garden (see map), but only for goods and boat traffic. The commissioners had a stormy debate on Tuesday May 30 and, relenting, made a new agreement on June 1, 1899 now assenting to a line from the Pavilion to the Palace and beyond to the quay, without the proposed toll, but with a flat rate charge of £10 per year against the IOMT & EP, which was also obliged to light the street intersections. The commissioners' debates revealed the proposed route to the quay as "across Parsonage Road and the old Pump Road and then below Mr Cruikshank's house, skirting round here and going down to Casement's on the Quay". A line along Queen's Drive to the Queen's Pier was also agreed, subject to Tynwald approval.

Meanwhile, much of the Douglas—Laxey section had been planted with ornamental shrubs, and further waiting rooms had been built (or planned) at Half-Way House, Garwick, Ballabeg and South Cape. Most of these still exist, but the Half-Way House shelter was later moved to Minorca. New cars for the Ramsey service arrived on May 13. The cutting at Ballagorry had been widened to take a double track and, by early June 1899, work was in full swing on Ballure bridge. This had two spans, formed by four girders 80ft by 9ft, in pairs, placed 10ft apart, with one girder under each track. The southern abutments carry a cast-iron plate bearing the names of the manufacturer (Francis Morton & Co, of Garston, Liverpool) and the erector, William Knowles, CE, and the date, 1899.

At last, on June 17, the line was reopened to Ballure, with an hourly service. By June 6, track had been laid to Parsonage Road, including some stretches in grooved rail at the behest of the land-owners concerned, and on June 9 the town commissioners (all forgiven) were taken to Snaefell, under the guidance of Dr Farrell. Then, on the afternoon of July 3, 1899, a saloon car bearing Bruce, Farrell, Joshua Shaw and Knowles, ran through into Ramsey, and the mail service began on July 11. At the Governor's invitation, Colonel Rich and Major Cardew officially inspected the new line, Rich on July 21, Cardew on July 20. Their reports are dated August 22 (!) and July 27 respectively. The 1,266-yard extension from 1898's terminal, the doubling at Ballagorry, and the new bridge all found approval, as did the new cars' performance. Cardew merely sought a regular earth check in Ramsey town.

IOMT & EP advertisements announced the planned Saturday July 22 opening, but this actually took place the following Monday. An advertisement in the Ramsey Courier of July 28 specified a service leaving town from 7am half-hourly until 9pm, and, on Sundays, from 9.30am until 8pm. The return fare to Douglas was 3s 6d (17.5p) (6d dearer than by carriage), and fell to 2s 6d (12.5p) after 4pm. Remarkably, it was still 3s 6d in the winter of 1965-6. On bank holiday Monday, August 7, bookings had to be suspended for a time because of the rush, and on Wednesday, August 16, the line brought about 4,500 people from Douglas. Bruce had invited the six battalions of the West Yorkshire Infantry Volunteer Brigade to hold their annual camp near Ramsey, on the Milntown estate, and their manœuvres around Snaefell culminated in a full-scale mock battle on August 9, held at a point only accessi-

Although taken after 1903, the general impression of the Ballure viaduct scene shown is that of 1899 but with some subsequent tree growth. (A Tranter collection)

Ramsey station layout. (DGC)

A site of station building 1899
B station & office 190? to 1964
C station building 1964

ble by electric car and which the public were invited to witness. The Palace station, a single-storey building 55ft by 12ft 3ins, was completed by August 25, and on September 26 the Bay Regatta had as its first prize a cup presented by the IOMT & EP. Former Governor Ridgeway visited the line on October 13. (The station had previously been erected at Ballure.)

On September 1, 1899, three road/rail wagons from the Bonner Wagon Co, of Toledo, Ohio, USA, entered service. Carried on a four-wheel 3ft gauge truck, or on their own road wheels, the transition was effected by means of a simple trackside twin ramp which, by transferring the load to the road wheels, left the rail truck free to be withdrawn. The appearance was that of an orthodox high-sided, five-ton, two-horse cart, measuring 13ft by 6ft by 2ft 6ins, with all four sides capable of being lowered. The Bonner wagons were intended for a shuttle service, taking coal from Ramsey harbour to Ballaglass power station, and returning with setts from Dhoon quarry for export, but loading ramps also existed at Derby Castle and Laxey. Soon after the service began, complaints arose in Ramsey at the noise caused during the night, and this was solved from September 5 by making the road/rail transfer at Queen's Drive instead of Ramsey station, using a portable ramp.

Meanwhile, there was fresh activity in the Laxey valley. Here meet the Laxey river and the equally swift-flowing Glen Roy stream. The former was already exploited by the mining industry, while the latter drove a large corn mill, but opportunity still existed for a water-powered generating station using the combined waters. The company saw in this a source of cheap winter power for the cars; the 1898 feeder system had been completed, and it was anticipated that all three traction batteries could be

43

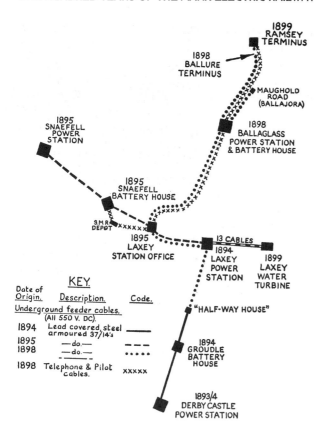

The electrical feeder system as evolved by 1899. (JCC)

kept charged by turbine, allowing the steam stations to be shut down each winter. At this time the peak summer load on the three power stations had reached 2,200hp, all produced from coal imported from South Wales. Even so, further extensions were contemplated, including an enormous brick chimney to be duly dated "1899".

The turbine power plant was designed by Joshua Shaw, with F Nell as consultant. Nell also supplied the turbines and pipework. The associated civil engineering was the responsibility of Harry Curphey, AMICE, who had been one of the company's 1894 apprentices. A headwork consisting of a concrete

Galloway boilers at Ballaglass, 1922. Those at both Laxey and Douglas were similar, but of smaller dimensions. (Rev B Kelly)

weir 40ft long and 4ft 6ins high was first built across the river, after which the water passed through a first settling tank, then 826ft of head race, a second settling tank, and 820ft of 3ft diameter x $\frac{1}{8}$-inch steel pipes. Considerable trouble was taken to avoid the entry of mineral residue. A total fall of 41ft was obtained by taking water some distance above the steam power plant and discharging direct into Laxey harbour. The fall from the level of the weir to the centre of the turbines was 26ft, the remaining 15ft fall being obtained by "draft tubes". A 10ft wide tail race, 624ft in length, took the water to the harbour.

The new equipment was housed in a turbine house, 30ft by 16ft and 13ft 3ins high to the eaves. Two independent Victor 70hp 12-inch horizontal turbines were provided, in a common casing with the shafts direct-coupled; at low water one turbine only could be used. The running speed was 720rpm, driving a combined bipolar dynamo and booster by the Electric Construction Co, giving 160 amps at 520 volts. The friction clutch drive permitted its use as an ordinary motor-driven booster in the summer when the river was very low. All the machines were provided with self-lubricating bearings. The mains from the generator and booster, and their regulating wires (totalling 15 cables) were carried overhead to

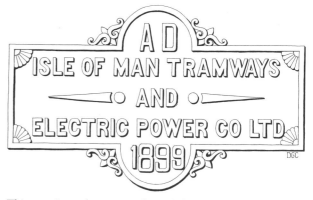

This cast iron plate once adorned the head box of the Laxey turbine plant — it was between three and four feet in length, and was only removed during the Sixties. (DGC)

the steam power station 1,100 ft upstream, from which the turbines were initially controlled, two Lundell $\frac{1}{4}$hp motors (powered from a small battery) being used to open and close the turbine regulators. Switch panels for the plant were thus included in the main switchboard in the steam station*.

The turbine plant was normally worked in parallel with the three battery substations, each now containing 250 cells of the Chloride 'R' type. The turbine generator thus assisted the batteries when under load, as well as providing charging current. During the night, the booster was put in series with the generator, and the batteries charged at a heavy rate through the underground feeders, enabling a full load to be maintained on the turbines over the 24 hours. It was hoped that the steam plant might now

---

* See *The Electrician* of January 26, 1900 for a detailed account.

be shut down for seven months of the year, but this was found to be over-optimistic. Plans were also prepared in 1899 for a similar plant at Ballaglass, with a weir below the tramway bridge and a 1,470ft trench leading at a gradient of 1 in 2,000 to the proposed turbine plant.

On December 17, 1899, Bruce performed what was to be his last public duty by starting the Laxey turbines; within a few months he was to be a dying man. The turbine plant successfully completed a 240-hour continuous test, and regular working commenced on December 27. In October, a six per cent preference and 7$^{1}/_{2}$ per cent ordinary dividend had been declared for the six months to June 30.

Nine months earlier, on January 6, 1899, W E Young had resigned the secretaryship, for the company was seriously overspent and he could not stomach the publication of the forthcoming balance sheet. But, he kept his complaints private other than to the auditors, and so when, at 10am on Saturday,

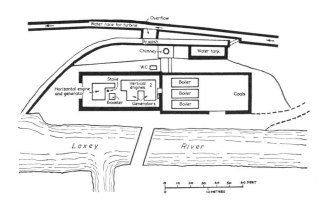

Laxey steam power station as evolved by 1899. (SB)

February 3, 1900, Dumbell's Bank suddenly closed, the entire Manx community was taken by surprise. The apparent cause was the withdrawal of an underwriting of February 1 by Parrs Bank, authorised by Bruce from his home when he was already seriously ill. The IOMT & EP immediately dismissed 100 quarry workmen.

On Monday, February 12, J A Mylrea had to tell his fellow bank shareholders that the "absolute, most implicit confidence" placed in Bruce and manager Shimmon had been "grossly betrayed". The bank had, in fact, two major undisclosed liabilities. By March 17 it emerged that the loan of £65,000 to the Laxey-Ramsey "separate undertaking" had not come from England, but from Dumbell's, which then borrowed a like sum from the English bank concerned, and the whole landslide apparently started when the mainland bank wanted its money back from Dumbell's. By May 12, the true cost of the IOMT & EP lines emerged — £518,000, of which only £366,000 had been raised. The general undertaking's share capital was only £165,000, and the IOMT & EP owed about £150,000 to Dumbell's Bank, while Ramsey line land claims await-

ing arbitration still totalled some £20,000. Payment of dividends totalling £15,646 had been made out of capital!

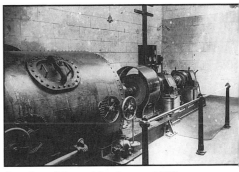

Interior of the turbine house, 1899. (MER)

By June 9, warrants were issued for Nelson, Bruce, Shimmon, W & H Aldred (the tramway auditors) and J D Rogers. Bruce (in bed since March) had been showing signs of recovery, and had written letters in his own defence, but now he experienced a severe relapse and the High Bailiff accepted without question evidence that his arrest would be fatal.

The IOMT & EP board had met on February 7 and, frightened by its financial position, called upon Turquand Young & Co to make a special audit, which took 59 days. This 51-page audit was based on the working for 1899, and it was a gloomy one. Dividends had been paid "other than out of profits" since 1896, and in December 1897, when securing the £65,000 loan, debentures had been issued with promissory notes as a charge against the separate undertaking (one for £35,000 and another for £30,000) for which the latter general undertaking was charged with £30,000 as collateral security. The year 1899 had seen a working loss of £402, and the constructional costs for Laxey-Ramsey now emerged as £111,750 for civil engineering and permanent way, and £41,662 for overhead, cars and power. The trolley conversion cost was given as £2,821. Unpaid calls on ordinary and preference shares totalled £7,113. No further scandals were uncovered, and the criticisms raised by Turquand Young were more an exercise in book-keeping logic. Despite all this, Aldred Sons & Turner produced an optimistic balance sheet for 1899 on May 5.

The company's meeting was held late, on Thursday, May 24. J R Cowell, a director since March 1899, presided, and with him were Mylrea, F G

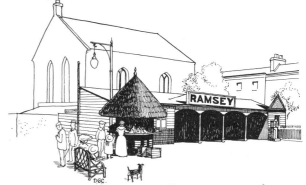

The wooden station once at Ballure, as re-erected at Ramsey. The kiosk conceals the second "gablet" — this type of sales point was another IoMT&EP lineside feature, appearing at Garwick, Laxey and Dhoon. (DGC)

Callow and Dr Farrell, along with Joshua Shaw and F Browne. Dhoon Quarry was by now completely closed, and the hotels let off. The railway service had been kept going, but all the time English creditors were proceeding against the company. A minor point of interest was the repudiation of Bruce's further order to Colonel Bonner for six more wagons. Cowell explained that while the audit had been in progress he had sought interviews with several English banks to whom money was owed, begging more time and asking for capital in the form of a loan, but this failed, as did requests for help from London financiers.

In desperation, Cowell had tried to sell the entire concern, so as to give a fair return to the shareholders — but potential buyers could see the likely opportunity of getting hold of the line from a liquidator for less. The total capital needed to put the concern on its feet was £150,000. Coming to the Snaefell Mountain Railway purchase, Cowell defended the transaction as a perfectly open and fair one, though he admitted that the Laxey and Ramsey section's earning power was inadequate to cover even the money already spent on it: ill tidings indeed for its shareholders. He then detailed the various debts on capital; until 1895 things had been kept straight, but overspending thereafter had been £533 in 1896, £22,587 in 1897, £12,010 in 1898, and £51,861 in 1899 — a total of £86,991. Excusing the board's apparent acquiescence, he blamed Bruce for everything, but praised Joshua Shaw who had latterly "carried" the whole concern, as both engineer and secretary.

A plausibly-explained rider by Aldred Sons & Turner to their accounts for 1898 was then produced, which effectively exonerated both themselves, and Cowell and his fellow directors. Cowell ended by proposing acceptance of the 1899 accounts, and suggested that a committee drawn from shareholders should look further into affairs with the board, which was agreed. Though his speech had been given a quiet hearing, Cowell's proposal to adopt the 1899 accounts was defeated; speakers condemned the board and Bruce repeatedly, but excused Cowell, who had been either busy in America or ill at home for much of 1899.

The Snaefell Association had clearly made a very smart deal for itself, the shares of members reaching one and a half times their par value at the time of sale. W E Young was present, and the facts of his resignation came out; he had first protested at a profit of £6,000 made by the general undertaking from a contract for the new line, which the board then relinquished, but when in September of the same year Bruce announced a £10,000 profit from the same source (and a 7^1/$_2$ per cent interim dividend), Young gave notice and left. After more exchanges on the subject of Snaefell, all adjourned until June 15.

The resumed meeting that day was as lengthy as that of May 24, and even more disjointed. The shareholders' committee held fruitless discussions with the board, and two factions now emerged; those who hoped to find more capital, and those who favoured liquidation, knowing that a liquidator and receiver would rescue all he could. The latter group, largely debenture holders, was accused of seeking to scuttle in its own interests. Meanwhile, a creditor (Robert Okell) had lodged a petition in court to wind up the company, and it was finally decided to adjourn until Tuesday, June 19, the day following the court hearing.

On Monday, June 18, the Clerk of the Rolls presided, and in his dealing with the petitioner showed that the company had at least some sympathy in the Island courts. By this time, however, the company lacked directors, as Mylrea had resigned (His Honour: "Who has he resigned to?"). Farrell, who was in court, later protested that he, Mylrea and Callow were still directors, but to no avail, and the Clerk of the Rolls adjourned the petition until Thursday. At the adjourned company meeting on June 19, Farrell was re-elected to directorship, with newcomers Messrs Ward, Harrison, Clare, Shackleton, Hodson, and Dr Edward Hopkinson, and a supporting committee of shareholders.

Appearing at court on June 20, the new board obtained an extension of grace until July 11, and were willing that a receiver (W H Walker) be appointed. Meanwhile, though, he was not to interfere with Shaw's management of the line, of which all approved. At the court hearing of July 11, no further progress had been made by the company towards self-salvation, and liquidation was enforced with W H Walker as receiver. His appointment was confirmed by the Clerk of the Rolls on July 25, and all the familiar names hereafter vanish from the scene.

The order for sale was not made until July 3, 1901, and by then a historically invaluable liquidator's book, largely the work of Mr Ramsey B Moore, later Attorney-General, was ready for circulation. Apparently, even in mid-1901, the company's paper affairs, especially concerning land purchase, were still in an appalling state.

The bank trial took place in Douglas from from November 5-19, 1900, and the five accused present were found guilty. Shimmon and Nelson each received sentences of eight years penal servitude, and Aldred senior, then 75, escaped with six months hard labour. Bruce was not there, for he had died at 2am on Saturday, July 14, the news of the liquidation being perhaps the last blow. His funeral the following Tuesday was an occasion for public curiosity, and some older Manx folk continued to believe that the coffin contained but stones, and that Bruce escaped. More realistically, and fairly, the Press admitted that "had Mr Bruce died a year ago, half Douglas would have followed his coffin".

Chapter 4

The Manx Electric Takeover

The popular OPEN and CLOSED ELECTRIC CARS along the COAST ROUTE, noted for its COAST AND MOUNTAIN VIEWS.
M E R publicity folder

AT 11AM ON SEPTEMBER 7, 1901, TENDERS for the purchase of the liquidated undertaking were opened. The offers, which included one from the British Electric Traction Company, lay between £188,850 and £225,000, the latter for all five lines (horse, cable, and three electric). Douglas Corporation's final offer of £50,000 for the horse and cable lines was accepted on September 25, but the liquidator was dissatisfied with the others, and things dragged on until January 1902, when a prominent merchant banker of Continental origin (representing himself as "a Manchester syndicate") offered £250,000 for the electric lines, and this was accepted. The sale was sanctioned by the Clerk of the Rolls on September 5, 1902, the final figure being £252,000, and completion was to be by November 14.

Royal journey inside No 59 August 25, 1902: Whilst still under the control of the liquidator, the line enjoyed a Royal visit which provided suitable publicity for many years. (Manx National Heritage)

A new company, the Manx Electric Railway Company, was incorporated on November 12, 1902. Its leading figures were Ernest Schenk (nominee for the purchaser), A G Kitching, William H Vaudrey, and Bernard E Greenwell, most of whom had interests in overseas railways, mainly in South America. The registered office was in London, at 78 Cornhill. Schenk, who changed his name in 1913 to Remnant, had a numerous personal directorships including the Crystal Palace Company, the South Manchurian Syndicate, and the Yorkshire Electric Tramways Construction Syndicate. The Greenwell family were noted London stockbrokers, and took up the lion's share of the new MER's capital. Boscawen and Vaudrey were later knighted, and Greenwell became a baronet. The purchase price paid by the new company to the "Manchester syndicate" on November 30 was £370,000....

Meanwhile, in December 1901, Joshua Shaw, general manager and engineer of the IOMT & EP since January 1899 had resigned. His successor as engineer of the future Manx Electric system was IOMT & EP employee Frank Edmondson, then about 27 years old, and earlier a product of Dr Farrell's Victoria College and Owen's College, Manchester. Later in 1902, the new owners appointed as manager Harold Brown, a young self-made Manxman who had begun his working career with the Steam Packet company, where he had rapidly risen to take charge of the goods department at Douglas. One of Shaw's last engineering tasks before departure had been the erection in 1901 of a three-span wooden footbridge over the line at Ballagorry cutting, replaced in the 1950s by a neat MER-built concrete structure.

On August 25, 1902 the coast electric line, then still administered by the liquidator of the IOMT & EP, was the scene of a royal journey. Landing from the Royal Yacht at Ramsey during their post-Coronation cruise, King Edward VII and Queen Alexandra drove in carriages from Ramsey to Kirk Michael, Peel, Tynwald Hill and Douglas, and returned to Ramsey by the electric railway. At Derby Castle, where the double-deck horse cars formed a convenient grandstand at 2d per patron, their Majesties were greeted by a guard of honour, Hall Caine, and a band, plus local dignitaries. Draped in royal purple, the saloon trailer No 59 was coupled to one of the 19-22 series motor cars, with the late Harry Quayle as conductor and William Hunter as motorman, and made a fast run to Ramsey, with Edmondson as accompanying guide. The MER still possesses a handsome brass plate commemorating this visit, and for many years used the Royal Route slogan in its publicity. The royal trip ended at Walpole Drive, from where an open carriage, drawn by fishermen, conveyed the royal party to Ramsey pier.

The authorised capital of the new Manx Electric Railway Company was £500,000, half in shares and half in debenture stock. Of the share capital, half was to be in ordinary shares and half in 5^1/$_2$ per cent preference shares. By March 1903, £200,000 of the share capital and £170,000 of the 4¹/₂ per cent debenture stock had been raised, largely by the Greenwells. The first statutory meeting of the new company was held in Douglas late in February 1903, under Bernard E Greenwell's chairmanship. The purchase agreement of November 13, 1902 included retrospective adjustment to August 18, and since that date £12,239 had been earned and £8,152 spent; debenture interest had absorbed £4,726. Mileage run had been 146,187 for passengers, and 16,556 for goods, including "company's service".

Permanent way superintendent Robert Newell reported on the entire coastal line, as inspected early in 1903. Alarmingly, there was scarcely one mile of "good" track between Douglas and Laxey, and no serious attempt at ballasting had been made until March 1900; instead, a dressing of stone had simply been put on top of the earth ballast. The drains soon filled with earth, due to vibration, and the sleepers had so deteriorated in six or seven years that Newell had already put in 6,000 new sleepers and reballasted accordingly, until stopped by the liquidation. Fencing repairs were another headache, especially as the sharing of the responsibility between Douglas Bay Estates and the tramway company had never been properly settled. Some of Newell's requirements must have caused rather a shock to the new owners — he wanted 120 tons of rail, up to 20,000 tons of stone ballast, and new sleepers to the tune of 5,200, for

Among the new company's inherited assets were the quarries at Ballajora and (after re-purchase) Dhoon. This is the layout at Ballajora and from which much stone was shortly to be taken for ballasting improvements (1904). (DGC)

Douglas-Laxey alone.

On the Ramsey section, less work was needed, apart from local ballasting and alignment of the 62¹/₂lbs per yard rail, and the sleepers were appreciably better. The new company disliked the partially cantilevered 1898 tracks at Bulgham, and its consulting civil engineer, Douglas Cooper, had met Highway Board officials at Bulgham the previous October. It was decided to move the tracks on to the solid rock (within today's sinuously curved retaining wall), and to move the public road in by a similar amount by cutting back the cliff. Leave was given to close the road for six months from January 1903, and the work was already under way by the end of February. In their first year, £1,240 was spent on this, and another £3,332 followed during the next; completion was delayed by a landslip, and was not finally achieved until October 1904. Some 46,735 tons of spoil had been removed from Bulgham by the end of 1903.

How many of Newell's other ambitions were fulfilled is a little difficult to say. He raised and ballasted the Douglas-Laxey track during 1904, and put in some very heavy rails at the various road crossings, about 100 tons of 85lbs per yard rail being bought for this purpose. He also advocated (and obtained) a crossover at Ballameanagh, where the locomotive had been obliged to run many dead miles in shunting during reballasting work. Another request remained unfulfilled; Newell was worried about the lack of catch points on the long up grades and, when taking a run, he had made a practice of riding in the last wagon of the train from whence he could (in case of run-back) apply a brake. During the next few years, the drains, hedges and platforms were completed or improved, and several interrupted curves were converted into easier continuous ones.

On the electrical side, the new company was also penalised. By 1902 Ferranti's work on AC supply had utterly discredited DC generation and distribution, and the slow reciprocating steam power plant was equally obsolescent. Immediately on taking possession, the new company asked the engineering consultants, Messrs Kincaid, Waller, Manville & Dawson, of Westminster, to report on how to bring the line up to modern (1903) technical standards.

Dhoon Quarry was first leased by Bruce in 1895, and later appears to have been purchased outright, then re-sold, as the MER recorded its re-purchase during the financial year 1902-3. The permanent way "department" had extensive facilities here, too (see plan details). (DGC/JCC)

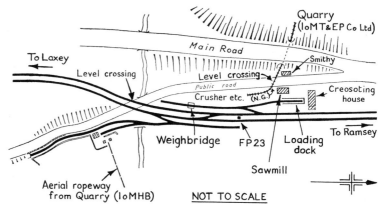

48

Mr Dawson's report, which was accepted in toto, recommended a change to AC generation and distribution, and re-equipment of the cars. Tenders were invited, and the major contract was awarded on February 16, 1903 to Witting, Eborall & Co, which submitted the lowest of three tenders.

Some specific points in Dawson's report are given attention in an article published by the Isle of Man Railway Society early in 1991. The consultants were somewhat surprised to find the tramway had neither a wheel lathe nor a press, and discovered that the ECC cars had in some respects a design fault, electrically speaking — their performance had accordingly been marginally improved by the conversion of the field circuits from parallel to series — the original arrangements had seen the cars most economic performance reached at about 17.5mph, whereas the cars frequently climbed at much lower speeds. At the time considerable effort was being devoted to a scheme for operating four-car sets, apparently with two trailers "sandwiched" between two motors. The consultants' wish to see air-braking was met when the Christensen equipment arrived: their remarks as to the complete obsolescence of the 1893-4 motor equipments stated the obvious.

Laxey steam power station, which lay nearest to harbour facilities, was selected as the hub of the new AC system, and the generating side was reconstructed in the five months to July, 1903. The Galloway boilers were augmented by two Climax cylindrical vertical water-tube boilers by B Rowland & Co of Reddish (Stockport), 12ft in diameter and 23ft high, which could raise steam to a level of 150lbs per square inch, in 30 minutes and produced 11,000lbs per hour at a working pressure of 165lbs per square inch. Each had a self-contained 75ft steel chimney, 44ins in diameter, and mild-steel steam pipes to the two new engines. The auxiliaries comprised a surface condensing plant by Mirrlees & Watson, and two Weir feed pumps.

The new engines were totally-enclosed Bellis & Morcom triple expansion machines of 400 horse-

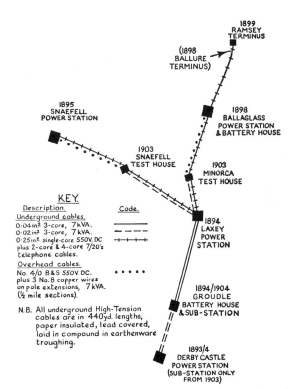

The new AC distribution system, as superimposed on the DC feeders of 1899. (JCC)

power, Nos 1702 and 1956, the three cylinders having respective diameters of 12, 17 and 26 inches and a 13-inch stroke. The working pressure was 155lbs per square inch, and the running speed, 375rpm. These drove two 300kW revolving field alternators with star-connected armatures, producing three-phase alternating current at 7,000 volts, 25 cycles. They were built to a special ultracompact design evolved by the Société l'Électricité et l'Hydraulique of Charleroi, Belgium, forerunners of the present ACEC company. The Galloway boilers and the Robb-Armstrong engine were retained, as was the water-turbine plant, but the 1894 Galloway/Mather & Platt sets were removed and offered for sale. The new high-tension switchgear was placed in a special fireproof annexe, and was remotely controlled from a nine-panel white marble switchboard erected above the old low-tension board.

On the distribution system, the work was divided between Henley's (underground) and R W Blackwell (overhead). The old underground DC feeders were retained as part of the distribution network, and were still capable of use in the 1970s — a wonderful tribute to their makers. The 7,000-volt supply was taken through the new AC feeders to rotary converter sub-stations at Douglas, Groudle, Ballaglass and Snaefell, and to similar equipment inside the Laxey power station. The sub-stations contained six-pole rotary convertors by

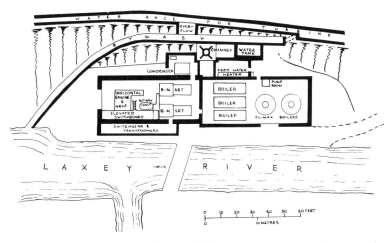

Laxey power station as revised after 1903's reconstruction of the generating plant. (SB)

The number of new vehicles seen among the six depicted suggests a visit by the Directorate, especially noting the winter vegetation. This is perhaps early in 1905: the canopy still carried the IoMT&EP's inscription. (NTM)

Kolben & Co, of Prague, with a speed of 500rpm and a rating of 150kW at 330/550 volts, 25 cycles, designed for alternative compound or simple wound operation, and fed through pairs of 75kW Kolben transformers. These were air-cooled when first installed but converted later to oil cooling. The rotary converter at Laxey was started from the DC side by means of the Groudle battery plant.*

At Douglas, the 1893-4 generating plant was taken out of use, and the rotary and its six-panel marble switchboard went into the engine room. The Galloway/Mather & Platt sets were dismantled and offered for sale. The Bellis alternator set used for the public supply was split, the engine being sold and replaced by a 75hp motor supplied by Witting, Eborall & Co. One rotary converter was placed in Laxey power station, and two more (each with a four-panel switchboard) in the Ballaglass one, of which one set was intended for Snaefell. The other converters were placed in a new stone substation building at Groudle, measuring 44ft by 30ft and completed by April 1904. The Groudle battery was augmented by a new 260-cell Tudor battery with a capacity of 560 ampère-hours, and by a new 72hp 160-amp Swiss-built booster set of R Thury type by the Electrical Industry Co of Geneva, which remained in use until 1944. An eight-panel marble switchboard completed the new plant here.

The new generating plant was first run in July 1903, and the AC distribution network was ready for tests in December. During preparations for these tests, No 1 Bellis alternator suffered a serious short circuit, consuming five coils; the culprit turned out

to be a mouse whose charred remains were later discovered in the machine frame. Late in December, the overhead high-tension lines to Ballaglass were commissioned, and withstood 7,500 volts for an hour without trouble, despite a wet day. These lines were carried on timber extensions from the overhead standards. The rule book warned the crews not to mistake the AC overhead feeder between Minorca and Ballaglass for a trolley wire! The new system was completed during 1904, when one Mather & Platt 1895 set was removed from the Snaefell mountain power station and the spare rotary converter from Ballaglass (with its four switchgear panels and twin transformers) was installed in its

The details of an MER repaint (especially on the older cars) were cleverly contrived to impose a marked "house style" irrespective of the varying body designs. (Manx National Heritage)

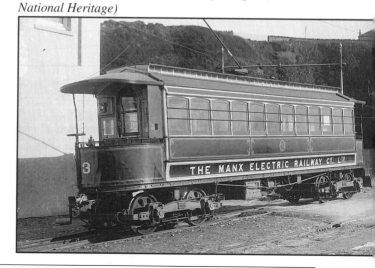

---

* Many of the details in this text are taken from the Light Railway and Tramway Journal of March 4, 1904.

place, fed by an already completed 7,000-volt pole-mounted line from Laxey; this line now carries 6,600 volts AC to the present-day rectifiers.

Coal for the Laxey power station was brought up from the harbour by cart, but in February 1904, Edmondson proposed a special electric railway from the quay to the power station. This would have been isolated from the main system, but in 1906 final surveys were made for a longer branch tramway continuing up to the main line. In the event, neither line was built. The Laxey station now operated from 6.30am until midnight during the summer, and in winter it was steamed intermittently to compensate for water deficiency at the turbine plant. The longest runs with turbines and batteries alone averaged three to four weeks. Ballaglass power station from 1904 ran only during the summer, and attempts were made (against Edmondson's advice) to sell off the entire Snaefell plant, but this plan was dropped and partial steam working at Snaefell continued until September 3, 1924, after which a second 1903 rotary converter was transferred from Laxey. This came into use in 1925.

Coal consumption was now reduced to between 2,000 and 3,000 tons per year. Staffing on the generation side remained at about 23; the Laxey steam station had two drivers (who in winter worked as fitters), four shift firemen, two shift trimmers, two switchboard men and one or two apprentices. Laxey

Trailers 40 to 43 carried this elegant Hadley Castle transfer in green, gold, black and bronze. (JCC)

turbine house now had a night attendant, Ballaglass had an attendant for the rotaries, an engine driver, a fireman and an apprentice, Snaefell had one fireman, an engine driver and an apprentice, the Groudle sub-station was manned on a shift basis, and Derby Castle had an apprentice tending its rotary converter and an additional man on the AC lighting supply plant. The staffing of the Snaefell plant seems to imply only partial working, probably on busy afternoons.

Re-equipment of the cars by Witting, Eborall & Co was spread over two years, for the successful summer season of 1903 demanded full use of the rolling stock. A welcome result was a reduction in the standard journey time for the Douglas-Laxey run to 30 minutes; before the four-motor ECC cars were brought in in 1898, the best time had been 35-40 minutes, reflecting the low power of the 1893 and 1894 equipments. The load was then limited to one

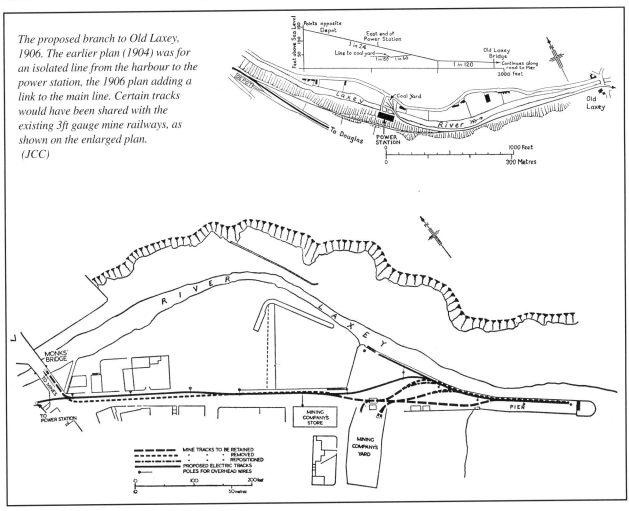

The proposed branch to Old Laxey, 1906. The earlier plan (1904) was for an isolated line from the harbour to the power station, the 1906 plan adding a link to the main line. Certain tracks would have been shared with the existing 3ft gauge mine railways, as shown on the enlarged plan. (JCC)

The Manx Electric Railway Company, Ltd.

Station...................................... Date.............................191

Quarry......................................

Goods Rolling Stock Daily Return.

	ON HAND			LOADED			
	Loaded	Empty	Required	In	Out	Station for	CLASS OF GOODS.
Vans Nos. 3 4 11 12							
Mail Vans Nos. 15 16							
Parcel Vans Nos. 13 14							
Freight Car							
Motor Cattle Wagon							
Sheep Trailers							
Dismantled Trailers Nos.							
Open Wagons Nos. 1 2 5 6 7 8 9 10							
O/149							

REMARKS ————————————————

Agent————————————

A page of the goods stock daily register, from which the then-current fleet may be deduced (See Chapter 9). (MER)

light trailer or a goods wagon, but not both. Joshua Shaw, before 1900, quoted the weight of a train as 8½ tons for the motor-car, plus three tons of passengers, and a 4-ton trailer with three tons of passengers, or a 1½-ton wagon with a 6-ton payload. The 1898 ECC equipment (as modified?) gave a better performance, recorded on test in 1901 with No 21 hauling two 1899 trailers from Douglas to Laxey at an average speed of 15.23mph, with an average current consumption of 104.72 ampères. If the average was calculated so as to include the periods of coasting, the consumption on this run worked out at only 65 ampères. Three-car trains, as in this example, were (in 1968) only run with empty stock (as when pairs of lightweight trailers were hauled to Ramsey for winter storage).

The first winter's working by the new company was somewhat unrepresentative. The new company's financial year ended on September 30, and the next annual meeting was held in London on January 26, 1904, to adopt the accounts for the period from August 18, 1902 to September 30, 1903. Car miles had been 448,639 (passenger) and 39,237 (goods and company's service), and traffic overall was 20 per cent up on earlier years. Earnings were £41,000 against costs of £20,435, enabling debenture interest and preference interest to be paid and the equivalent of 3¼ per cent on the ordinary shares to be carried forward to the following year.

On the capital side, the issued capital had reached £395,098, but expenditure already came to £400,042. The bill for new works now totalled £44,399, plus £3,332 spent on Bulgham and £1,508 in purchasing Dhoon quarry. A new 16-car depot 150ft 6ins by 40ft (by Carine) and a large goods shed were in hand at Laxey, and a goods shed at Ramsey, where the layout was altered. New waiting shelters were being erected at out-of-town locations, new trailer cars had arrived from the Hadley Castle works of G F Milnes, and much of the work on re-equipping the cars had been carried out. A further £20,584 was spent in the following year, bringing the total outlay to £420,455. By September 1905, this figure had risen to £422,605, of which nearly £6,000 was for new vehicles.

Below: The energetic development of goods traffic also produced this scheme for a siding to Corlett's Laxey flour mills, drawn by R B Newell in 1911. (JCC)

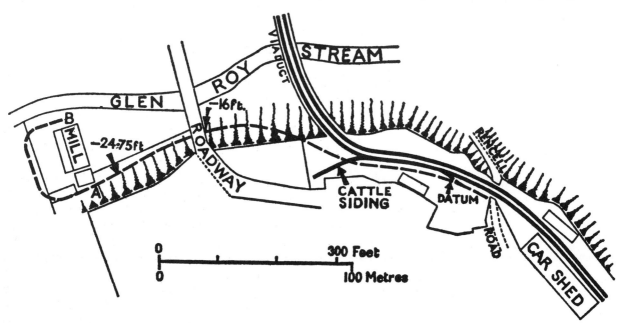

The company meeting of January 3, 1905 must have found the summer results of 1904 rather disappointing; only 472,556 passengers had been carried as against 557,346 in 1903. Car miles for 1904 were 378,721 (passenger) and 58,901 (goods). No ordinary dividend was paid, and the year's balance of some £780 was carried forward. The next year, 1905, was better, with 501,696 passengers and 359,960 car miles (plus 38,732 for goods), and the expenses/receipts ratio had improved from 56/44 to 47/53. Preference shareholders continued to receive their $5^1/_2$ per cent, and the debenture interest was always paid, but there was still no dividend on the ordinary shares.

The Preston works photographer (E Hoole) was typically on form when recording 28's debut in 1904 as indeed was an unknown Douglas cameraman with respect to 58. The style differences of 28-31 as to their Milnes' predecessors are fairly small (clerestory detail in large part) but with 57 and 58 the strongly emphasised Preston style is fully in evidence. (MER — top picture; Manx National Heritage— lower)

Perhaps fortunately, the majority shareholding, both ordinary and preference, lay in the hands of the Greenwells, who looked on the line as a family concern. In later years their losses were considerable, and theirs was a charitable financial dynasty from the Island's viewpoint. It was thus rather unjust that the line was now regarded as the disliked "outsider" in the corridors of Manx financial power. The 1905 payments of $4^1/_2$ per cent on £200,000, $5^1/_2$ per cent on £127,500 and nothing on £100,000 would, if rearranged as a flat rate, pay just under four per cent on the whole capital as at that date.

There had, in the mean-

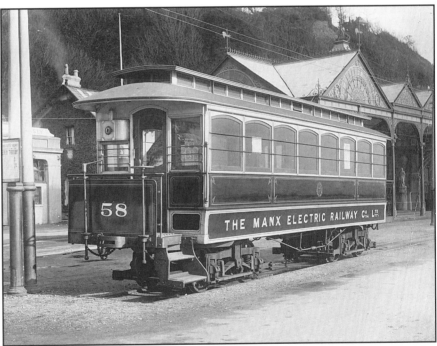

time, occurred a second attempt by the electric line to take over the Manx Northern Railway. By April 1904 the Manx Northern was rapidly drifting into the hands of the IMR, which had worked the line, with government approval, since February. Vondy of the MNR favoured the MER cause, and tried to have the sale to the IMR deferred for a month, though rumours that the MER had already made an offer were unfounded. Edmondson put up a case for purchase to MER secretary C A Huni, considering that, on a capital of £75,000, the line would be valuable as an adjunct to the MER and would confine IMR activity to the southern half of the island.

Following a wire from Huni, conveyed via

Edmondson, Vondy had met MNR chairman Todhunter, talking until ten at night, and had then arranged a further meeting between Edmondson and the MNR chairman and directors for April 12. However, they failed to appear, and later that day a shareholders' meeting, fearing an IMR withdrawal, rejected any postponement. Edmondson then suggested to Huni that the MER should advertise the fact that it could have improved on the IMR offer. Director Vaudrey sought to see the Attorney-General, and the IMR, now thoroughly frightened, was rushing its purchase through the House of Keys with all possible speed. On April 18, Huni wrote to Edmondson to say that the MER board had decided

No 57/8's interiors had all the refined detail of their Preston contemporaries, then appearing on tramways in several continents. (MER)

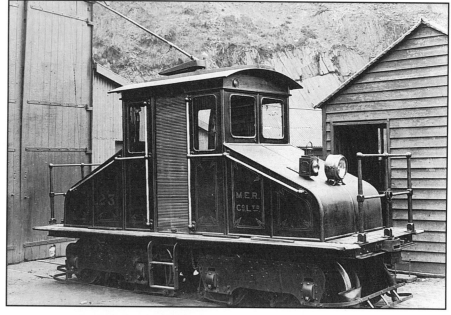

Locomotive 23 soon after re-lettering in MER style (as built it proclaimed "IoMT&EP". (MER)

MER staff, about 1907: Manager Harold Brown is fourth from left on the second row with engineer Frank Edmondson on his left. On the extreme right of the same row is Robert Newell, the permanent way superintendent. The two back rows consist of station-masters. (Rev B Kelly)

to withdraw, and the Act of Tynwald allowing an IMR takeover was passed on May 24, 1904. The two companies were finally merged as from April 19, 1905, and the price was a mere £60,000 — poor comfort for the MNR shareholders who got only 14s for each preference share and 9s for each ordinary share.

The construction in 1903 of goods depots for the MER reflected a determined effort by manager Harold Brown to offset the unbalanced working season. At liquidation, there were 12 orthodox goods vehicles (Nos 1-12) and the three Bonner wagons, together with a locomotive (No 23) which ran on bogies borrowed seasonally from a passenger car. Early in 1903, passenger car No 12 was converted to a bogie motor cattle vehicle, and further vehicles were added in subsequent years. During the agricultural peak period each spring, seatless 1893 trailers were pressed into service to carry bagged patent manure. The company was out for business in no uncertain terms, and traders' tickets were issued to Ramsey at 1s 6d return to those who undertook to send all their goods via MER. An even larger goods shed was built at Douglas in 1908, on the site of the 1893 boiler house, where it still stands (though recently modified).

By March 1912, goods stock had increased to 29 vehicles, excluding the Bonner wagons, which were never listed as stock by the MER, although certainly used for some years; their unrecorded demise is an exasperating mystery. Traffic had grown to cover a wide range of goods, and Mr William Duggan, former goods manager, remembers particularly the cattle rush for the Christmas Mart, horses for the Whitehaven boat sailing, up to 200 tons of flour for Corlett's mill at Laxey, and a regular 200-package total of luggage for the Steam Packet sailing on Friday night. The stone traffic from Dhoon quarries continued, usually in trains of two six-ton wagons hauled by locomotive No 23 and trans-shipped to road vehicles at Derby Castle terminus close by the booking office. Dhoon granite setts were exported to the mainland and widely used on the Island, and the quarries (latterly one on each side of the line) supplied lower-grade roadstone until 1961-3.

In addition to the goods and parcels traffic (including milk) provided by traders and farmers, the line was extensively used by the Post Office. The origins of this service go back to at least 1894, and an 1895 minute to the Postmaster-General refers to "Kirk Onchan & Laxey Posts; revised service by Electric Tramway". By 1897 postmen were using the line to travel to Half-Way House, and in 1899 bagged mail traffic was instituted between the Douglas and Ramsey sorting offices. From July 1903 the formal arrangements for the carriage of the mails became even more sophisticated, with MER conductors being recognised as Auxiliary Postmen (it seems likely that this simply formalised the "status quo", as timed collections from lineside

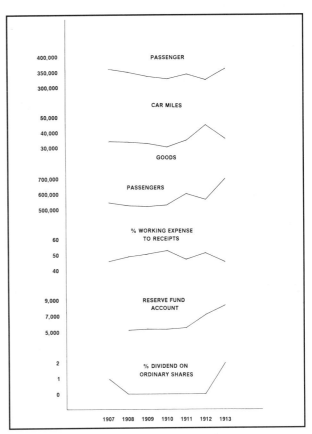

Traffic and Finance, 1907-13. Over this period, reserves hovered at around the £5,300 level, rising to £8,615 for 1913. (SB)

boxes had already begun). By the mid-1900s mail traffic saw three van journeys north and two south each weekday — the southbound trips also cleared the letter boxes. By the Thirties there were to be three van journeys each way, daily, during the high season. There were also formal arrangements for handling the considerable volume of mail posted at Snaefell summit, where the company had a non-GPO posting box, its contents being "transferred" to the Post Office at Laxey by adding the locked bag concerned to the afternoon load of mailbags destined for Douglas. The operation of mail services during the Sixties is detailed in Chapter 6, and their final years are covered in Chapter 8.

The Island's 1906 season was a record-breaker, and the MER carried 535,021 passengers and earned £34,279. Mileages run were 368,152 passenger and 43,541 goods. A reserve fund for special renewals was invested in securities or in South American railway shares; this totalled £4,066 15s by 1907. The capital structure was overhauled, £2,500 being cancelled, leaving £475,000. The new cars and trailers delivered in 1906, and the opening on August 10 of the new Snaefell Summit hotel, completed the physical re-equipment of the line, stabilising the capital account. Results for the years 1907-13 are, therefore, presented in the form of a graph. In 1907, a dividend of one per cent was at last paid on the ordinary shares.

In 1906, the company had bought Laxey Glen and Gardens. First-class military bands were engaged each summer, including the Royal Artillery (Portsmouth) and HM Life Guards, and traffic further increased as a result. The company's involvement in the "Glen Industry" was considerable, and dated back to an agreement of September 28, 1892 between Saunderson (as trustee for the Howstrake Company) and R M Broadbent (the future proprietor of Groudle Glen) whereby the sum of $^3/_4$d was payable to the company for each person entering the glen. Although the Howstrake company's private road began at Derby Castle, the portion to Groudle was free of toll, the toll-house being placed on the corner just beyond the entrance to Groudle Glen; tolls were charged until the late 1920s. Ballaglass Glen was at first rented and later owned by the tramway, and Garwick was the subject of an agreement like that for Groudle, with payments of 1d per head for adults, $^1/_2$d for children, no fare from Douglas to be higher than sixpence. Its importance merited a station 30ft 6ins by 14ft. Dhoon Glen was rented, with a payment of 1$^3/_4$d per head to the owners.

In July 1907, the MER brought in a motor charabanc service from the Bungalow to Tholt-y-Will, at the head of Sulby Glen, where it had built a large rustic tea-room. The licensing returns show two Argus vehicles up to 1913, registrations MN 67 and 68, three for 1914 (the addition being a De Dion, MN 479), and two again after 1917. After the first world war a change was made to 30-seat Caledons (MN 1053 and 1054), with a further change in 1926 to three Model 'T' Ford vehicles, replaced in 1937-9 by two Bedford 20-seat WLBs, MN 8685 and 8686.* In 1907, 42,500 people arrived in the Island over August bank holiday weekend, and the queue for electric cars stretched to the foot of Summer Hill, forcing horse cars to stop short of their terminus.

By this time, the company had resumed possession of all its licensed houses, some of which had previously been let out (and which from 1899 were tied to Isle of Man Breweries). A reference to the loss sustained from unsatisfactory tenancies appears in the liquidator's report of 1901. A hotels manager was appointed look after these activities, which at their maximum comprised six licensed houses, plus the refreshment rooms and a café at Laxey. They included the Strathallan hotel at Douglas, the Laxey Station hotel and the hotels and refreshment rooms at Bungalow, Snaefell, Tholt-y-Will and Dhoon. The large complex at the Dhoon burned down on April 3, 1932 and was not rebuilt. The Ramsey Palace concert hall, purchased in 1897, was always let out, and was finally sold off about 1938; it was later renamed the Plaza when it underwent a facelift as the town cinema. There was also a refreshment kiosk at Ballaglass Glen, with a lady attendant who also collected the admission fees.

The collector of transport ephemera is offered a vast field by the company's excursion publicity and advertising handbills, every possible event in Laxey and Ramsey, and the alluring features of scenes en route, being subjects of this form of advertisement.

A winter timetable from about 1908 provides a source of intermediate timings — note the effects of gradients.

	N'bound	S'bound
Douglas-Groudle	9	(13)*
Groudle-Half Way House	5	5
Half Way House-Garwick	4	6
Garwick-Ballabeg	3	4
Ballabeg-South Cape	4	4
South Cape-Laxey	(5)*	3
Laxey-Minorca	3	3
Minorca-Dhoon	12	9
Dhoon-Glen Mona	5	5
Glen Mona-Ballaglass	4	4
Ballaglass-Ballajora	7	7
Ballajora-Belle Vue	6	6
Belle Vue-Ramsey	(8)*	6

Note: Timings include an allowance for late running.*

Excellent sepia postcards of the line, the scenery, the glens and Snaefell were sold in their tens of thousands, and, as already mentioned, a special postbox was installed at Snaefell summit, with its own special franking (the letters being given a second, orthodox, postmark on reaching Douglas). Until 1914, the company retained a guide at the top of Snaefell, and even sold postcards of him. In later Edwardian years he acquired a fenced platform for about 75 people, from which to deliver his peroration.

During 1906, Frank Edmondson was offered a senior post in Delhi, but stayed with the MER following a salary increase. Mr E Barnes, later in life to return to the line as chief assistant engineer, went to Canada, and in 1907 Harold Brown followed him across the Atlantic. Frank Edmondson was promoted to the position of manager and engineer, and there now came to the MER as chief assistant engineer, Bertram G Kelly, a young Manxman who had previously studied at the Royal Technical College, Glasgow, and had gained practical engineering experience with Lowdon Brothers of Dundee, Cromptons of Chelmsford, the London County Council and the Midland Railway. His father, Captain James Kelly, had many years previously left the Island to become piermaster at Southend-on-Sea, whose pioneer electric tramway had its own power station long before there was any public electricity in the town.

---

* For details of these and later road vehicles, I am indebted to the late Mr W T Lambden.

Edwardian peak traffic, July 1906. (MER)

Earlier attempts to lease and electrify the Douglas horse tramway have already been described (Chapter 1). In 1911, the MER arranged the electric lighting of the promenade as part of a carnival, and the corporation was so impressed that it placed a contract with the Electric Street Lighting Apparatus Company of London for permanent decorative lighting, for which (until 1923) the MER supplied the current. This marks the start of the well-known summer and autumn illuminations.

The winding-up of the Isle of Man Tramways & Electric Power Company was not completed until 1908, when W H Walker made a final payment to creditors. Debenture holders were paid off and creditors received 13s 6d (67.5p) in the pound, but ordinary shareholders got nothing. The final payment to depositors in Dumbell's Bank had been only 3s 4d (16.5p) in the pound. Among those who had lost heavily in the collapse of IOMT & EP and all that it entailed was Frederick Saunderson, AICE, who spent his later years as manager o the Douglas Bay Estate and of the Groudle hotel. He died, aged 71, on July 9, 1911, and was buried in the borough cemetery at Douglas.

In the years before 1914 the MER ratio of costs to receipts reflected credit on its management. Although ordinary shareholders received only two dividends in seven years, three quarters of the stock was in debentures or preference shares, and the substantial interest payments on these underlines the sustained financial stability. The Blackpool and Fleetwood tramway showed better financial performance but had an easier route, a more balanced traffic and a much longer visitor season.

The 1914 season, up to July 13, had been ahead

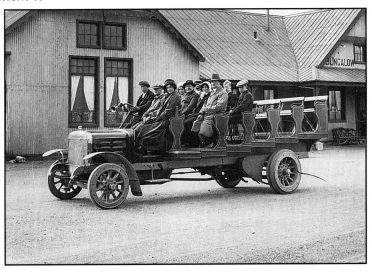

Right: *The charabanc service about to depart for Tholt-e-Will: Argus-built MN67 (or 68) of 1907 at the Bungalow. (NTM)*

of 1913's record performance, but this ended with the declaration of war, even though there was no sudden panic exodus from the Island. In 1914, the number of passengers carried fell to 496,568, and expenses rose to 63.15 per cent of receipts; no dividend was paid on either share category, and an item of £1,000 on further generating plant was to be the last capital expenditure until after the war. Recorded mileages were 305,732 for passenger trains, and 35,488 for goods. Large internment camps at Douglas and Knockaloe ultimately raised the Island's population, but brought little or no traffic. In 1915, passengers carried dropped to 104,224, passenger car miles to 114,373, and goods mileage to 19,346. The Snaefell line was closed, and a debit balance of £9,436 required the issue of second debentures to pay debenture interest for the second half-year. The chairman said that the "state of war entirely destroyed the holiday season in the Island".

The generating equipment referred to in the previous paragraph was a second-hand 750kW (1,000 hp) Parsons turbo-alternator, No 6999, purchased in October 1914, complete with condensers. It dated from 1906, but had been little used and would offer an output exceeding that of two of the Bellis sets, and a higher efficiency. It got as far as Laxey goods shed, and then the war immobilised the project. The restricted service operated in 1914-18 enabled the water turbine plant to sustain the batteries for much longer periods than hitherto, and the steam plant was really needed only at low-water times, when the Laxey Robb-Armstrong engine was used. To provide water for several battery houses, a water-tower was built in 1916-17 alongside the line between Laxey and South Cape, fed from Laxey power station, where the supply barrels could be filled. It is still in situ.

In 1916, the loss climbed to £19,171, and second debentures funded the debenture interest for the entire year. Two directors were at the war, so secretary C A Huni was elected managing director. In the course of the year, 109,959 passenger miles had been run and 111,982 passengers carried, goods mileage being 19,288. Colonel Boscawen left the Board in 1917 to become a member of the British government.

Passengers in 1917 rose to 119,683, with mileages of 111,595 (passenger) and 17,179 (goods), and only £52 was lost on working; the debit balance was now £28,222. On September 24, 1917, fire destroyed the large rustic refreshment room at Laxey, and it was not rebuilt. The year 1918 saw a working profit of £5,812 from 173,000 passengers, 134,315 passenger miles and 22,579 goods miles. Some plant and a charabanc were sold, and the debit balance increased by £3,189 to £31,411.

The bread strike of July 4-5, 1918 saw the MER service halted, in common with all other island transport. The position of the MER employees had shown a parallel slow improvement to that of the corporation tramwaymen; before 1917 wages had been 30s in summer (for any hours) and 24s 6d in winter, but from 1917 they secured a 56-hour week at sixpence an hour. According to Mr Alfred Teare, MBE, a pioneer labour leader, the company was by no means the worst of the Island's employers to deal with, although Frank Edmondson was a tough bargainer in the company's interest.

The physical status of the Manx Electric system had remained quite good during the war, but the accrued deficit of £31,411 was a formidable burden for the future, especially in the light of the increased costs of basic commodities such as coal.

The ultimate in rustic cabins. Erected at Laxey in 1899, it was destroyed by fire in September, 1917. The largest portion formed a refreshment room. (DGC)

Chapter 5

Manx Electric, 1919 to 1956

Everyone who has travelled abroad will recognise an old friend in this railway. It is the counterpart of innumerable friendly little continental railways, and shares their complete disregard for speed. It is like stepping back into the days of our forefathers to experience its pleasant, ambling motion, which is calculated to soothe the most impatient passenger to a quiet appreciation of the charm of this way of travel.
Miss Maxwell Fraser, In Praise of Manxland

WITH THE WAR ENDED, VISITORS WERE soon coming back to the Isle of Man, and to the Manx Electric. The Snaefell line, closed since August 9, 1914, reopened on June 10, 1919. No passenger figures are given in the reports for 1919 or 1920, but 295,426 passenger miles were run on the system in 1919, and 26,477 goods miles. Earnings amounted to £57,102 with a profit margin of £31,501 that enabled all past debt to be wiped off, though debenture interest was again funded by second debentures.

The modernisation of the power supply was now resumed. After a fruitless attempt in 1919 to sell the unused Parsons turbo-alternator in order to buy a diesel plant, it was decided to carry out the scheme envisaged in 1914. The turbo-alternator was installed in the winter of 1919-20 on a new overhead gantry in the Laxey power station, between the old engine room and a new boiler house, and an overhead crane was installed in the enlarged engine room thus formed. By 1921, a new boiler house, separated from the engine room by a wood-framed partition, contained a new installation by the Stirling Boiler Co Ltd, consisting of two 120lbs per square inch water-tube boilers of 8ft 6ins diameter, one with an evaporative capacity of 12,000lbs per hour and the other of 4,000lbs per hour. These replaced the Climax boilers, which were taken out of use as the new units became serviceable; the three Galloway boilers of 1894-8 had been removed before

commencing the new 86ft by 40ft building. The new boiler room was approached by a relocated bridge across the adjoining river, and the flues were connected to a steel plate chimney 135ft 6ins high on an 18ft 7ins plinth, tapering from 8 ft diameter at the base to 6ft at the top. A few years afterwards the chimney was shortened and given a forced-draught fan.

The turbo-alternator was a low voltage machine (400V, 25 cycles, three-phase), and thus required a 400/7,000V step-up transformer, which was supplied by the British Electric Transformer Company, of Hayes. Other auxiliaries were a $9^{1}/_{2}$hp 440V three-phase air pump rnotor by the Mechanical & Electrical Engineering Company, of Walsall, and a 50hp Brook centrifugal pump motor. In 1924 or 1925, the new installation was provided with Hodgkinson motor-driven mechanical stokers.

In 1920, car miles soared to 394,953 passenger and 34,195 goods, Snaefell passengers totalled 84,956, and the line earned £89,780, with a profit of £40,909. This cleared the interest on second mortgage debentures from 1915 to 1920, and enabled the company to pay preference share dividends for 1914 and 1915. The reserve for special renewals now stood at £13,535, and the company's investment account at £64,505. A three-car lean-to annexe was added to the Derby Castle trailer car shed; a consulting engineer's report on post-war policy had lately recommended four new motor cars and two trailers.

The following year, 1921, saw a more sober passenger figure of 667,178, with earnings of £63,708, but the operating ratio rose to 70.21 per cent and the net profit was cut by more than half. Preference share dividend was paid for 1916, and interest on the second mortgage debentures. These totalled £40,500 in 1921 but were then redeemed to £36,000. Only £915 was carried on to the 1922 accounts, and the investment account had shrunk by two thirds. The next year saw preference share interest paid up to 1918, 1923 paid for 1919, and 1924 cov-

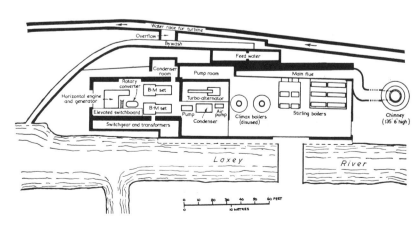

Laxey power station as finally developed and operated between 1921-35. The river bridge carried broad and narrow gauge tracks (for coal and ash?). (SB).

ered 1920; ground was being neither gained nor lost. The second mortgage debentures were now down to £22,500, and in 1925 to £18,000, when arrears of interest were paid up to the start of 1923.

Bertram Kelly, chief assistant to the engineer, left the MER in 1922 to take charge of the construction of Douglas Corporation's first electric power station at North Quay. Corporation supply commenced on May 18, 1923, and Mr Kelly was appointed borough electrical engineer. In October 1925 he gave a prophetic address to the Isle of Man Municipal Association which detailed an almost exact outline of the Island-wide public supply system which would be inaugurated by the Isle of Man Electricity Board in 1932-3. Mr Kelly's retirement, in 1947, was no more then a prelude to

Laxey power station as in 1922. (DGC)

full-time church work; an honorary diocesan Reader since 1919, his ordination 28 years later was the beginning of an intensive second career, for he served three years as curate and then 14 years, from 1950, as vicar of the large parish of Kirk Braddan, widely known for its open-air services — in his bishop's words, "a great work splendidly done".

In 1924, winter service on the MER gave nine northbound and eight southbound weekday journeys, some starting or finishing at Laxey. Saturdays had four extra services in all, but Sundays saw but two cars each way. One morning weekday journey north from Laxey was expressly for schoolchildren. Parcels were collected at 10.00 and 3.00 from a Times branch office in Victoria Street, from "Mr Newby's", Bucks Road, and from the Steam Packet Company's goods offices. The timetable's footnotes included "goods, merchandise, livestock and parcels conveyed between all stations". From 1928 to 1937 a once-daily Ramsey Express ran, taking only 60 minutes and carrying a special headboard.

It normally consisted of a 19-22 class car with a "parcel van" attached.

The remaining steam plant at Snaefell was last used on September 3, 1924 and was replaced by a second 1903 rotary converter transferred from Laxey. This in turn was now replaced by a second-hand BTH rotary converter, which differed from its predecessors in being started from the AC side. This left only two steam-generating stations, Ballaglass and Laxey. The 1904 AC distribution system continued in use, as did the supply of current to domestic consumers in Onchan and to Derby Castle and Douglas Bay hotel. This, too, was an AC supply, but dual wiring allowed the remaining consumers to use DC in winter so that the Douglas alternator could be shut down. It is said that the winter sermons at St Peter's church in Onchan were often punctuated by theatrical dimmings and brightenings as the MER cars took power!

Sir William Vaudrey, addressing the company meeting of December 16, 1925 saw matters currently as "very satisfactory". First debentures had been reduced by a sinking fund to £189,538, and the boom in textiles had been coupled with a fine summer. Sir William Vaudrey, chairman, and director C A Huni, both died in 1926, and Sir Arthur Griffith-Boscawen came back to the board. In 1929 he was to serve as chairman of the Royal Commission on Transport, parent of the mainland Road Traffic Act of 1930. The General Strike in Britain meant that in 1926 only half the

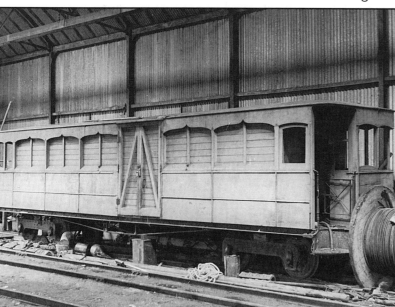

Ex-passenger car 10 as seen in 1954, in its stored condition as "withdrawn" freight trailer 26. In 1979 it was restored for the Isle of Man Railway Society, broadly to its 1918 condition.(JNS)

preference dividend could be paid, though the second mortgage debentures were reduced to £13,500. During the coal strike three-car trains were run, one car being a light 1893 or 1894 trailer, but this ceased when solder ran out of the controller terminals.

In 1927, Frank Edmondson, manager and engineer, was elected to the board. Second debentures were reduced to £8,000, and the first debenture stock, the subject of redemption payments for some years, now stood at £184,500, but there was no preference share interest payment. Motor-bus competition had now appeared between Douglas, Laxey and Ramsey. A plan was drawn up in 1927 to replace Bellis Morcom generating sets by diesel units, using 150kW Crossleys or 300kW Maldons, but this was not carried out. The following year, 1928, saw the only serious accident the line has known, when a trailer broke loose near Fairy Cottage and 32 passengers were injured (an earlier collision on September 17, 1908 also caused injury). The only fatal accidents to passengers ever to have occurred on the MER appear to have been one or two cases of inebriates falling from rear platforms into the path of trailer cars.

Mr J Rowe, later to become company secretary, joined the Douglas office staff during 1929. The Strathallan office staff at this time comprised a traffic superintendent, a clerk for goods, a typist, and two male clerks. All ticketing and cash were handled by this office, including the through tickets to Ramsey and Laxey from mainland railways, which had to be collected. In the economic slump of 1929-30 the MER was not too badly affected; the second mort-

gage debentures were completely redeemed, the debenture stock interest paid, and two per cent paid on the preference shares for the remaining half-year of 1923.

In the early hours of April 5, 1930, a fire at Laxey depot destroyed the building and 11 cars. It was probably caused by a cigarette end dropped behind the seats of a car, igniting the dust and dry waste that tends to accumulate there. The depot was promptly rebuilt, and three replacement trailers obtained from English Electric by midsummer; the fire claim was for £6,140.

On the night of September 17-18, 1930, a rainstorm and ensuing floods in the centre and north-east of the Island produced an accumulation of debris behind the weir of the hydro-electric plant at Laxey. Between 2,000 and 4,000 tons of debris filled the bed of the river, which took to the adjoining road, flooding the power station and other properties as far down as the harbour. The floods submerged the water turbine and much of the steam plant, but the water remained below the turbine's elevated platform and the switchgear. The following day, only the steam turbine was in commission, exhausting to the atmosphere; Ballaglass No 2 set was started up later that day, and ran until October

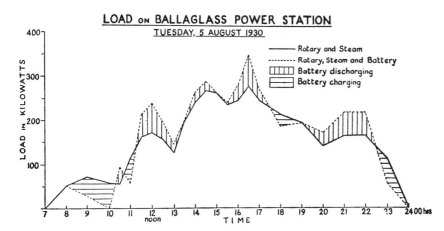

Loading diagram showing how battery equipment absorbed the excess peak demand, in this case at Ballaglass. The peaks occur as visitors leave and return to their hotels and boarding-houses for meals.(SB)

MANX ELECTRIC RAILWAY

Boat Passengers are notified that THE MANX ELECTRIC RAILWAY PASSENGER AND MAIL EXPRESS (stopping at Baldrine, Laxey and Ramsey only) and

Due in Ramsey within one hour from time of departure from Douglas

will not leave Derby Castle Station before 3.30 p.m. This is the quickest passenger service in operation between Douglas and Ramsey connecting with this steamer's arrival.

The Manx Electric Railway Company's Motor Lorry which is in attendance on the Pier at the arrival of passenger steamers will convey your luggage to Derby Castle at a nominal charge. Instruct porter on steamer to place your luggage on the Manx Electric Railway Motor Lorry.

F. EDMONDSON, General Manager

NORRIS MODERN PRESS LTD.

MER notice displayed in IoMSP steamers, circa 1930. (MER)

25. Water power became available on September 25, but the other plant had to be stripped and the parts dried in a heated box, larger parts being cleaned and dried in situ. No 1 Bellis set came back into use on October 22, No 2 on October 31, and the Robb-Armstrong No 3 set on November 20; the only

No 22 and its van in their "Ramsey Express" role, circa 1928. (NTM)

subsequent failures were of a wattmeter transformer and of an air pump stator coil. The flood repairs cost £3,472, including river clearance and road maintenance, for which an ensuing legal judgment placed responsibility on the company.

In charge of the Laxey flood repairs was Mr J F Watson, who was later to become a general manager and chief engineer. He had joined the MER as an apprentice in 1916 (his father had been with the IOMT & EP from 1897), and following war service and a period on the mainland, he returned to the MER in 1929 and became assistant to the chief engineer in 1936.

From 1930 onwards, the debenture interest payments were a veritable millstone around the MER's neck, particularly as motor-coach and bus competition became more intensive. The year 1931 was materially worse than 1930 and debenture interest went unpaid, the holders having agreed to a postponement until October 1, 1933 of the second half of the year's payment due to them, in view of the line's recent ordeals. The renewals fund stood at £20,752, and the debt to the debenture holders was £4,117 10s. In 1932 it grew to £12,352 10s, but the renewals fund also climbed to £20,854, less £1,125 written off on further flood repairs.

To eliminate painting and overhaul of Snaefell cars at Laxey, a three-rail, mixed gauge siding was laid in about 1932, on which Snaefell cars could be transferred by traversing jacks on to 3ft gauge bogie and taken down to the main Derby Castle works. The surviving

sector table at the Snaefell depot appears to have been removed at the same date.

In 1933, $2^{1}/_{2}$ per cent of the cumulative total of debenture interest of £20,587 10s was paid off, and the special reserve for renewals stood at almost £20,000. A further $2^{1}/_{2}$ per cent was paid off in the year to September 30, 1934. Public electricity supply was now becoming available throughout the Island, and the MER AC supply to domestic consumers in Onchan and to Derby Castle and Douglas Bay hotel through the 1894 underground mains came to an end between 1931 and 1933. The last such customer for MER power was the Howstrake holiday camp, dating from the 1920s. With MER generation costs at some £5,000 a year and the newest plant some 20 years old, discussions began with a view to taking current for the line from the Isle of Man Electricity Board, through a network of substations.

On November 7, 1934, an agreement was reached with the Isle of Man Electricity Board by which it was given a prior charge on the company's real estate for £15,978, the company being obliged to seek hire-purchase terms for the equipment and transmission lines involved. The new layout consisted of six rectifier substations, at Douglas, Groudle, Laxey, Snaefell, Ballaglass and Bellevue. Of these, Ballaglass, Bellevue and Laxey are fed direct from the public supply at 33,000V 50 cycles AC, while Douglas, Groudle and Snaefell are fed at 6,600V AC through the 1904 lines from a purpose-built transformer substation at Laxey; an emergency supply at 3,300V is obtainable at Douglas. To reinforce the

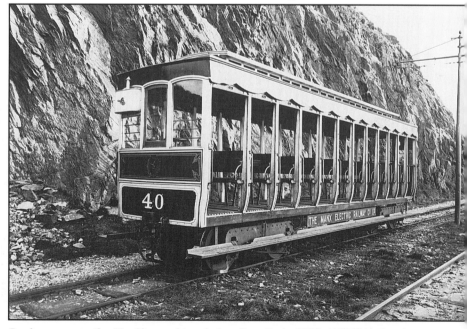

Replacement trailer No 40 posed just below Port Jack, 1930. (GEC/Alsthom)

550V DC feeders, an additional overhead line hung from ordinary ears was added from Douglas to Groudle, supplementing the 1894 underground feeder, while beyond Groudle it is carried on pole-mounted brackets all the way to Queen's Drive, Ramsey.

The transfer process (first initiated in 1932) for Snaefell cars requiring major body overhaul/painting. A 3ft gauge bogie is propelled towards the mixed gauge track.

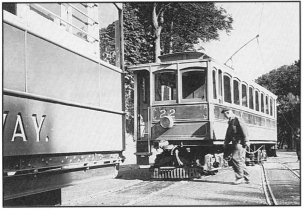

No 22, shepherded by the late Allan McMullen, moves down towards No4, by now jacked up and re-bogied to the narrower gauge.

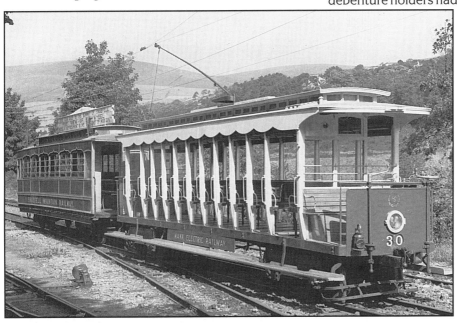

A photograph by the late C L Fry of a less "compatible" train (1961). (All above photos: A R Cannell/C L Fry)

The new rectifiers were fan-cooled, mercury-arc traction units by the Hewittic company, with Hackbridge transformers. At Douglas, one 200kW unit was placed in the former engine room, and two similar units were put in the existing building at Groudle. Laxey (two units of 200kW) and Bellevue (one of 150kW) were new buildings, at Snaefell (two of 150kW) part of the old engine room was used, while at Ballaglass the two 150kW rectifiers seem lost in the vast emptiness of the original buildings. The 1904 Witting, Eborall DC switchgear was re-used throughout, for white marble insulation does not age.

The steam generating plant at Ballaglass was by this time already idle, No 1 set being last used on August 16, 1934 and No 2 set two weeks later; the plant was dismantled in 1935. At Laxey, the steam turbine (No 4 set) ran for the last time on September 6, 1934, followed by No 3 set on September 22. This left the two Bellis-Morcom sets and the water-turbine plant to maintain the supply during the final winter. By April 1935, all was ready, and the water turbine plant, No 2 set and No 1 set were used for the last time respectively on April 28, 29 and 30, marking the end of all MER steam generation; the new supply system came into use on May 1. A book loss of £53,000 was sustained in disposing of the old plant but the shell of Laxey power station was eventually sold in 1944 for nearly £5,000. The new Laxey substation was near the site of the 1895-6 terminal, beyond the Rencell Bridge. Increasing UK prosperity made 1935 a better year. Passengers reached 543,126, the expenses ratio fell (through power economies) to 74.35 per cent, and mileages were 308,560 for passenger trains and 39,839 for goods. The reserve fund stood untouched at £23,582. Debenture interest was paid up to September 30, 1933, with two years of arrears remaining. The debenture holders had agreed to a postponement of arrears payment until October 1936 for the board, in a circular letter, held out hope of paying further amounts in that year. Increasing motor traffic on the Island roads made it necessary to instal trolley-activated traffic lights at three points, Half-Way House in March 1934, Ballure and Ballabeg, in June 1936. These have since been updated to modern standards.

Although they assembled every three months for a board meeting at Strathallan Crescent, the directors wisely made little effort to interfere in the working of the line. The operating methods were very specialised. Most visitors arrived on Saturday, and their first exploration on Sunday gave an opportunity to put out advertising literature; the general line in advertising was that of a (variously) "Manx Switzerland" or "Riviera coast" made accessible by the MER: a 1930s example of the former type is illustrated. The latter variety was a mainly post-war theme, visually represented by palm trees. Buyers of the 5s (25p) two-day Rover tickets were given a four-page explanatory leaflet, with the leading theme "If fine, go to Snaefell". In 1927, Rover tickets had allowed any number of Snaefell journeys, but this soon had to be stopped as the cars simply could not

FIRST DAY.

(1) After Breakfast proceed to Derby Castle Station at the Northern end of Douglas Bay and the terminus of the Corporation Horse Tramway and Buses.

(2) Board the Electric Car for Laxey.

(3) Arriving at Laxey, change into the Snaefell Mountain Car and proceed direct to the Summit.

(4) On the return trip break of journey may be made at the first stop known as the Bungalow Station and a 1/- Extension Ticket may be purchased for the run by Motor Char-a-banc to and from Tholt-e-Will, Sulby Glen, where, situate in the centre of the Glen, is a fully Licensed Hotel, to minister to the wants of the Tourist. This Glen, nestling on the Western slope of Snaefell Mountain, is known locally as the Heart of the Manx Switzerland. On returning to the Bungalow Station, rejoin a Snaefell Car for Laxey, travelling again on the Rover Ticket. The extension is here mentioned as the Rover Ticket entitles the holder to one return journey only on the Mountain Section.

(5) On reaching Laxey the remainder of the day may be delightfully spent in visiting the Big Wheel, the Beach, and Laxey Glen Gardens. ALTERNATIVELY to returning to the Bungalow, another route is open to the Tourist, viz: book a single Extension Ticket only on the Char-a-banc at a cost of 6d., and from the lower Entrance of the Glen continue by a walk of three and a half miles through the charming Vale of Sulby, all down hill and no climbing, which will bring the Tourist to the Sulby Glen Station of the Steam Railway, and the

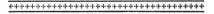

THE

MANX ELECTRIC RAILWAY

To the Holder of a Rover Ticket

How to use
the TWO-DAY
Rover Ticket
to the best possible advantage

It is available for any Two Days' Travel by the Electric Car (not necessarily consecutive days) within seven days of date of issue

Two Days are really required to visit all the Beauty Spots reached by the Electric Cars

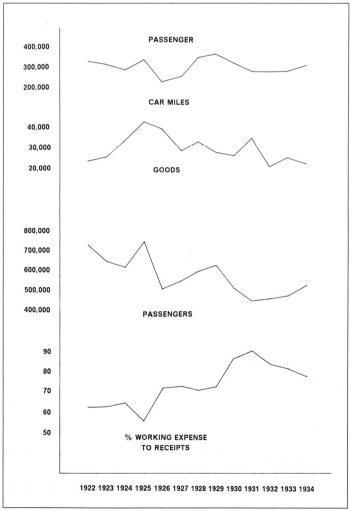

Operating statistics, 1922-34. (SB)

Above: Front cover and first page of a pre-war leaflet for Rover ticket holders. In 1955 the MER offered almost as detailed advice in a leaflet addressed to steamer day excursionist. (MER)

cope. Sunday afternoon, if fine, could be busy, and with Monday the rush was on in earnest; between 9.30 and 10.15 the cars were filled with Rover ticket holders, and a similar rush occurred between 1.45 and 2.30pm. Takings on Tuesdays were lower— the "rovers" were often on their second day, though Wednesday was an alternative choice. Thursday was bedevilled by a regular long-day Fleetwood excursion, whose arrivals congested Laxey, queuing for Snaefell. Friday and Saturday were relatively quiet.

Each week, the Saturday arrival figures were rushed to the office to allow an estimate of the crew requirements for the following week. Tide tables were also consulted, for the tides materially influenced the availability or otherwise of deckchairs on the Douglas beaches, a counter-attraction to MER excursions. The recent widening of the northern end of Douglas promenade had, however, brought business to the MER in the carriage of mines waste from Laxey, used in this and other civil engineering projects associated with public relief employment. Weather forecasts were anxiously studied, and on fine days queues formed from 8am onwards for the full-day Snaefell-Sulby Glen tours, on

The IoMT&EP made maximum use of contemporary publicity media.

DHOON GLEN HOTEL AND ELECTRIC TRAM STATION, I.O.M.

Left: No 3 climbs from Laxey in summer of 1894. The general colouring of this postcard is surprisingly accurate, remembering it was attained by tinting a photo-original. (IoMT&EP)

Below left: *Dhoon Glen Hotel, circa 1900 shows both a cattle grid and a gradient post and the rustic kiosk and shelter at the entrance to the Glen (left). The vast "eating shed" extending North from the hotel is also noteworthy. (IoMT&EP)*

Below right: *This view of Groudle is some years earlier (probably 1895-6) and includes No 12 and a nicely painted station building. (IoMT&EP)*

Right: *One of Dhoon Glen's waterfalls provides the subject for an attractive piece of postcard colouring which quite accurately conveys what a glen was and happily, in large part, still is. (IoMT&EP)*

DHOON GLEN. I. O. M.

Groudle Station, DOUGLAS. I. O. M.

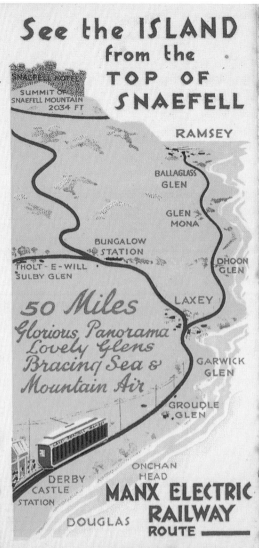

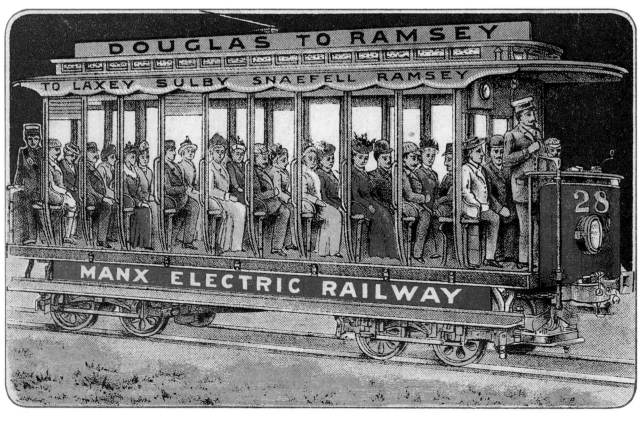

Top left: A typical leaflet of the late 1930s produced under Mr Barnes regime. Post-war variants were rather less aesthetic productions. (MER)

Below left: Front page of an attractive leaflet circa 1908 and typical of Edwardian publicity. (MER)

Above: A perhaps slightly more synthetic piece of colouring appears on this 1920s view of a typical MER catering establishment — that at Sulby Glen. In their then-pristine state, the garden surroundings were quite pleasant. (MER)

Top: An animated scene at the Bungalow in 1914 shows three of the MER's charabancs and a passenger car. The retouching artists seem to have been at pains to make the mountain appear as dramatic as possible. (MER)

Above: During a 1956 crisis in which the line's future hung in the balance, the company played host to a Light Railway Transport League Convention. Two cars were used — here No 1 and trailer 59 stand during a photo stop. (Electrail Slides)

Top Left: The Groudle booster survived long enough to allow modern colour photography of its red, orange and green paintwork — all the generating plant must have enjoyed similar colour schemes. The steel handrails were kept polished. (J B Matthews)

Top Right: G F Milnes lettering of 1899 from a 19-22 series car. (J B Matthews)

Above: A colour impression of No 1 in green livery circa 1958 produced by Stanley Letts. The result, on these cars, was moderately acceptable. (S Letts/W A Camwell)
Top: No 22 in green livery at Bulgham, circa 1958. (J N Slater)

Above: In this 1961 view of Groudle Bay can be seen the track of the Groudle Glen line, the roofs of the Howstrake camp, an MER goods lorry (at speed) and No 16 and trailer. *(J H Price)*

Inset: At about the same date, some MER passengers (bound for the Howstrake holiday camp, the entrance to which lay across the road to the right) receive assistance with their luggage. This has made the journey on the rear end of the trailer, (the shutters, on being pulled down, make the area adjacent to the bulkhead a useful luggage space.) The rather forlorn ornamental gates to the rear are a survivor of the one-time Howstrake Park development. *(J H Price)*

Below: Busy goods traffic at Derby Castle, April, 1966. *(JCC)*

Top: Surviving MER crest on an unidentified trailer circa 1966. *(JCC)*
Top right: This superb interior of No 5 epitomises the lovely late Victorian woodwork of these cars, and shows the pleasing moquette used by the MER for its upholstery in the immediate post-war years (taken 1977). (G K Whiteley)
Above: Enthusiasts grouped at short notice to fund this farewell present for Bill Jackson's 1987 retirement. (Model and photo by P Hammond)
Right: Sir Charles Kerruish, President of Tynwald, unveils the commemorative nameplate of loco No 23 at the ceremony held at Derby Castle on Monday May 25, 1992. (R Powell Hendry)

73

Above: *No 2 in what was its usual guise as works car, with the tower wagon on overhead repair. Service car No 21 passes, bound for Laxey, at Lag Birragh. (Stan Basnett)*
Top: *Jackson era winter cars with added headlights, 1978. (Roy Scott)*

Above*: MER No 22 on single-line working in the snow in 1965 on King Edward Road when all other public transport to Laxey and beyond was at a standstill. (Stan Basnett)*
Top*: Snow in Glen Mona, April, 1966. (JCC)*

Above: This 1978 view of No 58 represents the Jackson regime's house style most typically. (Roy Scott)
Top: The newly cleared Derby Castle site and the MER's yard, April, 1966. (JCC)

Above: The survey special of 1966 pauses at the site of the later landslip! *(JCC)*

Top: IMR loco No 4 hauling both saloon trailers during a "steam on the MER" rehearsal on December 5, 1991. *(IoMR)*

Above: An evening departure from Douglas. (Roy Scott)

Top: Newly rebuilt SMR No 3 sporting its Isle of Man Railways dual "crest" in summer 1978. The below-underframe board carried the "Isle of Man Railways" titling. (Roy Scott)

MER No 27 approaching Laxey Station from Ramsey. (Stan Basnett)

which lunch was taken at the Summit hotel, the Bungalow, or Tholt-y-Will. Both tours (Douglas-Laxey-Snaefell-Sulby, tour No 1, and Douglas-Laxey-Snaefell-Ramsey, tour No 2) were offered at 4s 6d (22.5p).

Staffing in the Thirties comprised station-masters at Douglas, Groudle, Laxey, Bungalow, Summit and Ramsey, assistant station-masters at Douglas, Laxey and Ramsey, booking-clerks at Douglas (two), Laxey and Summit, kiosk attendants at White City, Sulby Glen, Dhoon and Ballaglass, and a chief inspector supported by a team of four. Until 1930, a station-master was also positioned at Garwick. Platform staff comprised 24 double crews, a yard foreman to select cars and issue instructions,

The late J F Watson had a particular affection for the Robb Armstrong sets — here is one of those at Ballaglass. (Rev B Kelly)

	Passenger car miles	Goods mileage	Passengers	Profit £
1940	104093	33173	69004	—7,439
1941	115240	100227	104535	— 38
1942	?	?	?	1,434
1943	?	?	?	3,473
1944	?	10545	?	4,060

War time traffic. Results for the years 1940-44 are incomplete, but this table does convey something of the overall picture.

with a maintenance staff of a chargehand, two cleaners, an armature winder, two joiners, two painters, a blacksmith, and from four to six labourers; apprentice numbers varied between three and five. On the busiest days, the indoor staff would help out as drivers, a tradition which continues to this day. Each of the six substations was manned, but in winter the reduced load enabled the one at Bellevue to be closed from September to May. In summer, it operated from 10am to 6pm.*

On the death of Mr Edmondson in January 1936; his assistant, Mr E Barnes, was appointed manager and engineer. The year's passenger figure climbed to 552,815, though the expenses ratio still hovered at 74.93 per cent; car miles were 315,338 (passengers) and 36,627 (freight). The debenture interest debt at September 30 was £24,705, but a further £5,000 was paid off a week later. The next year, 1937, was even better; 570,833 rode the line, and the car miles (307,890 and 30,914) showed better loading, and thus an improved profit ratio, the expenses ratio falling to 63.83 per cent. Of the debenture arrears of £20,000, £7,316 was paid off on October 1, and the capital charges owed to the Isle of Man Electricity Board had already been reduced by £2,663, roughly a sixth.

At Groudle, the traction battery continued in use, due to the "maximum demand" tariff charged by the electricity board. In 1938, an ingenious form of traffic and traction load control was introduced in an

The Bellis sets and elevated switchboard at Laxey. (Rev B Kelly)

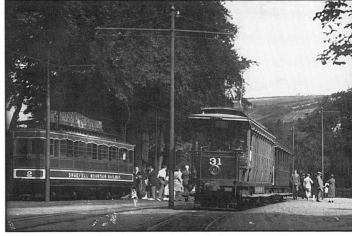

Above: This view of No 31 and an "umbrella" appears to date from the thirties and shows the motor car to have been given varnished (or grained) posts like an ECC (contrast with views of 28 as new). The umbrella trailer to the rear is even darker (see view of no 60 in Chapter 9). A "known date" view (1934) of sister car 28 shows it in, broadly, 1904 style, with white posts and bulkhead detail. (W A Camwell)

Left: Rebuilt car No 22, 1992 with interior inset. (Andrew Scarffe)

* The 1993 MER official guidebook contains some excellent employee reminiscences of this period.

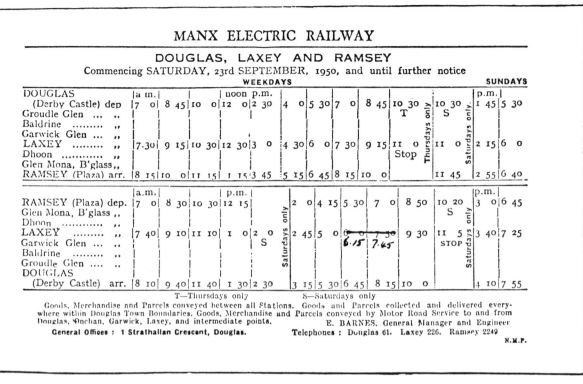

MANX ELECTRIC RAILWAY

DOUGLAS, LAXEY AND RAMSEY
Commencing SATURDAY, 23rd SEPTEMBER, 1950, and until further notice

	WEEKDAYS													SUNDAYS	
DOUGLAS	a.m.			noon	p.m.									p.m.	
(Derby Castle) dep	7 0	8 45	10 0	12 0	2 30	4 0	5 30	7 0	8 45	10 30 T	10 30 S			1 45	5 30
Groudle Glen ... ,,															
Baldrine .... ,,															
Garwick Glen ... ,,															
LAXEY .... ,,	7.30	9 15	10 30	12 30	3 0	4 30	6 0	7 30	9 15	11 0 Stop	11 0			2 15	6 0
Dhoon .... ,,															
Glen Mona, B'glass ,,															
RAMSEY (Plaza) arr.	8 15	10 0	11 15	1 15	3 45	5 15	6 45	8 15	10 0		11 45			2 55	6 40

	a.m.			p.m.										p.m.	
RAMSEY (Plaza) dep.	7 0	8 30	10 30	12 15		2 0	4 15	5 30	7 0	8 50	10 20 S			3 0	6 45
Glen Mona, B'glass ,,															
Dhoon .... ,,															
LAXEY .... ,,	7 40	9 10	11 10	1 0	2 0 S	2 45	5 0	6 0—7 30 (6.15 7.45)		9 30	11 5 STOP			3 40	7 25
Garwick Glen ... ,,															
Baldrine .... ,,															
Groudle Glen .... ,,															
DOUGLAS															
(Derby Castle) arr.	8 10	9 40	11 40	1 30	2 30	3 15	5 30	6 45	8 15	10 0				4 10	7 55

T—Thursdays only   S—Saturdays only

Goods, Merchandise and Parcels conveyed between all Stations. Goods and Parcels collected and delivered everywhere within Douglas Town Boundaries. Goods, Merchandise and Parcels conveyed by Motor Road Service to and from Douglas, Onchan, Garwick, Laxey, and intermediate points.   E. BARNES, General Manager and Engineer

General Offices : 1 Strathallan Crescent, Douglas.   Telephones : Douglas 61. Laxey 226. Ramsey 2249

N.M.P.

This timetable for winter, 1950 illustrates the substantial service then still provided for residents. (MER)

attempt to even out power consumption. Cars were despatched according to the passage of marked counters on an electrically-driven belt — representing the line from Douglas to Laxey — timed to complete the journey in 30 minutes. The intention was to avoid simultaneous uphill starts from different points on the line. The device was disused after the 1939 season, but came back into use from 1954 to 1956. On the hillside above the car sheds, an electric sign proclaimed "MER for Scenery"; a gorse fire later damaged it, and when re-erected the wording was changed to "Electric Railway for Scenery".

In 1938, however, passenger numbers dropped back significantly to 514,360; the expenses ratio rose to 72.6 per cent, and passenger-miles declined to 296,573. The figure for goods was 23,043. By October 1, 1938, the debenture arrears were further brought down to a little over £12,000, and it seemed a fair assumption that the debt might be wiped off by the early 1940s. A little ground was being gained each year, and a fifth of the debt to the electricity board had now been cleared.

But with the outbreak of war in 1939, a third of the traffic vanished, leaving just 489,621 carried, expenses at 78.12 per cent, and miles run down to 279,119 and 15,748. The debenture debt climbed back to over £16,000. Sir Bernard Greenwell, chairman since 1926, died on November 28 that year, and was replaced by Mr A W Bolden, whose major interests were in South American railways. This only left Sir Arthur Boscawen, Ernest Remnant, and secretary A D Foster of the original team of 1902. The debenture holders, by resolution of December 19, 1940 waived all interest due to them from September 30 the previous year (leaving arrears frozen at £16,459), and the War (Local Conditions) Committee similarly waived repayments to the electricity board, to which the company still owed £10,000.

By March 1940, MER staff had fallen to 30.

Left: A Groudle short working in 1947. The ECC's used on this shuttle had their open gearing lubricated while standing at Derby Castle by an "oiler" stationed there for the purpose. (By this date grass may also have made its contribution to the lubrication arrangements). This is perhaps the most austere of MER liveries. (J H Meredith)

Already the Manx government had been obliged to assist distressed hotel and boarding-house keepers. The MER staved off its immediate crisis by selling 1939's remaining stocks of liquid refreshment, and by selling the Strathallan Brows and the glen below Summer Hill, now Calvary Glen. Later, it applied to the War (Local Conditions) Committee for a loan of £6,000, estimated to cover the following year's working. In the event this was never used, for new wartime traffic arose from the need to convey interned "aliens" to farm work sites. There was also peat-cutting traffic from Snaefell, and the haulage of mine waste from Laxey to Ramsey to build the runways at Jurby air station. A siding was laid at Laxey for this traffic, from the northbound track to the mines' deads heap, passing between the Agneash road crossing and the IMRS garage. The Snaefell line closed from September 20, 1939 and did not reopen until June 2, 1946. All the company's investments (chiefly in South American railways) were frozen for the duration of the war but, in any event, their ultimate sale realised far less than their book value.

Mr Remnant died in May 1941 and Mr Bolden the following month. They were replaced on the board by Messrs A D Foster and A G Hunt; S A Young (a business associate of Foster's) became secretary. Under the Isle of Man Defence Regulations, the accounts for 1942 and 1943 were not published, and no figures for passengers and goods appear. In 1944 the maximum-demand electricity tariff ceased to apply, and after August the Groudle traction battery was abandoned. The building still contained the disused Thury booster of 1904, and another (archaic) booster of the 1895-6 era was used in the Snaefell car shed for drying out cars each spring.

By March 1945, Messrs Boscawen, Foster and Hunt were able to resume publication of the company accounts. Happily, the overall debit balance of September 30, 1941 had been reduced from £17,482 to £8,514, and 1944 had brought a working profit. The debt to the electricity board was a little over £5,000, the pre-war debenture arrears about £16,000, and the Isle of Man government was owed £6,000. In 1945, with a mini-boom sparked by war-weary visitors, 216,080 passenger miles were run, with 12,306 goods; the line made £11,636 working profit, and the overall balance for the year was £3,121. The moratorium on debenture interest continued, and the debt to the electricity board fell below £5,000. The company report mentions the

intention to catch up on renewals neglected during the war.

Next year, 1946, saw even better results with an incredible 1.5 million passenger journeys. The Snaefell line re-opened, the through return fare from Douglas now being 5s (25p). Miles run climbed to 327,944, with goods at 15,941. Of the profit of £32,699, £15,000 was put aside for "repairs" and the credit balance carried forward for the year was £9,713. The reserve fund for special renewals still stood at about £24,000, and £12,000 now appeared in the capital account for rectifier equipment, on which the hire-purchase debt had been cleared. Another link with the 1902 board was broken by the death of Sir Arthur Griffith Boscawen, leaving only ex-secretary A D Foster, who became chairman. A G Hunt had also died, and new directors Robert Holmes (of the Greenwell concern) and G B Parker, a barrister with Manx connections, took their place.

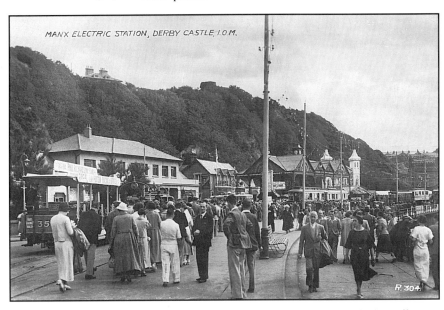

A 1936 view of the morning queue. The unwidened promenade saw little traffic, fortunately — this typical scene would be at around 9.30am. (MER)

The same year also saw the resumption of the circular tours to Sulby Glen. Before the war, the No 1 tour was Douglas-Laxey-Snaefell-Sulby, and No 2 tour Douglas-Laxey-Snaefell-Ramsey, both offered at 4s 6d (22.5p). After the war the tour numbering was reversed, with No 1 tour at 7s and No 2 at 6s. The vehicles used for the road journey were the two 20-seat Bedford WLBs of 1937, MN 8685 and 8686. The tours ran for seven seasons, but with the end of petrol rationing, increasing coach competition began to affect results and the operation ceased after the 1952 season and the vehicles were sold the following year.

For 1947, the year's profit was £28,858, leaving £10,071 to be carried forward, even though the government loan was repaid in full and half the 1939 debenture arrears paid off. Miles run were 320,400 and 14,398 (goods), and £3,037 was spent on renewals. The capital structure of the company was adjusted to clear the £53,000 loss on power plant, leaving the issued capital at £409,826. A commission on public transport reported in July 1947, and acknowledged the need to retain the MER and the social value of the year-round service. In 1949 the Manx government brought in outside experts; the railway study was made by G B Howden of the Great Northern Railway (Ireland), and that of the road services by Messrs Arnold, Robinson and Wright, of the Tilling group. Their report foresaw the MER's impending crisis and raised long-term doubts about the Laxey-Ramsey route. But the Island's road services did not escape criticism, especially on fare levels. The Tilling men were anxious to "omnibus" the entire island, as might be expected. The chief effect of these surveys was to rationalise the bus service to the detriment of the MER.

The wave of prosperity still rode high in 1948. A working profit of £22,402 (£16,859 net) made possible the payment of renewed debenture interest, legally due from January 20, 1948, and the final clearance of arrears. Mileage had been 321,243 passenger, 13,971 goods. In his annual statement of March 1949, chairman A D Foster explained the intended transfer of the company's direction from London to Douglas, and proposed a "scheme of arrangement" to reform the its financial structure. Mr E Barnes, general manager and engineer, was brought on to the board, joining Messrs Foster, Holmes and Parker. Incidentally, the year had seen a trail of Ferodo centre-rail brake-shoes on a Snaefell car, without positive results.

In 1949, the MER had to go to court to contest Douglas Corporation's ambitions to run buses beyond the boundary along King Edward Road to Groudle. The threatened Groudle licence was not granted and the buses ran only to White City, with a DCT payment to the MER in respect of the consequent traffic loss. The service ran from 1950 to 1957 (compensation in 1957 was £344), and recommenced in 1959, when the fee payable to the MER was re-negotiated at 0.525 pence per passenger.

From October 1, 1949, the secretary's office, at River Plate House, 10-11 Finsbury Circus, London EC2, was transferred to Douglas and merged with the registered office at 1 Strathallan Crescent. A D Foster retired for health reasons, and Holmes became chairman, J Rowe secre-

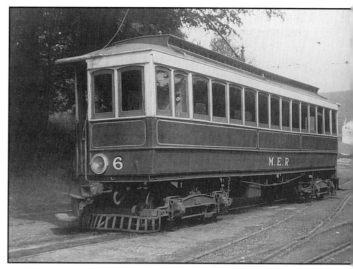

A 1951 shot of No 6 at Laxey perhaps exemplifies the "poor but proud" aspect of the company in its final years. (FKP)

tary, and the former secretary, S A Young, joined Messrs Holmes, Parker and Barnes on the board. The capital reconstruction scheme approved by the Manx government on November 26, 1949, wrote down the company's issued capital from £403,231 to £310,731, of which £140,200 was in 10s ordinary shares and £170,531 in 4½ per cent first mortgage debentures. Presenting his first report in February 1950, Mr Rowe stated that the 1949 profit was £14,006, which permitted payment of debenture interest and two per cent on the reconstructed ordinary shares. Miles run were 303,403 and 15,278 (goods) and £6,176 had been spent on renewals. The reserve fund now stood at £29,122.

In 1950, the Island's post-war boom abruptly collapsed, and visitor numbers fell by 75,000. Mileage was but 284,583 (goods 17,147), and profits were £4,732, of which £2,974 was spent on renewals and £2,158 carried forward to 1951. Only the aid of the previous year's net revenue balance enabled debenture interest to be paid. The renewals fund still stood at a nominal £29,122, but the grass-grown 1894 trackwork now needed major renewals. De-

No 16 at Garwick in 1954. The bulkhead is varnished (or grained — certainly the seat backs were and are) on its front face but the outer pillars are otherwise white as are all the intermediates. (B Y Williams)

spite this, the 1950 winter timetable (as in other post-war years) showed early and late runs timed for 70 minutes, and the entire timetable for the winter of 1951-2 was so timed. In that year, for the first time, the winter Sunday service was withdrawn because of lack of traffic.

In 1950, construction of an Air Ministry radar station on the summit of Snaefell called for winter journeys by a Snaefell car. This meant that the overhead line on the upper section had to be left in position despite the risk of ice damage, whereas normally it is taken down in winter and tied to the Fell rail chairs. To avoid the need for the line to be left up in subsequent years, the Air Ministry in 1951 supplied a four-wheel Wickham railcar with a Ford V8 petrol engine and a centre-rail clasp-brake, so that the radar operator could drive to and from the summit station. This vehicle weighs 2¹/₂ tons, and was fitted with Fell guide wheels in 1954-5 because of its instability in high winds. In 1957, Wickham's supplied a larger four-wheel car with a 28hp Ford diesel engine; this vehicle was Fell-equipped from the start and has a one-ton goods portion and detachable snowploughs. Both cars are kept in a separate shed at Laxey (extended in 1957) and both can carry four passengers as well as the driver. Their summer operation is limited to Sunday mornings, when the electric cars do not run. The 1951 car was re-engined in 1964-5. Both were in blue livery until 1966, but are now brown and yellow (for later changes see Chapter 8 and table appearing in Chapter 9).

During 1951, Mr R J Clutton was appointed to the board from Schroeder's Bank, inheritor of the debenture stock trusteeship. Mr Clutton had some (perhaps ominous) prior experience in "disposing of" several South American railways, bargaining in Spanish. New trustees were appointed, including Mr J R Quayle, then chairman of the Isle of Man Bank. Car mileage was much the same as in 1950, at 284,524 passenger and 15,928 goods, but the profit was a mere £2,244, and a £5,000 transfer from the general reserve was made to meet debenture interest. The £1,852 spent on deferred renewals was hardly significant.

In 1952, the MER obtained from the Isle of Man Highways and Transport Board a quantity of rails and overhead poles salvaged from the former Douglas Head Marine Drive tramway. Earlier, poles on the Snaefell line's upper portion had been replaced by timber substitutes. During the Thirties, replacement of the original poles with a Stewarts &

Lloyds stepped pole had begun, but some of the ancient tapered poles of 1893-4 still survive, as do most of the 1898-9 poles on the Ramsey line, now minus their decorative collars. The DHMD poles, although equally old, had lasted well, thanks to their galvanised top section and rust-resistant lower parts. The first DHMD rails, when laid in 1955 near Lonan Old Church, were found to be unduly noisy, owing to head corrosion, and no more were obtained, but further poles followed in the next few years.

Mr Barnes died on November 2 1952, and November 12 saw the start of joint management by J Rowe and J F Watson; Mr Watson had been assistant to Mr Barnes since 1936. The 1952 operating profit was £4,318; mileage run was 282,021 (passenger) and 10,213 (goods). Repairs and renewals totalled £1,767, and old stock valued at £942 was written off, which left the renewals fund at

On May 30, 1955 an LRTL special employed No 32 for a "sprint" from Douglas to the Dhoon quarry sidings. Steamer times were tight but 32 had a few minutes respite on the return journey to produce this pleasing study. (J H Price)

£27,274. Material ordered but not yet delivered accounted for another £1,484. A further £3,000 had been transferred from the general reserve account and, with the holders' agreement, only six months' debenture interest was to be paid. Late in 1952, Mr Barnes's place on the board was taken by the late R C Drinkwater, a member of an old Manx family, whose affection for the Island's most scenic transport amenity was to be of great help in ensuring its survival.

The year 1953 saw an operating loss of £863, and a further £7,000 transfer exhausted the general reserve. Miles run had totalled 268,806, plus 8,480 for goods, and all repairs had been charged against revenue. The only bright spot was the sale of property amounting to £5,660, which went to the trustees for the debenture holders; this included the

The SMR's No 3 makes a "photo stop" at Lhergy Veg on Sunday May 20, 1956. The white corner post of these cars originally continued up to the eaves board — this distinctive feature was to be reinstated in the 1970s. (NTM)

debt on debenture stock had been allowed to grow, by further moratoria, to £9,145. The debenture holders had it in their power to realise the assets and wind up the company, but they took the opposite course; the chairman pointed out that they were now providing an amenity for the Island from their own resources.

The Island's loss in popularity after 1950 might form the basis of a whole series of essays, and one is tempted to cite the negative part of the *Manx* character as in part responsible: changes called for by the advance of tastes and fashion came hard to many hoteliers, shop and boarding-house keepers. The fall in the Island's permanent population between 1951 and 1961 (from 55,253 to 48,150) underlined the general exodus of the more ambitious. Recognising that the post-war boom in the holiday industry had evaporated, to be succeeded by a long and painful decline, the Island government in 1955 appointed a Commission on the Visiting Industry. The commission reported on January 13, 1956 and among its recommendations were the continuance of both the coastal tramway and the Snaefell line, with implied government assistance.

With good weather and higher fares, 1955 saw a working profit of £4,075, though the final result was a debit balance of £10,542. Car miles were 259,693 passenger and 8,744 goods, and debenture interest arrears were now £22,974. Every effort was made to get maximum results for the least expense, and an interesting publicity effort was a leaflet for long day-

glens at Dhoon and Ballaglass, whose new owner was the Isle of Man Forestry Board. The newer of the two Dhoon quarries had already passed to the Highways Board, which used it until 1961-3. A total of £2,213 had been spent on track material, principally a new crossover installed the following winter on the Snaefell line below the Bungalow to make possible normal up and down working during Tourist Trophy race weeks. Before 1954, these events (which closed the mountain road crossing) saw a two-car shuttle on the upward track and three cars on the downward, with a single car working to and from the summit.

The company promoted a Bill seeking winter closure at any date between October 31 and May 3, and authorising fares beyond the limits imposed in the original Acts of 1892-7. In the June 1954 debate, Advocate McPherson pointed out for the company that the two-car winter service was costing £3,538; winter passengers totalled about 37,000 out of 814,357 for the year, plus journeys by 200 contract holders and the 40 pupils of Dhoon school. Winter receipts were about £2,500, and the service employed 20 men. But although efficient operation of the Douglas-Ramsey bus route by Isle of Man Road Services had robbed the MER of its once substantial residential traffic, for people in the Maughold peninsula it was still their local transport artery, and winter closure was defeated 12-10. The fare increases were approved, but too late for the 1954 season to benefit. Mr H C Kerruish, speaking in the Keys debate on behalf of his Garff constituents, said that "they thought there was a greater degree of civility and courtesy from this service than from any other company in the Island". For 1954, the working loss grew to £2,005. Car miles were cut to 253,503 (passenger) and 7,026 (goods), and the

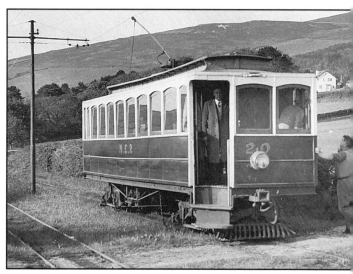

Robert B Parr's evocative view of the MER in its role as a "country trolley". Writers have repeatedly called the line an "interurban" but this is really a misnomer — country trolley is a far more accurate description. (NTM)

excursion steamer passengers, explaining how to reach Snaefell and return in time for the boat. Maintenance work was limited by lack of funds, but it included the cropping of dropped rail ends near Laxey and their Thermit welding, as shortened, on site, as well as repairs to the timbers on Ballure bridge. This last job required single-line working between Lewaigue and Ramsey, during which a collision occurred on August 3; four passengers were taken to hospital, but were not detained. The 60th anniversary of the Snaefell line on August 21 was marked with special headboards and posters and some useful press and television publicity.

In December 1955, the MER directors wrote to the government stating that they could not continue in business beyond the end of the following season. They were willing to sell the line for £70,000, excluding the Douglas and Laxey hotels

What must really, one supposes, be called "vesting day" — June 1, 1957. Sir Ambrose Dundas Flux Dundas is at the controls of No 32 accompanied by Sir Ralph Stevenson. Standing nearest the car is Mr T W Kneale, M. Eng., with Howard Simcocks to his left. To be glimpsed inside, in silk hat, is Deemster Sir Percy Cowley. Sir Percy was among those who encouraged the retention efforts of Whitsuntide, 1956. (Manx National Heritage)

and suggested the formation of a new company with a capital consisting of the sale price of £70,000, plus working capital of £30,000. The Island's Executive Council* appointed a sub-committee of MHKs, comprising J B Bolton, J F Crellin and H K Corlett to look into the whole question. They, in turn, imported three specialists from the London Midland Region of British Railways, R Varley, MIEE, M Inst T (formerly manager of the Mersey Railway); D A Paterson and J H Fowles. The specialists produced an estimate of £674,000 for the complete renewal of cars, track and nearly everything else, to be spread over 16 years. They considered that it would be cheaper to use double-deck buses, and soon afterwards certain other parties were to be seen lurking at MER stations and along King Edward Road gathering information for their anticipated replacement bus services.

Whitsun 1956 saw a well-attended Light Rail Transport League convention in Laxey, with an exhibition opened by the lieutenant-governor, and jointly arranged by the Douglas Society of Model Engineers and the author. Speeches at the convention dinner included noteworthy contributions from J E Ellison (chairman of the Laxey Commissioners) and R C Drinkwater of the MER, and much favourable publicity resulted.** Another guest was H C Kerruish, MHK, who on June 5 took 18 of the 24

members of the Keys for a trip up Snaefell, where they weighed the view against the cost and affirmed their belief that the Island could not afford to let the line close.

The sub-committee presented its dismal report in the Keys on Tuesday June 19, and recommended that no assistance be given. After a pungent debate during which the line's chief detractor was seen to be J B Bolton (who wanted a road up Snaefell), the report was put aside, and the House agreed to a proposal by Mr Kerruish that a new committee be appointed to investigate the possibility of continuing to run the railway at a reasonable cost. Its members were Deemster Sir Percy Cowley, MBE; Sir Ralph Stevenson, KCMG; H C Kerruish; J B Bolton; and G Taggart. They were to report back in October.

On July 10, the company petitioned Tynwald for leave to introduce an abandonment Bill, which was rejected by a small majority; the alternative solution (in October) was an indemnity against losses to September 30, 1957, under which the company agreed to continue for another 12 months. Track renewal, the last carried out by the company, was begun south of Baldromma-Beg. The direct loss on working in 1956 was £3,169, and car miles were 253,603 (passenger) and 8,536 (goods). S A Young died in February, 1957, and the final directorate

---

* The Executive Council's purpose was (in a 1961 definition) "to consider and advise the Governor upon all matters of principle and policy and legislation" — it had evolved over many years and only became a Statutory body after the MacDermott Commission of 1958. The Governor presided over its meetings (usually held weekly) until 1984, and continued to attend and participate until the major changes of 1990 in which Exco itself disappeared. This is a convenient point to recommend perusal of Appendix 5 where the general mechanism of Tynwald's activity is outlined.

** An excellent account appeared in *The Ramsey Courier* of May 25, 1956.

consisted of Messrs Holmes, Parker, Clutton and Drinkwater.

The Committee of Tynwald sought a further expert report, this time with two members chosen from tramway, rather than mainline railway, fields. An inspection followed on July 2-3, 1956 by J W Fowler AM Inst BE (chairman of the Light Railway Transport League); C T Humpidge, BSc, M Inst T, general manager of Bradford City Transport; and (once more) R Varley of British Railways, all of whom found that the line could indeed be kept going for far less than the sum previously quoted. They considered that the line could not be constructed at that time for less than 20 times its sale value, if at all, and that its intrinsic worth was incalculable. A difference of opinion survived between the two new investigators and Mr Varley, who seemed convinced that new rolling stock would be essential.

In August 1956, the Tynwald committee met the directors, and entered into a provisional agreement for the sale of the line to the government for £50,000, or about £2,000 per mile. The company, influenced by the views of those directors who put the island's interests before their own, made a very real sacrifice in agreeing to this figure, for the reduction of £20,000 brought the price down to about the estimated scrap value of the plant, ignoring the land value.

The committee reported on November 6, 1956 in favour of purchase, recommending a ten-year renewal programme for Douglas-Laxey and Laxey-Snaefell. The proposals came up for full debate on December 12. Deemster Sir Percy Cowley earnestly put the case for the line's acquisition. His main opponents were J B Bolton and a new member, J M Cain, a director of the IMR and IMRS. Mr Cain suggested that his own company could carry all the MER traffic with ten extra buses, which could be taken to mean that only one passenger in three would bother to make the journey at all if it meant going by bus. Telling points in the railway's favour included the fact that 70 per cent of visitors rode on it, the degree to which its existence helped Ramsey, and the annual disbursement of £31,000 in wages.

The ensuing vote was 17 to 4 in favour of purchasing the line and commencing the initial ten-year programme of renewals, and by April 17, 1957 the necessary Bill was signed in Tynwald. It was a historic decision, and in this way the Manx Electric system came to survive, and now approaches its centenary. Its prime function as a "vehicle" of collective enjoyment happily continues!

As a parallel, consider the Hill of Howth tramway in Ireland, replaced by buses shortly after its closure. Traffic promptly dropped by about two thirds, with the result that the buses, although cheaper to run, still lost nearly as much money as the trams.

A splendid view of No 14 and trailer in full (red and white) livery, taken by the late H C Casserley in July, 1933. This typifies the style of cross bench cars when varnished posts were abandoned.

Chapter 6

Nationalisation and After

Established services and attractions such as the Manx Electric Railway and Snaefell Mountain Railway should be preserved and developed.
Commission on the Visiting Industry, January 1956

This text relates to the status quo in about 1968. Where contradictory to current facts, this originating date has been mentioned or implied by the use of the past tense, or (as in the route description) the obsolete elements omitted.

ON THE MORNING OF SATURDAY JUNE 1, 1957, the Lieutenant-Governor, Sir Ambrose Dundas Flux Dundas, drove a flag-bedecked MER No 32 in brilliant sunshine from Derby Castle to Groudle, to mark the transfer of the undertaking to the Manx government. Aboard the car were Deemster Cowley, Mr Kerruish, Tourist Board secretary L Bond and the joint managers, with Sir Ralph Stevenson, first Chairman of the new Manx Electric Railway Board, set up in May 1957 to manage the undertaking.

Boards of Tynwald in those days were composite bodies consisting of elected members from the House of Keys and non-Tynwald members appointed by the Governor. The new MER board had three Tynwald and two outside members. The Chairman was Sir Ralph Stevenson, GCMG, MLC, the Keys members were R C Stephen and A H Simcocks, and the nominated members T W Kneale, M ENG, and T W Billington. Mr Stephen was concerned with traffic operation, Mr Simcocks with publicity, Mr Kneale with permanent way and engineering, Mr Billington with accountancy. T W Kneale was a former divisional executive engineer of the North Western Railway of India, and although professionally retired, in his MER capacity he spared none of his still considerable energies. The Board's first term of office extended to November 30, 1961.

The intention was to relay the Douglas-Laxey section in the first seven years, followed by Laxey-Snaefell in the next three, the work to be financed by an annual grant. On June 18, 1957, Tynwald voted £40,000 for the first two miles of new track, and orders were placed for 200 tons of 60lb flat-bottom rail, specially rolled at Workington. The new track used 6ft x 9ins x 4$\frac{1}{2}$ins sleepers and such sophisticated devices as elastic rail spikes, rubber pads (on one stretch) and proper transition curves; the noted curve at Groudle lost a dog-leg of particularly vicious character. On October 10, 3,000 sleepers arrived at Ramsey aboard the Ben Ain, followed a few days later by the 200 tons of rail, delivered to the lineside site at Queen's Drive which Bruce had bought in 1899 during the dispute over the Ramsey terminus.

Mr Fred Comaish, the Permanent Way foreman who had worked on the line since 1899, retired on January 15, 1958, and in view of the heavy work programme (with 110 men at work) the board created a new post of engineering assistant, filled by A R Cannell from the Harbour Board, who had previously served an MER apprenticeship.

Help was also made available to the MER board between 1961 and 1965 under the winter employment schemes, by which the Island government sought to offset the seasonal nature of tourist employment. The amount of work which could be accomplished each year depended on the level of employment provided through the schemes. Work under the schemes saw the three lines completely weeded, and the fences and drainage works repaired and cleared. The Ramsey line revealed itself as far from life-expended, thanks to a good original design of rail section and generous ballasting. The line was thereafter treated with a selective weed-killer and in parts with a brushwood killer, applied by a special tank wagon of 1958 with a small petrol engine providing pressure spraying at 5mph. Other winter work schemes saw Laxey and Ramsey stations resurfaced in Tarmac, and the same treatment was later given to Derby Castle yard. The Forestry Board also greatly improved Dhoon and Ballaglass glens.

Passenger figures in 1957 had shown a drop of some 56,000, and on December 10, Tynwald voted £9,000 to offset the consequent loss of

The new station at Ramsey, 1964. (DGC)

income and cover rising costs, as well £3,820 for track work. By this time, the Board had decided to adopt a new colour scheme of green and white for the cars, and the first of 14 green cars appeared on Christmas Eve. This unhappy choice is further referred to in Chapter 9, and was abandoned after 1959. Attempts were made to obtain the Laxey-Douglas school contract, and late cars were run to Douglas and Ramsey for people enjoying evening entertainment, but they attracted few customers.

Annual estimates were presented to Tynwald by each Board by March 31. The MER board in its first year found that adding renewals to operating losses would require an annual £45,000 instead of the intended £25,000, and would mean a 2s 10d (14p) subsidy for every 5s (25p) fare, according to a report from Sir Ralph on April 18, 1958. A storm broke over the heads of the Board, and proposed remedies included the permanent closure of the Ramsey line. On May 22, a vote of 11:10 resolved (just) to stay in business, but to run the line purely as a scenic railway, with no early or late cars and with complete closure from September 13 to May 16 each year. The next stage of track relaying would be financed by a loan, and this involved the issue of £20,000 of Manx Electric Railway Board five per cent guaranteed stock. This 20-year loan had been recommended in the second advisory report of 1956, and in July 1958 the Board was granted borrowing powers up to £110,000. The completion date for work on the Douglas-Laxey stretch was now extended to 1965.

The MER duly did as it was told, introducing an 11-journey 10am to 6pm service in June 1958 and, as might be expected, uproar ensued. The unfortunate chairman and three of the four Board members resigned on June 18, and Douglas Corporation and Isle of Man Road Services promptly sought licences to run to Groudle and points en route, on the grounds of the inadequate MER service.

On July 8, the courageous survivor, Mr Kneale, found himself joined by a new board comprising H H Radcliffe, JP, MHK; W E Quayle, JP, MHK; Lieut-

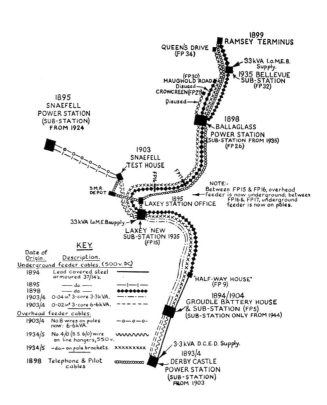

The feeder system as extant in 1968 — changes since 1985 or so are detailed in Chapter 8. (JCC)

Cmdr J L Quine, MHK; and R Dean, JP. The new board stated that it would try and run the line within its subsidy ceiling of £25,000, and would maintain a winter service. The full 20-journey timetable was restored from July 12. In Mr Radcliffe, the new chairman, the MER had found a vocal champion, and in the ensuing debate the line's chief adversary, Mr Bolton, was told that the railway would last long after he had ceased to grace the Tynwald chamber.

In 1957, the Board had bought two Leyland Cubs from Douglas Corporation, and experimented with a renewed Sulby service. For 1958, a more grandiose conducted tour was evolved, with IMR cooperation, modelled on one of pre-war years. For 14s (70p), it offered a full day tour, Douglas to Snaefell, a five-course lunch at the summit, bus from Bungalow to Tholt-y-Will and on to Sulby Glen station, steam train to Ramsey and MER to Douglas. Participants were limited to 50, and bad weather refunds were offered. This excellent tour attracted only moderate support, and was not repeated in 1959, officially because of the difficulty of keeping the two elderly buses serviceable. The vehicles had a useful last outing on August 7, 1959 when they ran a shuttle service in Ramsey from the Plaza to the Royal Manx Agricultural Show at Lezayre Road. In 1960 they remained disused, and were sold in 1961. The Post Office contract, which might have been lost if the line had closed in winter, was successfully renegotiated in 1959 at improved rates. The Snaefell

Conductor Duggie Sanderson collecting the 4.10pm post at Ballajora, August 1955 — sadly, 20 years on, mail services finally ceased. (FKP)

Entering Ramsey in the evening sunshine, No 22 presents an idyllic picture, 1961. (W G S Hyde)

Summit hotel was re-equipped and redecorated for the 1958 tours, to the designs of architect T H Kennaugh, and maintained a really excellent standard of catering thereafter. Good business was also done in the sale of such items as Snaefell souvenirs, leather goods and headscarfs, and the Board introduced an excellent range of colour postcards. The Bungalow hotel was closed and demolished early in 1958, and was replaced by a public shelter and conveniences (to whose cost the Board contributed) after unsuccessful attempts to obtain tenancy of an RAF building alongside the mountain road.

Another 200 tons of new rail arrived at Douglas in September 1958, and a further 100 tons a year later. By 1962, the total bought had reached 600 tons, of which 539 had been laid by 1964. In January 1960, Tynwald made a special grant of £9,000, and a further £3,000 was voted in June 1961 to cover a wage increase, but good traffic results enabled the board to report back that this sum was no longer needed. In 1959-60, a reduced working deficit left £6,000 of the basic £25,000 grant available to finance further relaying, and when Colonel Robertson of the British Ministry of Transport visited the Island in April and May 1960, the MER track passed his inspection with flying colours. The year 1959 saw the repainting of Ballure bridge, which absorbed 40 gallons of paint and six man-months. MER efforts to obtain the school contract beyond the Maughold area were still unsuccessful; Isle of Man Road Services opposition was vehement, and (as contractor for the rest of the Island) all too effective.

The years 1959 and 1960 saw an overhaul of MER publicity. Press advertising, which had much increased in 1958, now ceased again, and was replaced by advertising spots in cinema programmes. A 20-minute 16mm film was made, based

on a full-day trip from Douglas to Snaefell and Ramsey, and was shown to the public on summer evenings at the Sefton booking office, a shop on Douglas promenade. MER advertising began to appear in Douglas Corporation buses, and walled panels were used to screen Derby Castle yard (in 1964, a similar wall was put up to screen Laxey goods depot). From 1966, the MER sponsored weather forecasts on Manx Radio. The results of the Board's publicity and of the generous distribution of timetables for display in hotels, boarding-houses, offices and shops can be judged by comparing the post-nationalisation Snaefell traffic figures with those for six earlier years:

1948	77,000	**1957**	92,000
1949	76,000	**1958**	68,000
1950	60,000	**1959**	94,000
1951	56,000	**1960**	96,000
1952	61,000	**1961**	124,000
1953	48,000	**1962**	111,000

Renewals were also made from 1958 onwards to the overhead line, using traditional round-section trolley wire and phosphor-bronze overhead parts. An arrangement was reached with the Colton Electrical Equipment Company for the continued manufacture of round wire fittings. In 1958-62 the overhead poles received a very thorough repainting in dark green, as did the lineside buildings, while new white paint on accommodation gates further improved the line's appearance. In 1968, the overhead line gang had two tower wagons, normally based at Laxey shed, a convenient centre from which to reach any failure. In November 1961, Mr Alfred Callister retired from his position in charge of Derby Castle car sheds, after 38 years' service, and was succeeded by Mr Lewis Gale, with Mr Alan McMullen as assistant.

From winter 1959-60 co-ordination of timings at Derby Castle with the promenade buses was arranged, each car being met by a connecting bus. In summer, horse-car timings were also matched to MER arrivals. To eliminate the costly part-day manning of the substations at Ballaglass, Snaefell, Bellevue and Groudle, automatic switchgear by

No 15 poses at Derby Castle, 1961. (W G S Hyde)

J E Cull captured the Snaefell depot point in its more interesting position in this 1961 view.

Bertram Thomas (Engineering) Ltd was ordered in 1962 and installed in 1963-4, together with self-resetting circuit breakers. These units differ in their functions, that at Bellevue having a total operating cycle of 95 minutes. These automatic time switches have introduced several new and hitherto largely unknown phenomena in the behaviour of the line as an electrical entity!

In 1962 Mr Radcliffe and Mr Quayle were promoted to board chairmanships which carried membership of the Executive Council. Thus, on March 8, 1962 a third MER Board came into being, with T H Colebourn, MHK, as chairman, Major-General Sir Henry Sugden, MHK, as vice-chairman, and E R Moore, MHK, as the third Tynwald member. Mr Kneale and Mr Dean were reappointed by the Governor as the non-Tynwald members. Mr Colebourn soon showed himself as staunch an MER defender as Mr Radcliffe had been. Incidentally, an Act of 1962 modified the permitted constitution of Boards of Tynwald, including the MER 's. Boards from 1966 onwards were appointed under their new legislation.

By 1962, operating and renewing the MER had cost the Manx taxpayer about £180,000. Meanwhile, the ultimately abortive reconstruction of the Marine Drive, minus its tramway, had already cost £216,000, or almost as much as the MER/SMR system, which was eight times as long. However, recent negative factors included the withdrawal of the Fleetwood steamers after September 1961, reducing afternoon riding and similar negative developments were to occur over the next decade. During 1962, the road bridge across Glen Roy at Laxey was reconstructed, and foot passengers were allowed across the MER viaduct, which was partially paved for the purpose. A timed commentary on the scenery on the Snaefell route, with attractive background music, was introduced in the mountain cars, two receiving the equipment in 1962 and the other four in 1963; the tape was recorded by Mr Howard Lay, now Attorney-General, and was played on the uphill journey, with occasional humorous side-ef-

fects in case of delay or mist. In 1963, a grandstand was built at the Bungalow for the TT races, with a mobile licensed bar, and a footbridge was erected in 1965. The short-lived green and white livery finally disappeared late in 1963, and the senior staff were issued with uniforms closer to MER tradition than those of 1958-9, with their Ruritanian embellishments and exaggerated green lapels.

In 1963 the combined totals of deficiency and winter work grants became subject to a new accountancy practice whereby any unspent monies at the end of the year were repaid to the Treasury. Good seasonal earnings could thus no longer be used to boost the Board's civil engineering programme for the ensuing year. The total allocated for 1963-4 was £39,683, to which must be added the cost of a new shelter at Laxey (54ft by 10ft) for intending Snaefell passengers, and an entirely new 39ft by 24ft station building at Ramsey. A scheme for a new Laxey coastal line station, and a chairlift across Douglas harbour (for operation by the MER) fell victims to a budget deficiency. Poorer weather in 1963 put income £3,000 below the estimates, and rising wages brought the year's operating deficit to £32,682.

The Board pressed on with track relaying, duly completing Douglas-Laxey by 1965. Some resleepering was carried out on the Ramsey line, mainly between Dhoon and Ballaglass. The next task was the Snaefell track, whose 24ft Fell rails had corroded at their fishplates and were heavily worn across their working dimension, especially on curves. The running rail was less worn. The rail features a head which is quite good, but the section is poorly designed, with over-thin foot and web; some was relaid in 1961. The United Steel Companies, at Workington, were willing to make new Fell rail, but the cost (when known) provoked another sharp debate.

At Derby Castle, Douglas Corporation had bought the former entertainment complex, and the scheme's advocates now mounted a powerful attack on the supposed incongruity of MER and horse cars passing the planned swimming pool and solarium. They sought to expel the MER depot and terminus to the heights of Oncham Head: reputedly, representatives were found surveying the Board's yard without permission, and were duly given suggestions as to where they might go instead. At one stage it was suggested that MER cars might run behind the new centre in a tunnel, but final plans published in August 1964 showed the MER and its depot undisturbed, with the new building cantilevered over the tracks, a footbridge crossing to the seaward footway. The site was cleared in 1966 and construction began in 1967, with the swimming pool scheduled for completion in 1969 and the solarium in 1971.

Mr J Rowe retired from the position of secretary and joint manager at the end of 1964, concluding a 35-year association with the MER.* Mr J F Watson

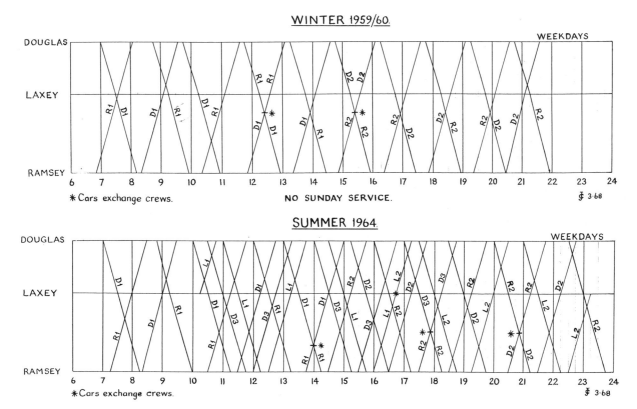

Winter and summer train diagrams. The prefixes D, L and R refer to the originating depot. (JCC)

now became general manager, engineer and secretary, Mr H Gilmore became chief assistant engineer and traffic manager, Mr E Halsall accountant and Mr A R Cannell engineering and traffic assistant. Sunday July 5, 1965, saw HRH Princess Margaret and Lord Snowdon make an evening Snaefell summit trip from the Bungalow by special car, accompanied by the Lieutenant-Governor. In April 1965 Onchan Commissioners bought Groudle beach for development, with the prospect of some additional traffic for the MER. This later turned out to comprise holiday residences.

Snow usually treats the Island lightly, and blockages have been chiefly one-day affairs. On March 3, 1965, No 9 on the 2.45 pm from Ramsey became lodged in a drift at Ballafayle when the power failed, but the line was open again by next day, and a shuttle service, Douglas-Laxey and Ballafayle-Ramsey, was maintained in the meantime. Mr and Mrs H C Kerruish (the Speaker of the Keys and his wife) were among those who accommodated the stranded passengers. The only regular movement on the Snaefell line in winter is by the diesel cars used by the staff of the Ministry of Defence radar station. These have often found their path blocked by the snow, and the operator has sometimes been marooned on the mountain for several days.

The Board maintained the MER goods service until 1966, with collection and delivery in its area and in the town of Douglas, by lorries based at Douglas and Ramsey, which transshipped their loads to covered vans (or open wagons) at the termini. Payment was "weigh and pay"' or by monthly account, and the rates remained low, for certain categories only 1s 6d (7.5p) per ton. Parcels were also collected from Mr E Hudson's shop, King Street, Douglas. By 1965, the lorries needed replacing, but this was considered uneconomic, so service was withdrawn on April 1, 1966, after Isle of Man Road Services had proved unwilling to provide connecting haulage. Goods brought to the termini are still conveyed (on a station-to-station basis), and it is common for Ramsey traders, finding a desired item out of stock, to have it sent up from

Van 3 descends from Ballaragh as the Royal Mail constituent of a typical Sixties train. (J Edgington)

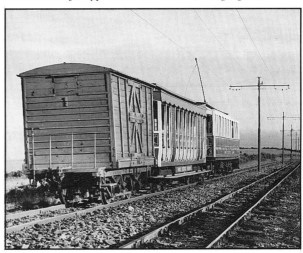

---

* Mr Rowe was the patient bearer of many of the author's queries and, with his MER colleagues, fought the line's case with great zeal during 1955-6.

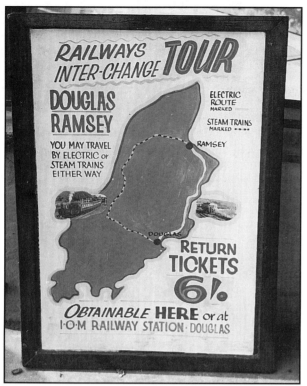

The MER's poster for the steam and electric circular tour of 1964. The IMR produced a well-scripted (but more economic) chalkboard equivalent. (Stan Basnett)

Colebourn emphasised the successful absorption of a £4,000 wage increase and £3,000 underspending on the deficiency grant. He saw an increased role for the line as the Island's roads grew more crowded. However, by his casting vote, the MER Board had decided to seek Tynwald permission to close in winter, since a mere 550 customers used the line each week and the winter loss was now £5,200. This would require a winter Maughold service by Isle of Man Road Services, which it was ready to provide. The court's critical remarks caused Mr Colebourn to refer this back to his board, and no further action was taken.

MER fares, which had remained low for many years, were increased to perhaps more harshly realistic levels in 1964, when the cost of a Douglas-Snaefell return was raised to 12s (60p) and Laxey-Snaefell to 8s 6d (42.5p). Reductions were granted on production of vouchers distributed by hotels and boarding-houses, but from 1965 these were re-placed by privilege rates made available on specific days (Tuesday, Friday and Saturday). An innovation of August 1964 was a railways interchange tour between Douglas and Ramsey for 6s (30p) — one way by IMR and the other by MER, but this was not repeated. A further five per cent fare increase was brought in in 1968, without adverse effect on traffic, and the best bargain was still the two-day Rover ticket (by now 16s (80p)) which allowed unlimited travel on the coastal line and one trip up Snaefell. Fares were differentiated in favour of the longer-distance rider, and books of residents' tickets (known as "name" tickets) were sold at a substantial dis-count. In winter, lower ordinary fares applied — the Ramsey return at 4s (20p) was probably the lowest priced 35-mile ticket anywhere in Great Britain, only 6d ($2\frac{1}{2}$p) more than 1899's summer return for the same journey.

In April 1965, the Isle of Man Government set up

Douglas by the next tram. Isle of Man Road Services took over the lorry work over the whole distance, and a bus had to be pressed into service on April 4, 1966 to cope with the parcels traffic.

March 23 of that year had seen a vigorous debate in Tynwald on the Snaefell relaying, now estimated to cost £145,000. Mr Bolton again mooted his road-to-the-summit proposal, and sought to delete from the Board's 1966-7 estimates of £106,977 the first £12,500 instalment for the Snaefell task. Nonethe-less, the estimates were passed, and Chairman

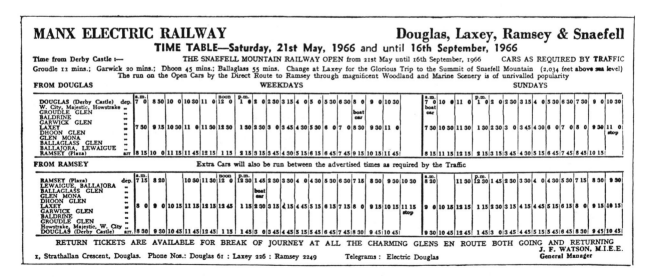

Typical Sixties' MER summer timetable. In some years a separate timetable applied from Whitsun to early July. (MER)

a commission to investigate public transport to and within the island. It comprised two members of Tynwald who had formerly sat on the MER board (Mr Radcliffe and Mr Quayle), together with D R Hunter (shipping manager of ICI, Liverpool), G E Lambert (transport consultant) and Captain J C Kelly Rogers, of Aerlinte Eireann, Dublin; Mr Radcliffe was chairman. Mr Colebourn gave evidence to the Commission on January 31, 1966, and said that the MER board planned to retain all its lines, but to run them as a scenic railway. He also remarked on the punitive effect on MER trade of "breakfast-table tour soliciting" by coach proprietors, and revealed a 3¹/₂ per cent rise in passenger numbers for 1965, which looked good against the reduced patronage reported by the steam railway and the buses, the former then on the verge of closure. The examination of coach operations was one of the Commission's chief functions, and the major coach proprietors were to some extent brought to heel by the institution of a Traffic Commission and licensing system. Coach stands in Douglas were consequently restricted, and stopping time at

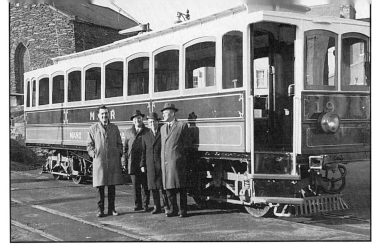

On April 2, 1966, the MER provided the author and his illustrative helpers with a Douglas-Ramsey "special", pictured here at Ramsey with (L to R) Messrs. Cannell, Gale, Gilmore and Watson. (JCC)

other loading points was limited to three minutes.

The Commission's 125-page report appeared on May 31, 1966, and was largely concerned access to the Island by sea and air, but it also proposed the amalgamation of all internal transport into a single authority, with the sole exception of the Douglas horse trams. It proposed the retention of the Douglas-Laxey and Snaefell lines (and part of the steam railway), but advocated closure of Laxey-Ramsey route. Much space was devoted to discussion of the merits of hovercraft, and, certainly, renewed day excursion traffic from the Lancashire coast by some new form of rapid service would certainly have improved — and indeed still would — the MER's position, especially if fed from its mid-point at Laxey. It is the perfect day-tripper ride, and a Laxey terminal would spread delighted patrons

The survey journey of April 2, 1966 produced some excellent camera work:
Above left: *A tramcar's view of snow in Glen Mona, taken from Ballaglass.*
Above: *From the same source, No 19 on the Bulgham "shelf" during the return journey. (Both Stan Basnett)*
Left: *A glance back at Laxey Head, late in the afternoon. (JCC)*

both north and south (and up to Snaefell) within the confines of a short visit.

The Commission's proposal to close Laxey-Ramsey was not adopted, and events in 1967 confirmed the line's continuance. But some remarks on the proposal may not be out of place. The Commission considered the MER's function to be the provision of a service calculated to attract visitors to the Island, and implied that this could be achieved wholly by keeping Douglas-Laxey and Laxey-Snaefell, but it overlooked the fact that Snaefell's seasonal capacity is limited to about 120,000 passengers — that of its six cars. The MER was attracting about 500,000 riders every year, and in 1965 one in six rode to Ramsey, or bought two-day Rover tickets which entitled them to do so, and which would not have been bought had their only objective been Snaefell. Instead of taking two MER rides, they would take only one, and the effect of closing Laxey-Ramsey would have been a reduction of perhaps one third in the traffic between Douglas and Laxey — the reverse of the Commission's aim. These prognostications were to be fully borne out by the results of closure of the Ramsey line in 1976. A better way to increase the traffic figures was surely to revive visitor interest north of Laxey, providing some new attraction in the Bulgham-Dhoon area, which has no equal in scenic terms. A cliffside restaurant and viewing terrace would be a possibility here, where the scenery is

The Bulgham bulge: this sketch was prepared from a photographic source and is dimensionally accurate "as existing" in mid-January, 1967. (FKP, after Stan Basnett)

The Bulgham repair in full swing early in May, 1967. (J H Price)

the equal of that on the Marine Drive.

Mr T W Kneale died on January 12, 1966, and after the 1966 elections a new Board was appointed in October. Major-General Sir Henry Sugden, KBE, CB, DSO, MHK, returned as chairman, with Miss J C C Thornton-Duesbery, JP, MHK, as vice-chairman. The number of non-Tynwald members was increased to three, Mr J R Gelling, Mr E R Moore and Mr M F Strickett. That year, 1966, saw the Island disaster of the seamen's strike, during which two late cars were deleted on the Ramsey line, and little use was therefore made of a revived facility — a ticket allowing travel between Douglas and Ramsey one way by MER and the other by the Ardrossan or Belfast steamers of the Isle of Man Steam Packet Company. Further losses by Isle of Man Road Services brought a cut in the winter Ramsey bus service and some extra winter business for the MER.

The following year, 1967, was to provide a prime example of the MER's resilience under stress. At Bulgham Bay, the seaward embankment wall at its southern end crosses a deep natural cleft in the 600ft cliff, containing a mass of material lying largely on shale. Since 1965, a bulge in the masonry at its base had caused concern, and in mid-afternoon on January 20, 1967 it failed, shortly after the 1.25 pm Ramsey-Douglas and 1.15 Douglas-Ramsey (car No 21) had passed. Services were maintained to each side of the failure, and passengers walked the track for the intervening distance. Parcels traffic was next diverted to road van, with a rail van serving as transshipment warehouse at Derby Castle. Motor cars Nos 7 and 21 were isolated north of the failure. By January 27 the M E R had built steps into the dividing wall to allow passengers to transfer along the parallel road, closed since the previous day, but renewed structural movement caused further anxiety, and that evening a hired Road Services bus replaced the cars between Laxey and Dhoon Glen, using the top road through Ballaragh. The wall above the initial fall collapsed

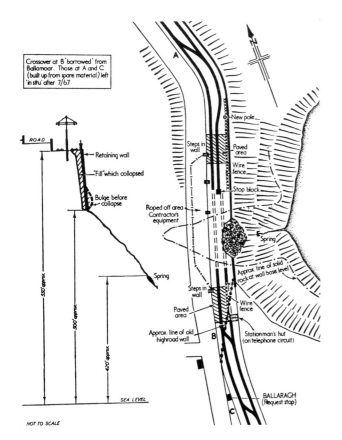

Crossover at 'B' 'borrowed' from Ballamoar. Those at A and C (built up from spare material) left 'in situ' after 7/67

Left: Traffic working at the Bulgham slip, with cars reversing on either side of the gap. When regular trailer operation commenced on May 20, north-side cars used the seaward track south of A for both arrival and departure, and their empty trailers were gravity-shunted into the terminal track while their motors withdrew to north of A. On the southern side, conventional run-around shunting was used, with the inner track serving as the terminal. Through running was resumed on July 10. (JCC)

Below: The Bulgham reconstruction, 1967. A shows the appearance of the original dry stone wall, B is a part section showing the lattice effect of the piles (116 in all) and C shows the detail of one row, with C1 representing penetration by the liquid grout poured down the bores. D shows the interlocking pre-cast units inserted where the parapet wall was removed; 40 were used, of which 24 spanned the failure. The end section shows how 16 extra vertical piles Z were sunk to a greater depth. Zone Y was filled with concrete after the pre-cast units were erected. (FKP)

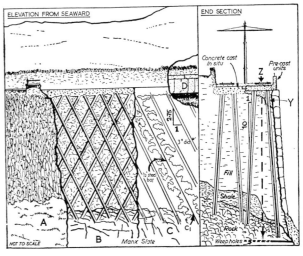

next day, but things now stabilised, and an all-tram shuttle service recommenced on February 1. A newly-printed timetable added five minutes to journey times and modified five departures to synchronise the Bulgham connections.

Repairs were the joint concern of the Highway and Transport and MER Boards, and C S Allot & Sons, of Manchester, were brought in as consultants early in February. Meanwhile, No 20 "ran the gauntlet" of the failure and replaced No 21, and by March 30 Nos 6 and 9 had gone north and several trailers were brought back from Ramsey for summer requirements. The MER prepared to build up a northern section summer operating fleet, and to provide transfer station facilities on a scale commensurate with summer traffic.

On March 22 Highway Board chairman R E S Kerruish announced that quotations for the repair work were awaited and that this would include the restoration of the tramway. The repair employed a method known as "reticulated pali-radice", an Italian technique carried out in Britain by Fondedile Foundations Ltd, of London. As can be seen from the drawing, the effect may be likened to that of burying a net in a mass of otherwise unstable material, and in this case 116 three-inch diameter concrete piles were used in four parallel double rows, with some later additions to give additional assurance. The contractors began work on May 1, and with a third of the job complete by May 18, grout had already appeared on the face of the wall. Night work commenced in mid-May, with completion scheduled for June 15. The MER built the stations

shown on the plan by May 20, when the special summer service came into operation, so arranged that an empty car always awaited an arrival at Bulgham between 10.00am and 6pm, thus avoiding conflicting flows of passengers. These special arrangements were to see 66,000 transfers by July 10, more than the whole year's passenger total on the reopened steam line. Further car moves had been made on April 23 before the contractors lifted the tracks, motor cars Nos 16, 19 and 27 and trailers Nos 36, 41, 43, 44 and 48 being sent north, and No 20 coming south with a trailer and three vans; the trailers were hauled past the work site on the end of a rope. Mid-June saw the work nearing completion, and on June 29 prefabricated track was positioned by a Highway Board crane working from the adjacent roadway. The overhead lines followed, and at 7.00am on Monday July 10, the first through car

97

Two studies by R J S Wiseman of, respectively, the northern and southern stations at Bulgham, 1967.

(No 21) left Douglas for Ramsey, complete with van, and the 7.15am (car No 22) left Ramsey for Douglas. There was no special ceremony — the M E R was simply "back to normal".

In 1967 Island visitor numbers rose to 489,000, and the MER 's new full-scale timetable (July 10 to September 18) was fully justified. It provided $17^1/_2$ daily journeys in each direction, and gained good traffic in spite of renewed IMR competition. The rise was greatest in longer distance journeys: queues for Ramsey cars were seen at Laxey for the first time for some years, and Ramsey station ran specials to the Dhoon at 9.45 on weekdays and 12.45 on Sundays

In the legislature, another battle had been fought. The Isle of Man government estimates for 1966-7 had included provision for the first instalment of Snaefell track repairs, but in the final estimates of May this had been deleted. Following a Tynwald excursion to the summit on June 6, 1967, attended by the Governor and Lady Stallard, Sir Henry Sugden brought the issue to the fore by a motion in Tynwald asking for a Finance Board vote on essential maintenance on the Snaefell line, and in the debate of June 20, Sir Henry carried the day. (The author cherishes a triumphant note from Sir Henry to that effect!) Progressive renewal of the downhill braking rail was authorised, a typical Manx compromise, being a slower execution of the original project. MER technical skills saw the prompt production of a rail-bending rig carried on spare bogies, and 100 tons of centre rail were produced at Workington in 1967; work commenced on the Summit-Bungalow section in October, 1968.

The Board's senior officer, Mr J F Watson, C ENG, FIEE, retired at the end of 1967 after 38 years' service; he had held the posts of rolling-stock superintendent (1930), chief assistant engineer (1936), chief engineer and joint manager (1952) and, since 1963, had been general manager, engineer and secretary. His successor in that post was

Mr Harold Gilmore, with Mr A R Cannell as chief assistant engineer and Mr J R Gordon as traffic superintendent; Mr Watson's brother, Douglas, became ways and works superintendent. Mr J F Watson now became inspector of seasonal railways to the Isle of Man Government in place of Mr H Maxwell Rostron; previous holders of this post had been Mr R Varley (1963-5) and, earlier, Mr T W Kneale. (Mr Watson died in 1972.)

A rather disappointing episode involving the author was the attempt, between winter 1967-8 and late August 1968, to establish a broadly rail-based transport museum on the Island. Encouraged by the Tourist Board secretary and by the obvious enthusiasm of the Laxey Village Commissioners, a 2,000-word report was submitted to the Government on May 14. By this date, both Lord Ailsa and the MER Board had offered potential sites at (respectively) St John's and Laxey. However, the writer was informed of the Executive Council's negative decision late in July and, although the Laxey Commissioners continued enthusiastic until the early autumn, the lack of any official funding made the scheme a non-starter. By this date the various mainland preservation groups fully "consumed" the available resources of money and manpower (of a scale sufficient to create an entirely new museum project), but it did prove practicable to rescue and reconstruct a Douglas cable car over the period 1968-76 and, with the MER Board's help, an electric railway museum did eventually open in 1979, a steam railway museum having opened at Port Erin in the meantime.

Readers are now reminded that the remainder of this chapter summarises operations as in 1968, and completes the administrative story to that year. Chapters 7 and 8 take up the story from that date, and are intended as a normal progression from that point.

The operating year at that time (1968) was divided into summer and winter timetable periods,

The failed drystone wall at Bulgham in late May, 1967, photographed during removal of the loose stones. (Stan Basnett)

changing in mid-May and mid-September, and occasionally with separate early summer and peak timetables. The winter service (weekdays only since 1951) required four two-man crews. In 1959, for example, No 1 Douglas crew booked on at 6.40am to work the 7am to Ramsey, and finished at 2.40pm. The corresponding times for No 2 Douglas crew were 2.15, 2.45 and 9.40pm. No 1 Ramsey crew

booked on at 6.30am to work the 6.55 to Douglas, finishing at 2.30pm, and No 2 Ramsey crew took over the 2.55pm (booking on at 2.30) and finished with the 8.45pm from Douglas. Each turn included one changeover duty, in which cars exchanged crews as they passed (normally between Bulgham and Ballaglass), the 11.45am from Douglas changing with the 11.55am from Ramsey, and the 2.25pm from Douglas with the 2.55pm from Ramsey, to ensure that crews finished at their home stations.

In summer, Douglas provided three regular sets of men to Ramsey's two, and two sets of men worked from Laxey. In 1964, changeover duties were the 1.00, 5.00 and 8.00pm from Douglas, and the 1.45, 5.30 and 8.30pm from Ramsey. Sundays required five crews, two each from Douglas and Laxey and one from Ramsey. Crews for the then numerous extra cars were held on call according to estimated requirements, and these special cars were inserted at intervals determined by demand. Traffic control was carried out by telephone between station-masters, and the double track made any more complex arrangements, such as signalling, unnecessary.

On blind corners there are pole-mounted boards, red at entry and white for exit, and should a car stop there the conductor must be sent back as lookout. Single-line working during winter track renewals is catered for by staff and ticket — a red, a white and a blue staff covering the three sections Douglas-Garwick, Garwick-Dhoon Quarry and Dhoon Quarry-

Below: Graph showing MER passengers in relation to island visitors and island summer climate (the 1968 passenger figure was 551,000). (SB)

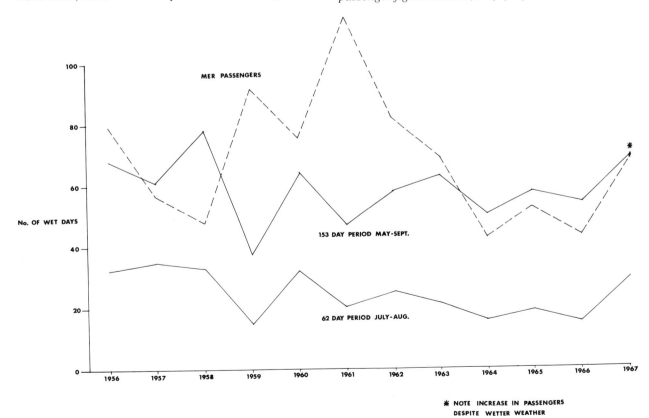

Note: graph labels: MER PASSENGERS · No. OF WET DAYS · 153 DAY PERIOD MAY-SEPT. · 62 DAY PERIOD JULY-AUG. · ✳ NOTE INCREASE IN PASSENGERS DESPITE WETTER WEATHER

Ramsey. The 64-page rule book had its last major revision in 1926. As well as general instructions, it has sections for station-masters, inspectors, motormen, conductors, linesmen, permanent way staff, and those working the Snaefell line.

The sheer physical extent of the MER saw the inclusion of some orthodox railway practices, and another reflection of the "distance" element was in the comprehensive spares allocated to each motor car and those held in the linesmen's emergency boxes at Douglas, Laxey and Ramsey. MER cars carried external oil lamps in case a power failure should see them marooned without lights, though the former internal oil lamps were largely incomplete, at least on summer-only cars.

On the Snaefell line, the first car, at about 8.45am, was reserved for hotel staff and supplies, and stopped at the mountain substation while its crew switched on the upper section current. The first service car on fine days left Laxey at about 10.30am, the subsequent frequency being determined by the weather and the loading reports telephoned from Douglas. On Sundays, first departure from Laxey was normally at 2pm. The last departure from the summit was at about 6.00pm, and again was partly filled by catering and station staff. Bungalow station had become important again, as in the Sulby Glen era, but now with road-borne visitors who left their cars there and took the mountain line to the summit; special cars were sometimes sent up from Laxey to pick up coach parties, those on certain tours taking their lunch or tea at the Summit hotel. Surprisingly,

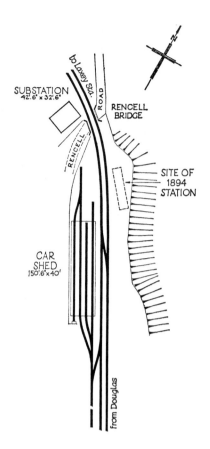

Laxey depot trackwork. (DGC)

Snaefell crews took only about a week to learn the road and the various lineside "marks" where brakes were applied or released. The maximum service frequency was ten minutes, with six cars.

The mail contract covered both lineside collection and bulk loading. The box locations are shown on the route maps, and were listed by the Post Office as follows:

Location Monogram	Type
Onchan Harbour VR	Wall, type B
Groudle VR	Wall, type C
Half-way House VR	Wall, type C
Baldrine G VI R	Wall, type B
Laxey Station G VI R	Pillar, type B
Glen Mona E VII R	Wall, type C
Ballajora VR	Wall, type C
Bellevue E VII R	Wall, type C

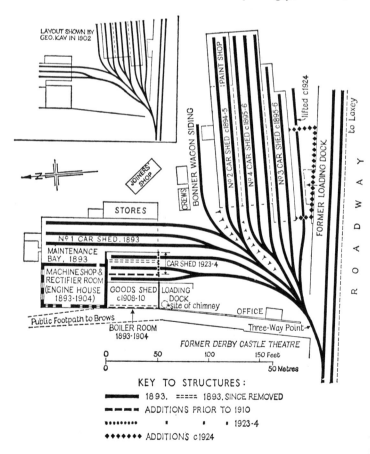

Left: Derby Castle depot as in 1968. Later changes are described in Chapter 8. (DGC)

For the summer of 1965, the collections were by the conductors of the 7.15am and 2.55pm cars from Ramsey, for the following winter those of the 7.20 and 11.55am. The Snaefell summit box was a private one, and was cleared before the last car; the mail being transferred in a locked bag at Laxey for transmission to Douglas. The practice ceased when the mail vans stopped running.

At the same dates, bagged mail travelled in summer by the 12.00 noon, 1.45 and 7.15pm from Ramsey to Douglas, the 7.00am and the 5.30pm from Douglas to Ramsey, the 7.00am Douglas-Laxey, and the 6.15 pm Laxey-Douglas. In winter, the runs were 7.25 -am Monday to Friday and 4.25pm Saturday, Ramsey-Douglas; 6.35pm, Laxey-Douglas; 7.00am and 5.45pm, Douglas-Ramsey; and 7.00am Douglas-Laxey. The mail travelled in locked four-wheel vans and was trans-shipped at Derby Castle to or from Post Office motor vans.

Ten supervisory and engineering staff were added in 1958 to the Derby Castle shed team, including three apprentices, giving the line a much changed air from its crisis days. The company's rather venerable selection of motormen (one ex-Marine Drive tramway) were now joined by several younger men, aided as usual in summer by student conductors, while older and more senior staff still attended to station matters. Conductors' duties include gravity-and-push shunting of trailers at Douglas, Laxey and Ramsey, aided by slight gradients. Outside work on track and overhead lines was (and is) the responsibility of two specialist gangs, which, given the lack of a special works car, then had the use of Nos 1, 2 and 9, which ran in this capacity (minus seats) each winter; in 1959-60 Nos 5 and 7 were also used, and an ECC-class car was commonly on overhead line duty, with ladders on the footboards. Since the reconstruction of cars 1 and 2, only cars of the 4-9 series are now normally employed on the works duties (see later remarks in Chapter 9).

At Derby Castle, all classes of repair were (and are) undertaken, and many parts are made on the spot. Periodic inspection by long-experienced staff allows faults to be rectified in good time, and averages include wheel profiling at 60,000 miles and new armature bearings (on 1903 motors which were not rebuilt) at like intervals. Brake-shoes last for about two months in winter, trolley wheels one month. Axles are tested ultrasonically, using equipment installed by the company. Car painting, to the traditional high standard, took place in the rearmost portion of depot No 2, where internal doors and a heating boiler and radiators were provided. The 1968 permanent winter staff numbered ten, and the more settled staffing made possible the retention of

men with special skills who might otherwise, if only employed seasonally, have tended to drift away. In later years the political crises did see some staff losses but most recent years have been less unsettling.

Imagine now that you are aboard a Manx Electric car at Derby Castle, with a ticket for Ramsey. The car starts away easily at the imperceptible foot of Saunderson's embankment, going into parallel at the second crossover and climbing vigorously past the depot, now on a gradient of 1 in 23.6. In 1968, looking back, the builders were hard at work on the ill-fated Summerland site*. Formerly that of the Derby Castle Variety Theatre and Dance Hall, the writer well remembers the sound of passing trams during the variety performances. There is now no regular uphill stop at Port Jack, and the line sweeps round the rocky bluff, which until 1988-9 was crowned by the once noted Douglas Bay hotel, giving a glimpse back across Douglas Bay. The gradient is 1 in 23.6, as the long straight vista of King Edward Road opens up ahead. In 1968 this brought the already wearied buildings of White City amusement complex into view (its wooden big dipper ended its days encased in an ad hoc collection of steel scaffolding tubes, by way of reinforcement) with Onchan Head station buildings on the landward side of the tracks. The gradient now, temporarily, eases.

Looking back, the site of 1894's trailer siding on Onchan Lane could once be seen; beyond, the bungalow residential development of recent years becomes apparent. Sustained climbing recurs before Far End, and as the open headland with the gaunt remains of Howstrake Park's former entrance comes into view, the overhead line is silhouetted against open sky. On reaching the level summit track at 258ft a splendid view of the rocky coast north of Groudle Bay to Clay Head opens out. At Groudle, the substation seen is that formerly standing behind the now-vanished Howstrake Estate toll house. This originally guarded iron gates across the road.

After the viaduct, virtually invisible from above, a good rear view of Banks Howe is obtained, and the car starts the long climb to Half-Way House traffic lights. This is a broad inland plateau; ahead are Lonan Church and the inland hills of Mullagh Ouyr, Claugh Ouyr and Snaefell. About half a mile north of Baldrine, the car passes the site of a trailing-connected siding formerly used to assist in handling the traffic once generated by Garwick Glen. The ensuing acutely curved embankment (itself shaded by trees) leads abruptly to the more open site of the one-time Glen station: Garwick once rivalled Groudle in its popularity. At Ballagawne, the line runs on a high shelf above the road, leading to Ballabeg

---

* Partly destroyed by a fire in 1973 in which 50 people died. The disaster brought changes in the Island and in Britain to legislation governing fire safety. A full account can be found in *Mann Ablaze!*, by Stan Basnett, Leading Edge, 1991.

crossing, again with traffic lights. An ancient grave-yard, Kist Vaens, was cut through in forming the line at this point, and was marked in 1894 with a wooden cross, white stones and a notice.

Now Laxey harbour and Head appear, with the Ramsey line just distinguishable, and the line begins its long cliff-top descent to Fairy Cottage. At South Cape, the abrupt turn into the Laxey valley leads into a secluded run through tall ivy-clad timber. Below, to the right, are the various survivors of the steam power and turbine plants. On these long descents, 28-30 mph running is commonplace, with the close-spaced rhythm of rear motor and lead trailer bogies as a staccato accompaniment. The car-shed briefly amplifies our sound to a roar, and we cross the Rencell bridge and the main Laxey viaduct into the SMR interchange station.

Leaving Laxey, 1898's retaining wall and the adjacent site of the 1897 Snaefell station are briefly glimpsed before the car crosses the former washing floor, curves to the right, and soon begins to climb the shelf leading to Minorca and on over Laxey Head. Minorca's high road bridge and stream now follow, increasingly wild vegetation on either hand. The harbour and Old Laxey are now seen spread out below, with Clay Head beyond. Curving north-west, and still climbing, the steep slope to the cliff-edge frames a splendid view out to sea, the view often including the Cumbrian coast and hills. Approaching Skinscoe, the line turns a little inland and parallels Strooan ny Grogee (Bobby's River) until this is crossed beyond Ballamoar. The fields on either hand, although more intensively farmed, are still full of coarse vegetation and reeds.

At Ballaragh, the high overall level of approach to Bulgham's cliff-edge viewpoint disguises its true nature. Only as the car runs on to the shelf does the line's real situation become apparent. Suddenly the most splendid tramway spectacle in these islands comes into view, with the line approaching the 600ft contour — higher than Blackpool tower — and the visitor interested in civil engineering will be looking out for the site of 1967's slip, now neatly repaired.

Beyond the Bulgham summit, the scene changes abruptly. The tramway now runs into the first of a succession of heavily timbered valleys nestling below North Barrule. A multitude of stopping places serves the farming community, and the gradients between Dhoon Glen and Dreemskerry are so varied that reference to the gradient profile is essential. When opened, the Ramsey extension had gradient posts throughout, and some survive here and there. The wider expanse of Glen Mona, leading away inland, is best seen by glancing back when entering the Corony stream's Ballaglass ravine, immediately after Ballagorry cutting. The heavily wooded country masks the sharply curved track at Cornaa station, where the line commences the wide southward detour which separates it from the road as far as Lewaigue. To seaward, on most days, the Sellafield nuclear complex is clearly visible.

After Ballafayle's two farms, the scenery is more open, with Port Mooar visible to the north east and, beyond, the green massif of Maughold Head and its white lighthouse. Inland, the little domed hills about Ballajora and Dreemskerry afford equal pleasure. Beyond Dreemskerry, the long straight run to Lewaigue offer views across the sheltered inland valley in which nestles the Crowville farm. Now the eye is drawn ahead by the returning seascape, with all Ramsey Bay, and the Point of Ayre beyond, coming into view.

From Bellevue to Ballure, the cliff-edge location almost rivals that approaching Laxey, with the added interest of Ramsey pier, now (1992) bereft of its tramway, and often yachts in the bay. Plunging among ancient trees, Ballure viaduct is crossed, with a brief glimpse of the stream in the green depths. Until the grooved rails and unique scroll-ornamented bracket arms of Walpole Drive are reached, the line winds its way across open fields, but it as suddenly becomes a roadside tramway once more, until at Queen's Drive it begins its final back-garden approach to the Plaza terminal.

No parallel scenic ride now exists in Britain, and few anywhere in the world. When (as ultimately must surely be the case) the island fully regains the appreciation it deserves, the MER will offer the most attractive possible medium for its exploration (as its contemporary patrons already wholeheartedly aver).

Milnes 1899 builder's plate, dimensionally identical with its predecessor on page 23. (JCC/FKP)

Chapter 7

Politics, Survival and Improvement, 1967-91

The substantial proportion of this chapter's content arising from the proceedings of the Tynwald Court and of the associated Governor's Executive Council has prompted the addition of Appendix 5, which summarises the machinery of Government on the Isle of Man. The changes in recent years have been complex and considerable, and the general reader is invited to pursue the topic to whatever depth he (or she) feels necessary.

WHEN THE PREVIOUS CHAPTER WAS FIRST written more than 20 years ago, its relatively optimistic tone seemed an accurate reflection of the situation in 1967. Yet the succeeding decade was to prove one of the most turbulent in the lines' history. Island politicians are still, by and large, "independents" in political terms and no clear-cut party divisions arise. However, groups do coalesce with common purpose and senior members come to exercise substantial influence on, for example, budgetary matters. The various public bodies have to compete for public funding, much as elsewhere, and periods of Government benevolence towards the railway have been matched by times when contrary sentiments applied. The manner in which the MER Board reports were presented came to be changed so that statistical material relating to different periods may be presented in a different manner, and a succession of consultants (with diverse backgrounds) came to examine the line and drew often conflicting conclusions. Principal changes in the technical field are mentioned en passant, but detail in these areas is left for the next chapter.

Meanwhile, it is useful to present a brief overview of the dramatic changes in the Island's lifestyle over this period. Looking back as far as the mid-Fifties there were already those in Government who foresaw the need to diversify the economy, so that consistent efforts to establish viable light industry formed an element of official planning thereafter — the modest rate at which this was achieved was probably all that could be hoped for, given market conditions, the relatively high cost of raw materials and the additional effort required to market a product, remembering the higher transport costs involved — the days of electronic communication and the roll-on roll-off heavy goods vehicle had yet to arrive. By the Sixties, efficient agricultural practice had also made its mark — Charles Kerruish (from 1979, Sir Charles, and a noteworthy Speaker, and ultimately President, of the House of Keys) was in the forefront of this advance at his Ballafayle farm. Regrettably, agriculture was one of the casualties of the late Eighties recession — the difficulties in relation to mainland practice are self-evident.

In 1961, faced with a declining population, the Island chose to use its independence in taxation matters (income tax was first levied in 1918) as a "residential incentive", with the aim of attracting better-off Britons and ex-colonials to the Island. The effects were not immediate — residential growth over the first five years was only about 2,000, but from 1970 the low tax regime, coupled with events overseas, saw the desired growth take real hold. Further specific incentives to finance and insurance operations were made available from 1981 onwards. The population today (as mentioned in the introduction) is almost 70,000 (69,788). The first obvious effects paralleled those already seen in the Channel Islands — an influx of "when I's"* of significant means and close social cohesion began to erect "compounds" of bungalows where they could resume their lately-lost colonial lifestyle, though with an absence of "ethnic" servants. A small influx of banking and "financial services" also took place — the Island laws in this area were still a little "wobbly" and periodic uproars ensued as the more gullible (and sometimes the not so gullible) "lost out".

As recently as 1964, the visible cornerstones of the traditional Manx economic scene had seemed much the same as ever — the Steam Packet Company and Isle of Man Railway Company continued to operate in their accustomed ways, the "Palace and Derby Castle" was still a major company, several brewers enjoyed their continued reign over much of the Island and Douglas still had a generous traditionally-operated bus undertaking, as also was the Isle of Man Road Services wing of the IMR). Mass "bucket and spade" tourism continued but there were soon to be ominous signs. The Isle of Man Railway "closed for the winter" in November 1965, and saw a succession of operators over the next 13 years, variously full and partial resumption of services and (in 1968) two major permanent abandonments. The disastrous Summerland fire of 1973 marred the early Seventies and really, but for the brief respite brought by the Manx "Parliament's" Millennium Year (1979), the traditional long-stay visiting industry slipped into accelerating decline

---

* A curtailment of "When I was in Rhodesia/Nyasaland/Singapore etc

thereafter. This was, after all, the era of cheap flights to sunny places.

The author's first awareness of coming change came with the loss of much of the traditional hotel accommodation at Ramsey, to be replaced by blocks of flats and shopping facilities for residents. However, it was only with the Eighties and the electronic revolution that the growing presence of the financial sector became physically apparent, as mini tower blocks and wholesale "refronts" began to occupy much of the inland end of Victoria Street, Douglas, and most of the older sections of Athol Street (and parts of Prospect Hill). Indeed, there were complete redevelopments of some properties, often dating back to Regency times. This visible presence was late evidence of an activity which had already overtaken tourism in earning capacity as early as 1970-71.

Over the following two decades the earlier-mentioned pillars of the Manx economic establishment began to crumble. The Steam Packet Company came under the control of an American, James Sherwood, for a while trading as "Isle of Man Seaways". By 1992 it had an operational fleet of but two vessels, one secondhand, and one purpose-built. The port of registry is now Nassau, in the Bahamas. Happily officers and crew are still, substantially, Manx.

Similarly, the Isle of Man Railway has become a nationalised fragment of its once-extensive self (albeit a substantial fragment in a progressively improving state), with the two bus undertakings likewise made one under Government ownership. More visually obvious were the wholesale closures of promenade hotels in Douglas — many of these had, by 1987, already been closed for more than two years and, with the onset of recession, remained boarded up, "pending redevelopment", at the time of writing. Initially, some of the more architecturally significant buildings seemed to be faced with a demolition — a fate already accorded some of the major buildings on the south side of Victoria Street — but more recently conservation pressures have helped make preservation, or near-replication of façades a more desirable aim. Many of these reconstructions are intended as business premises or for permanent residence — the substantial proportion of Island income once derived from tourism, put as high as 50 per cent by some sources, is most unlikely to see repetition. In 1985 visitor numbers were down to 351,240, and by 1989 the figure was 322,970. In such circumstances, a smaller number of visitor beds is inevitable.

More optimistically, 1989 brought 87,185 business visitors to the Island, of whom 66 per cent stayed more than one night. Collectively, these people spent about £1.80 for every £1 spent by "ordinary tourists". These more sophisticated visitors often make recreational railway journeys while on business, as do participants in various off-season holiday programmes.

Reference to changes in the mechanism of Government appears later but, returning to our subject proper, the 1968 MER Board results did seem encouraging — the passenger figure reached 551,000 and with the Bulgham affair now history things seemed to augur well for the future. This was not to last, however. In January 1966 Board member T W Kneale, M Eng, had died and (in retrospect) his considerable professionalism in seeking high standards in trackwork and mechanical engineering matters generally, found no early replacement. As older men retired a tendency towards lower standards could sometimes be discerned: in about 1969, the writer remembers observing some very rough fitting practice being applied to the already "delicate" bronze castings of a Snaefell car's motors when under hurried seasonal repair.

In Tynwald, members given to anti-M E R sentiments continued to challenge the Board. The chief adversary was still Mr J B Bolton, who had proved himself an astute controller of Government finance. However, his tramless Marine Drive reconstruction has been a failure — he also persistently (as earlier) advocated a road to the Snaefell summit. In addition there has always been a degree of criticism from members whose constituencies are remote from the line — self-interest on the part of constituents is not confined to mainland politics. Sir Henry Sugden's Board (in office from 1966) was nonetheless still able to challenge its critics to such effect that it had gained (as described in a previous chapter) the funds necessary to tackle essential relaying work on Snaefell, although in the process committing the line to the continued use of Fell technology. Meanwhile, however, Mr Gilmore was to be faced by a near-exponential rise in the occurrence of motor failure on the Snaefell line, resulting, by 1972, in some motors having to be rewound after as few as 700 miles (the topic is dealt with technically in the next chapter). MER Board action to deal with this finally came about in autumn 1975.

During the late Sixties the Board had been receiving volunteered designs and specifications for new vehicles from a transport enthusiast, Mr A M Goodwyn (who later became the major editorial contributor to one of the rival enthusiast society magazines which were initiated in 1973-4). The same person now set up a company on the Island, entitled Rapid Transit Technical Services, apparently with the intention of manufacturing traction equipment. Now, however, late in 1971 RTTS came to seek a lease on the electric lines as operator — later reportage, however, came to reveal among other things an RTTS request for a Government indemnity against revenue loss for seven years, to an unspecified level. The Government's Executive Council was by now deeply concerned at the apparent (see later) costs of the MER and announced its intention of having outside consultants report on the line and its management, and on the RTTS proposals. During the ensuing interval, RTTS made a tactical withdrawal on the grounds that the time limit on its proposition had expired. But its proposal must still have been in mind when the Government appointed British Rail's consultancy arm, Transmark, on November 10, 1972. Transmark's work seems to have been substantially completed in 11 months, but its conclusion remained unpublished until spring 1974.

Meanwhile, at a more traditional level, Mr J H Price and Light Railway Transport League associates had continued to offer advice about possible replacement electrical equipment from the Continent until late in 1970, when (with Snaefell motor problem now acute) the reverse circumstance began to apply. Mr Gilmore now wrote asking for information on excellent ex-Vicinal equipment then on the market, but in reply it was (again) pointed out that the SMR track dimensions made them unusable. Earlier, "good possibilities" of acquiring suitable equipment in 1958, 1959 and even in 1970 had been allowed to fall by the wayside. Some Maley and Taunton equipment was obtained as a trial project, via Blackpool, in 1971 but its advanced nature was beyond MER expertise at the time and it soon lay abandoned.

Sir Henry's Board had ended its term of office in November of 1971 and the new Board once again had as chairman Mr H H Radcliffe, MLC. "Hughie" was a deservedly popular figure and epitomised the best in Manx politicians — his career had been with the Mounties in Canada. He was now faced with a Government intent on economies. As hinted earlier, Board costs had risen, and the public mind was ill-equipped to make the necessary corrections to the raw figures to allow for inflation.

This is well illustrated by the following table:

Year	M E R Deficit	Corrected figure (1958-9 prices)	Real increase (as to 1958-9)
1958-9	£25,000	-	-
1965-6	£31,621	£26,026	4.1%
1971-2	£55,542	£33,120	32.5%

(Figures in part derived from those published by the Isle of Man Railway Society in 1981)

In the middle year quoted, British Rail's deficit grew by 60 per cent and, over the longer period from 1959 to 1980, BR's loss was to climb by 227 per cent, the MER's by just 41 per cent.

In the run-up to its publication in May 1974, leaks from the Transmark report had seemed far from encouraging. People like Ramsey Commissioner, Mr J L Kneale (also a Board member), countered with statistics of a more hopeful kind. In spite of failures, the mountain railway notched up 61,000 passengers in 1973 (the Board's best ever

and an increase of 14 per cent), with northbound passengers on the Ramsey line also rising five per cent to 50,000. However, the evening of May 15 saw Transmark's selected option revealed by Mr Percy Radcliffe, Chairman of the Executive Council. Transmark had presented its report on February 7, in the presence of the MER Board, and by mid-May Mr Radcliffe had provided Tynwald members with a resumé of all three principal Transmark options, and their probable financial implications, as seen by the Council. In his statement of May 15, Mr Radcliffe outlined savings which would result from the chosen option, set against a supposed requirement for capital expenditure on the Laxey-Ramsey line of £663,000, and an annual operating deficit of £121,000. This option thus called for the winter closure of the entire MER system from the end of September and the permanent closure of the line north of Laxey.

Mr Radcliffe's proposed motion provoked a storm of protest throughout the line's catchment area. In the Tynwald debate on May 22, Mr Radcliffe spoke at length on the genesis of Transmark, mentioning its detailed dismissal of RTTS's leasing proposals as "untenable".

However, Charles Kerruish, now Speaker of the House, but who — unlike his British counterpart — nonetheless retained his voting rights — at once questioned the totality of the Transmark information earlier made available to the House. The previous day had seen the Keys set up a Steering Committee on Transport with the objective of examining the effects of Government control of the remaining transport undertakings. Now Mr Kerruish argued that an early re-examination of the Ramsey line question should be a priority for the new committee. With the recent public uproar as background, the amendment to Mr Radcliffe's motion was passed 12-10, with the Legislative Council subsequently adding its backing by four votes to two

The general tone of Transmark seems to have been very lukewarm towards the MER, inevitably contrasting 1972's 347,000 passengers carried with the 580,000 of ten years previously. The corresponding figures for visitor arrivals on the Island (446,578 and 499,658, respectively) were not specified. One Transmark train of thought seemed to suggest the Snaefell line as the only surviving operation.

By now the stresses on the Board and MER staff must have been considerable and Mr "Hughie" Radcliffe fell ill. Retiring in December 1974, he was hospitalised early in 1975 and died in April of 1976. His successor was Mr John C Clucas MHK. The late Mr Clucas (a chartered accountant) was a conspicuously active member of Tynwald for six years (1970-76), seeing service on a total of five Boards, including a turbulent chairmanship of that of the MER. After his period in the House, he continued to be active in Manx public life, typically in connection with the Health Service and the Manx Museum and National Trust. The substantial attendance at his funeral on May 20, 1991 indicated his continued public esteem and collective regret at his early death.

Events during 1974 were otherwise unexceptional but after further alarming "hints" the Steering Committee came out in March 1975 with a renewed recommendation for closure of the line north of Laxey. On March 18, the Keys devoted three hours of debate to the matter but essentially repeated the indecision of the previous year, rejecting a five-year retention by the odd vote in 23. The Legislative Council was more "positively negative" — only the Lord Bishop supported retention. Mr Clucas, unhappily, voted for closure, along with a fellow Board member. A report by Mr Maxwell Rostron, now Government Inspector of railways, seemed very pessimistic, certainly so in the Committee's interpretation.

A tidal wave of protest arose once more — critics pointed out that saving £30,000 to £40,000 would have little impact on an Island budget already topping £16m. Of this, the Harbour Board alone was looking for some £299,000.

Next, a notice appeared in the Press (under section 17 of the 1957 Act) announcing closure of the Ramsey line on October 1, 1975 and the cessation of all other MER services from then until April 30, 1976 (a casualty was to be the remaining mail service — see next chapter). Secretary Gilmore had to receive objections by May 15. Tynwald members were now subject to continuous pressure from constituents and a new debate was arranged for July 8. On July 4, a Press statement revealed that winter closure would go ahead but the actual physical abandonment of the Ramsey line would be deferred. By this date many Islanders had been saddened by the melancholy visual reality of the dismemberment of the IMR's Peel and Ramsey lines (closed since 1968) and this was no doubt reflected in the minds of the Keys' members.

On July 8, with (as already implied) a growing volume of protest from both within and outside the Island, a resolution already on the Keys order paper was rapidly substituted by another. There were than two proposed amendments (both defeated) before there emerged a two-part resolution. The first section deleted the reference to summer closure north of Laxey contained in that of March 18, the second clearly spelled out:

"That the Manx Electric Railway Board be and at the same time is hereby authorised to terminate wholly its transport services on all sections of the line from the October 1, 1975 to April 30, 1976, and for the same period in every subsequent year."

Had the March 18 abandonment resolution been sustained unchanged the Ramsey closure would have stood, but the above revisions were duly passed by 9-0 in the Legislative Council and 18-4 in the Keys.

Meanwhile, the Board had bought five miles of permanent way forming part of the "Manx Northern" section of the IMR (rolled in Barrow, 1930) for £25,600. Other track elements were later retrieved from Northern Ireland where a scheme to reconstruct the Giant's Causeway tramway had collapsed, and a team was soon at work lifting the IMR rails (see later chapter).

After a relatively good summer, October 1 now drew near. For the first time in 102 years, the Island's railways were to be totally inert. On September 30 (a dismal day) the 16.25 departure from Ramsey saw Nos 19 and 58 leave well-filled (followed later by 21 and 57 running empty). A crowd of townspeople and several Commissioners watched, and recent events prevented the atmosphere from being too funereal. "Three per weekday" substitute buses began work the next day. Ramsey Grammar and Dhoon School pupils lost their tram ride home — roaring downhill towards Laxey in a crowded "winter saloon" full of these buoyant young people was a memorable "time warp" experience, at well over 35mph, in winter's near-darkness.

On October 9 and 10, Tynwald's Steering Committee reported on its original brief. It recommended national ownership of both IMRS and Douglas bus services, with a suggested takeover at the start of the following April. This would at least see the end of subsidising the IMRS operation while its parent IMR still paid a dividend to shareholders. In the event, the new manager of Isle of Man National Transport, the late Mr W T Lambden, only took office on September 1, 1976, with vehicles and operation transferred a month later.

Adding to the plethora of comment, the UK-based Tramway Museum Society's "Services Ltd" subsidiary now had its (mainly volunteer) consultants prepare a report for the Ramsey Town Commissioners. Their report finally reached the Commissioners on St Valentine's Day, 1976. It was of massive proportions and contained a great deal of first hand observation but it was criticised for being too general. The MER management, having already suffered Transmark, was by now perhaps a little weary of consultancies. However, the TMS liaison with the Commissioners was to continue until early 1977.

Returning to autumn 1975, the catalogue of Snaefell motor failures recorded for the past season had reached proportions which demanded remedy (only on six days had six cars been serviceable). One of Transmark's team had been seconded from London Transport and must have established a degree of rapport with railway staff, if only through shared technical interest. Mr Clucas now grasped the Snaefell nettle firmly and obtained sanction for a London Transport (Railways) consultancy at a cost of some £9,500, with an estimated follow-up expenditure of between £50,000 and £100,000. This would see the end of the 1895 motors and even,

Aachen cars awaiting their fate at Lots Road (LTE), 1976. (Author's collection)

hopefully, included a "float" of spares.

By December, decisions as to the content of next season's publicity literature made a firm decision on the 1976 operation essential and it was now decided by Tynwald (resolution of December 10) that the Ramsey line would remain closed for the 1976 season. The arguments continued at full strength — Ramsey's J L Kneale prophesied revenue losses which were to prove very close to reality. There were still "ghost trams" — car 7 remained at Ramsey and made a journey to Laxey each morning, returning in the late afternoon. This "inspection car" was to vanish early in March when the Press noticed its secondary function as free employee transport!

The summer closure decision gave the management the task of organising a different kind of service, with much reduced opportunity for "special promotions" like the Rover ticket. These seasonal operations of 1976 duly fulfilled Mr Kneale's dire expectations. There was a token service for 27 days commencing on May 3, then full service until September 17, then again a curtailed schedule until the end of the month. Evening cars ran only between July 5 and August 20. With no Rover tickets, traffic plunged by 27 per cent (Douglas-Laxey 207,000, SMR 54,000, in round figures).

Meanwhile, tasks set in hand late in 1975 still needed Tynwald's attention. What was by now known as London Transport International Services Ltd had reported on the Snaefell question and had indeed found suitable modern equipment in Aachen, West Germany. In July, Tynwald duly voted a global £150,000 to cover the modernisation work. London Transport's Acton works seems to have become genuinely intrigued by this offbeat assignment and a trial car was to be ready by May 1977.

With a General Election looming, Tynwald last sat on October 18-19, 1976. Mr Kerruish fired his final shot when he presented the Court with the Redress of Grievance* petition brought to Tynwald's July 5 ceremony by a Ramsey resident, Mrs Bella Callister, asking for a reappraisal of the Ramsey line closure. This was accepted and referred to the (new) Steering Committee. A final speech by Mr J B Bolton (in which he drew parallels to 1956-8) included the valid point that he didn't really hate the trams — he was simply "concerned" as a financial professional.

On a more optimistic note, J C Nivison, Transport Steering Committee Chairman, reported the anticipated resumption of Isle of Man Railway steam trains from Douglas to the south (following two seasons of truncated shuttle service from the Port Erin southern extremity).

The 1976 election campaign was a lively one, and the fate of the various railways was well aired — the enthusiasts' organisations, the Board and others often found themselves engaged in acrimonious public debate. The important fact was that the final session of the Keys had clearly left the Ramsey line's future for its successors to decide, and when the 24 new MHKs (out of a field of 60) first met on November 23, the question surfaced immediately, the Speaker seeking a "declaratory motion" giving authority for re-opening. This was not at first achieved — the matter was to be twice deferred, first to mid-January, then to February 16, to allow the new Transport Steering Committee to complete its report.

The next few weeks saw some decidedly heavy "in-fighting" involving Mr Clucas (who remained Board Chairman until his successor Mr John J Christian took office on December 21), the Treasury Department, Mr Christian and various MHKs.

Mr Christian was professionally a lawyer, but had

---

* The Redress of Grievance procedure permits Manx citizens to petition Tynwald directly once a year at the ceremonial sitting on Tynwald Hill, St John's, when Acts passed by the Tynwald in the previous year are read out in English and Manx.

experience in both hotel and newspaper proprietorship. His membership of the Keys spanned from 1967-81, throughout which period he was to be MER Board Chairman, as well as a member of the Tourist Board.

The Keys session on December 21 now saw the new MER Board's Vice Chairman, Peter Craine, move a declaratory resolution both to nationalise the IMR and to create a new Joint Railways Board. This amalgamation took another four years to achieve but the IMR takeover was agreed. The following day, the new Transport Steering Committee announced its intention to commission a northern line inspection, which ultimately took place between January 10 and 13, employing the Government Inspector, Maxwell Rostron, and his colleague William Jackson. Next, to round off an extraordinary year, the Manx Electric Railway Society found a friendly permanent way engineer to make another inspection on "its" behalf. The said Mr Ryan managed to put in 11 days over Christmas and his resultant report was handed to Mr Christian on January 12. In all fairness, Mr Ryan "reads" like a professional but it seems unlikely his findings could have been seriously at variance with Mr Rostron's.

The new Board, meanwhile, had met Ramsey Commissioners and TMSS Ltd personnel at Ramsey on January 8, returning on car 19. On January 13, the MER Board and members of the Finance Board rode to Ramsey — events seemed to augur well. However, a final decision still hung on the Steering Committee's report which, as stated earlier, was not to emerge until February. Tynwald eventually debated the report on February 16, but the Steering Committee appeared to have left the final decision on re-opening to the MER Board.

Mr Christian had meanwhile put on a virtuoso performance in a public statement on January 18, having obviously "done his homework" since Christmas. Using Mr Rostron's up-to-date data, together with figures from his own management sources, he proceeded to demonstrate how pessimistic had been the earlier figures from the "Clucas/Treasury axis". He continued to point to the previous season's operating losses stemming from the northern line closure. In terms of then values, the Ramsey line re-opening would mean spending about £600,000 to £700,000 over 20 years. Conversion to a "single line and loop" operation was intended.

Returning to the Tynwald debate of February 16, Mr Kerruish's Declaratory Resolution of November now came to be accepted overwhelmingly by the Keys and the Legislative Council, albeit with an amendment stipulating a three trial seasons caveat). The Finance Board (new Chairman Mr Percy Radcliffe, MLC) were next given the task of examining the MER's estimates on March 22. Following acceptance, Tynwald's final approval followed on May 17. By employing railway contractor Henry Boot on a £19,000 contract it was hoped to complete the necessary works in eight weeks, from May 18. Mr Gilmore (who should have retired in March) must have felt re-inspired after all the miserable uncertainties of the past few years — he volunteered to stay on to help with the new work, finally handing over to the new Chief Executive on January 6, 1978. Mr Gilmore thus had the satisfaction of seeing the Snaefell re-equipment brought substantially to completion. All the staff shared, one feels, in the feeling of renaissance.

Mr Rostron acted as Government Inspector of Railways in his own right, but was also a partner in the Liverpool firm of Sloan Lloyd Barnes, Consultant Engineers. He had brought to the Board's notice a colleague, William Jackson, C Eng, MCIT and it was happy to engage his services as Engineering Consultant. He promptly visited Acton works in connection with the Snaefell project, then made his own "up to date" Ramsey line inspections which duly led to the Henry Boot contract. His energetic approach obviously made its mark, and when the post of Chief Executive (a new position arising from Government's widening involvement in transport) came to be advertised Mr Jackson was among the six candidates interviewed on October 29. With his recent activity as clear evidence of his attainment, he was successful and began his ten-year tenure of the post in December, 1977.

Mr Jackson's régime was not without its critics (though one might question their own experience) but, speaking from first hand experience, his breezy manner and enthusiasm for innovation were attractively constructive attributes. It happens that the writer and a technical colleague undertook quite extensive track repairs for Douglas Tramways in spring, 1980, and a significant amount of work was performed for us by MER engineering personnel, as "sub-contractors". Throughout this exercise Mr Jackson offered every possible help and courtesy. As we approach 1993, the existence of a complete "MER" as inherited by Robert Smith, the present Chief Executive, seems to justify his approach entirely.

The early spring of 1977 saw two sad losses — former chairmen, Sir Henry Sugden, in March, and Mr T H Colebourn, in April. Henry Boot's work on the Ramsey line had begun as scheduled in mid-May, and forged ahead to such purpose that re-opening was brought forward to Saturday, June 25. Laxey and Ramsey were en fête. At Laxey (after the arrival of Douglas participants at about 1.35pm) speeches were followed by a tape-cutting ceremony carried out by Speaker Kerruish, with Mr J J Christian in attendance. Car 20 then led off, hauling trailer 57, and driven by Lieut-Governor, Sir John Paul. Succeeding pairs were 19 and 58 and 5 and 47. With service interval spacings, the first public car left at 3.15. Ensuing business was excellent, in spite of poor visitor figures generally. At the same time, re-equipped Snaefell car No 1 had begun public service, the first pair of London Transport bogies having arrived from Acton during May. The performance was more than adequate, the power available having increased by about 240 per cent!

The former Douglas Corporation Transport offices at Derby Castle were now secured as the future headquarters of the MER Board. The move was to be completed on December 1, with 1 & 2 Strathallan Crescent being sold. With the Isle of Man Railway soon to become Government property a welcome step was the institution of a £5 joint seven-day "rail Rover" ticket covering both lines. The IMR's purchase negotiations were for a while stormy, but agreement was finally reached on August 18.

By the end of the season on September 30 there had been good MER operating results (for a curtailed season, only nine per cent down on 1975)* and the re-equipped Snaefell car continued to show fully adequate, indeed even excess performance. Tynwald now voted the IMR purchase at a figure of £250,000 on October 19, later agreed by the company at an extraordinary general meeting on November 23. The actual takeover took place on January 13, 1978, with the MER Board to run both lines for the time being, under Chief Executive Jackson. By December, the new corporate title, Isle of Man Railways, was in use, Mr A R Cannell was Engineering Superintendent, John Gordon, Operations Superintendent, and Maurice Faragher, Workshops Superintendent. This team worked well, and the writers's co-operation with Mr Faragher in 1980 was a mutually cordial one.

A new image (happily less destructive than in 1958's "green and white" era) was promoted by the use of a dark red background to new Isle of Man Railways titling in a strong yellow. On the trams this appeared on a below-underframe board on some of the cars and on the rocker panel of others. A dual

crest (of self-adhesive material) also appeared — this was perhaps a less happy choice, deriving from that of the IMR . An Isle of Man Railways Bill was now rumoured to be in the offing, with the new joint undertaking intended also to run the IoM National Transport bus services. By April 1978 the new timetables for both railways (with services commencing on May 1) had appeared. New bold typefaces, logos and layout were adopted and a separate enclosure provided supporting information about Snaefell services. Various engineering innovations of the period are described later.

Late in Mr Clucas's term of office the Board's efforts to sell most of the now substantially surplus "ECCs" and some little-used 1893/4 trailers had become the subject of some very controversial press reportage. Somewhat insubstantial contacts seem to have continued, and after Mr Jackson's appointment late in 1977 a properly prepared sales brochure (by then for four cars and four trailers) was produced — the writer's own copy had a tendering date of October 31, 1978 superimposed. The period saw the competing availability of more orthodox equipment (of US origin) from Portugal, and interest in the Manx cars seems to have slowly faded, the main potential for sale lying in American museum operations.

Mr W T Lambden, Manager of IOMNT, died suddenly on July and he was succeeded by Mr J Oates. The 1978 season was a good one so far as visitor arrivals were concerned, but bad weather saw a rise of steam railway patronage at the expense of the MER , especially Snaefell. By 1979 it emerged that 1978's losses well exceeded those of 1977 (both railways then lost about £200,000) but considerable works on both railways were in progress and Government seemed willing to foot the new bill of more than £850,000. The Isle of Man Railway

Right: Charles Kerruish, Speaker of the House of Keys, cuts the white tape in front of car No 20 at Laxey station during the reopening ceremonies for the Laxey to Ramsey section, June 25, 1977. (J H Price).
Below: The special train on which the MER board and guests travelled from Douglas to Ramsey for the reopening. (J H Price)

---

* Ex-Douglas, 118,459; ex-Snaefell summit, 60,444; ex-Ramsey, 31,856.

Society now appeared as impending co-sponsor of the electric railway museum developed at Ramsey, and opened on May 31, 1979. This complemented the society's earlier support for Port Erin's IMR museum.

1979, as a part of the Millennium of Tynwald celebrations, the Board organised a Centenary of Electric Traction* celebration at Laxey, with an extensive procession of cars on May 31. Substantial repaints had seen many of the cars revert to turn-of-the-century lettering and (reasonably) accurate accompanying liveries. Mrs Callister (whose Redress of Grievance petition of July 1976 has already been mentioned) made a repeat appearance at the July Tynwald Ceremony with the intention of pressing for renewed all-year MER services and acceptance of continuance beyond the three-year trial period. Unfortunately, with the Queen present, she fell foul of possibly over-zealous police and was bundled off. Happily, however, the season was a good one — a repeat of 1978 would have been discouraging. By October 17, this success this was reflected in Tynwald's agreement to continue northern line operation for another five years. The new 1979-80 estimates lacked a figure for the 1977 proposal to convert the northern line to single-track operation, as the cost of the new signalling this would require was now seen as excessive. The steam line continued to "use" substantial sums of money, and some significant further expense was planned on coast line car equipment and on completing the re-equipment of Snaefell cars.

Thus, the October 17 Tynwald debate seemed to show a gentler attitude on the part of past adversaries, including Sir John Bolton, MLC (Knighted 1977) and Mr Percy Radcliffe. Sir Charles Kerruish and Mr Swales (MHK for Ramsey) presented some telling (though simple) figures which showed Ramsey line revenue as $2^1/_2$ times its maintenance costs and a three-year rise in patronage, southbound, from 31,000 to 69,000. Essentially, the Board was embarked on reconstruction from revenue rather than capital resources, a move duly perceived, but not entirely condemned, by the chairman of the Steering Committee on Transport, J C Nivison.

By March 13, 1980 Tynwald was to put into effect the amalgamation of the two railways with IOMNT's buses under the title Isle of Man National Transport, which status was to continue until 1983. The bus undertaking's General Manager, Mr J Oates, remained in office with correspondingly enlarged responsibilities (see Chapter 8), Mr Jackson's continuing rôle as Chief Executive having been confirmed in Tynwald on March 16. The controlling Board was legally still the Manx Electric Railway Board.

The Eighties

The advent of a new decade brought with an easing of the political pressures facing the railway. Government resources were improving, thanks to the increasing offshore financial activity mentioned at the beginning of this chapter, but the tourist industry's decline was to become acute, the real

Below: No 6 in IoMPT lettering, 1982. (R Powell Hendry)

Isle of Man Passenger Transport

---

* The pioneering Siemens and Halske line opened in Berlin in 1879 is commonly regarded as the world's first electric railway.

sufferers being the owners of hotels and boarding houses.

Railway traffic for 1980 was not expected to reach the levels of the preceding Millennium year. Poor weather, as so often, affected Snaefell earnings but, nonetheless, a significant improvement over 1978 was attained.

The Board, by now sensible of the service they could offer residents, reintroduced winter services, although on a much reduced scale from those of 1974-5. The first timetable was dated October 6, 1980 and underwent major revision on December 8. There has been a winter service ever since. "Winter break" holidays have thus been able to include a tramway journey in their itineraries — the Island winter landscape is a lovely one.

Following resumption of winter services, the Board's position as subject of a annual Government "seasonal" railway inspection (in the obligatory sense) no longer applied, but the Board chose to pre-empt possible criticism by appointing Michael Lockhart, of London Transport, to inspect on its own behalf.

With 1981's General Election, Mr Christian had by now (no doubt) had enough of politics for a while and did not stand again for the Keys until 1984. Following the election, and after some curious Keys vacillations (December 15-16) a new MER Board duly appeared, headed by Dominic Delaney, a Douglas MHK. Happily Mr Delaney's Board was to have a less contentious existence than those of Messrs Clucas and Christian — his colleagues now included J C Nivison, who proved a constructive addition. Visitor figures for the decade were to make a dismal reading,* but the railways' share of the available passenger "cake" has continued to be generous.

This sustained tourist attraction value has obviously influenced Government substantially. Current improvements to the line's infrastructure, and the extensive programme planned for 1993, clearly evidence the constructive attitude now prevalent.

At long last, an Isle of Man Passenger Transport Bill managed to get through the Keys and Legislative Council, being passed early in 1982. A car in the paint shop — No 6 — was duly lettered in this style and looked almost as "verbose" as those carrying "Douglas, Laxey and Ramsey Electric Railway" (27 letters versus 37!).

The resultant Isle of Man Passenger Transport Board administration finally became legally effective from April 1983, still chaired by Mr Delaney (the new IOMPT Board now had three members against the MER's previous five, their tenure being until November 1986).

Returning to the spring of 1982, the Highway Board was now looking into the problems of coastal erosion just south of Ballure. Happily, it was seen as a communal matter — road and railway were equally at risk — and repairs were ultimately put in hand by the Highway Board. It will probably have been realised by the reader that the various discussions on finance which have punctuated this chapter were, by 1983-4, rendered totally obsolete by the general level of inflation. The railways' (IMR & MER) budget for that year had ascended to £1.3m. Meanwhile, the Island's overall budget had climbed to more than £78m. Currently the Highway Board was spending about £100,000 at Ballure.

On November 16, 1983 Mr Delaney sought to remove the imminently approaching "five years of operation" caveat by a resolution allowing the Board to operate "for such period as the Board may determine, in accordance with the Board's statutory powers". His supporters included the Chairman of the Finance Board — changed days indeed. The resolution was approved with little or no dissent. Thereafter the controversies of the preceding 26 years were less prone to repetition...

By 1986 (another election year) the Island's governmental structure was substantially revised, with a new Ministerial format. The new "Ministerial Government" concept in some ways sought to insulate the activities of the various predecessor Boards from the lobbying to which their members had previously (at times) been subject, Ministerial authority being seen as less "accessible". At the same time, what seemed to be an undesirable proliferation of Boards was to be brought under control, with their replacement by only nine main "Departments".

The prime element in the Ministerial structure is that of Chief Minister, a choice made by the elected membership of the House of Keys. The Minister then selects his own "team" of nine from among members of the Keys, and it is this ten-strong "Cabinet" (The Council of Ministers) which has the task of running the everyday business of Government. It is (effectively) a strengthened version of the former Executive Council from which it can be seen as a logical derivation. As can be deduced from Appendix 5, the Executive Council — "ExCo" — had already become increasingly entangled in the daily business of Government, in spite of its declared "advisory" role (its existence only finally ended in 1990 when the Council of Ministers was formally established).

The railways and buses now became a "wing" of the Department of Tourism and Transport, with Allan Bell, MHK for Ramsey, as its first Minister. The three-man IOMPT Board administrative structure continued to exist under the new scheme with Mr Bell as Chairman and two MHKs as colleagues.

In July 1987 Mr Jackson elected to retire (his title was by now DoT&T's "Chief Officer"). The success-

---

* The experience was not unique to the Island — Cornwall's 1981 tourism statistics showed an even bigger fall than those of the Island.

ful applicant was Robert Smith, BA, MCIT.

Mr Smith joined London Transport as a graduate trainee in 1978. After widely based initial experience, he was attached to the LT consultancy "arm", London Transport International. Later, he was appointed Senior Commercial Development Executive, concerned with joint re-development schemes (with the private sector) arising from the reconstruction of LT stations.

His strongly-felt personal interest in the coordination of transport operations continued and when the Island post was advertised it seemed a classic opportunity to put these ambitions to practical effect — this leading to his taking up his new post in December, 1987.

During Mr Smith's regime, the IoMT Board at first continued three-man. Mr Bell's original (1986) colleagues were MHK's B May and Dr J R Orme — the former was later replaced by another MHK, Mr D C Cretney. Following the elections of November 1991 the Minister of Tourism, Leisure and Transport, Allan Bell was joined by MHK Mr A F Downie to form a new two-man Board. The sad death of General Manager Oates is referred to in Chapter 8. Following the retirement of John Gordon in June 1990, a new management structure resulted, which appears below (Mr Warhurst inheriting Mr Gordon's position). Incidentally, the Inspector of Railways is now Mr J H Taylor, succeeding Mr M A Lockhart.

Apart from his work in seeking to establish a truly integrated Island bus and rail network (a typical example was the institution of the Island Freedom Ticket in 1991, this covering *all* island bus and tram operations, and the steam railway), Mr Smith and his team have been occupied in advance planning for the Year of Railways (1993) centred on the MER centenary.

Alan Corlett was appointed as Centenary Coordinator in April, 1991. Work on the railways from that date may conveniently be divided as for "general infrastructure" and "centenary orientated".

In the first category is to be included the annual

expenditure of c£100,000 on the depot and workshop areas on both steam and electric lines — Derby Castle is in hand in 1992-3. Major improvements at Laxey station come in the same category, as is a new "drying out unit" — not for inebriates but for tramcar motors! Nos 18 and 31 are current "patients" with planned use in 1993. The coincidental rebuild of fire casualty MER 22 is mentioned in the next chapter. There has also been significant improvement at Ramsey and Laxey stations, the latter already earning an award (1987)

In the second category might be mentioned the special upgrading currently being afforded Groudle station, and the imminent conversion of No 9 to an illuminated tram — this last sponsored by Brian Horner. Throughout the latter part of 1991 and thereafter the railways have made repeated publicity appearances at mainland transport events, both amateur and professional, latterly using a specially converted bus as an exhibition and information centre. Considerable interest by the truly international clientèle of the November 1991 Light Railways exhibition held at Manchester's G Mex centre represented one tangible reward for the railways' team.

The latest publicity handout from the railways is able to list a 1993 programme of railway "happenings" between February 3 (when special postage stamps appear) and the end of October, with particularly important MER commemorations in June, August and September (and substantial enthusiast orientated provision in May, as has become traditional). Readers will join in wishing all the MER staff a successful year. Hopefully, reading the present text may inspire at least some to "go and see for themselves" — their welcome will be as warm as that the author has enjoyed for many years!

If a favourable verdict is given by the Council of Ministers, a specially constructed visitor centre may yet be able to be provided to assure a fully-integrated introduction to the history and present "reality" of the MER — this would be of particular value to visitors from the continent and the United States.

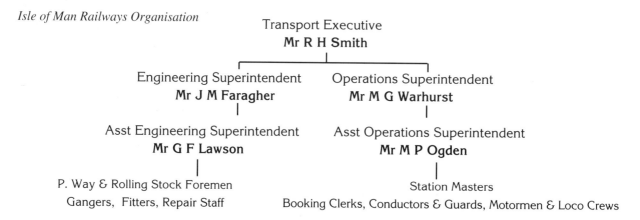

Isle of Man Railways Organisation

Transport Executive
Mr R H Smith

Engineering Superintendent
Mr J M Faragher

Operations Superintendent
Mr M G Warhurst

Asst Engineering Superintendent
Mr G F Lawson

Asst Operations Superintendent
Mr M P Ogden

P. Way & Rolling Stock Foremen
Gangers, Fitters, Repair Staff

Station Masters
Booking Clerks, Conductors & Guards, Motormen & Loco Crews

Administrative Staff work jointly for the Transport Executive, Engineering Superintendent and Operations Superintendent.

Chapter 8

The Line, 1968-92

Trackwork

Readers will recall that, at the close of Chapter 6, sanction had been obtained to commence major renewals on the Snaefell line, particularly of the downhill Fell rail, which was by this time showing appreciable wear. The implied commitment to the continued use of the contemporary technology is obvious — at this time, the near exponential rise in serious motor faults which developed in the early Seventies had yet to emerge. The running rails on the Snaefell line also caused difficulties, not through wear, for the head of the rail was generous, but because of an over-thin web and foot, on which corrosion had made serious inroads. Typically, 500 yards (460m) of track were relaid in winter 1972-3 and another 100 tons of Fell rail were delivered.

Continuing funding for the project was agreed the following winter, to the tune of £9,500, but by the spring of 1974 the work had fallen behind and only 17 lengths of the running rails had been replaced. There had been exceptionally poor weather, and the Board had also elected to renew track and timbers elsewhere, on the seaward side of the Ballure viaduct. Regrettably, by autumn the cost of materials for both these repair projects had risen by £2,500. Some 4,000 sleepers were shipped from Glasgow in mid-November.

Meanwhile, there continued the ongoing "battle of the poles". The use of ex-Douglas Head Marine Drive tramway poles has been mentioned previously. The annual toll of pole "casualties" on the Douglas-Laxey section of the MER has long been an accepted fact of life, and things are little better today on the Ramsey section (on the whole route from Douglas to Ramsey there are 904 poles in all). Acute ground level corrosion long ago necessitated the fitting of heavy cast reinforcing collars, while more recent repair techniques have seen the poles filled with steel angles, bars and concrete. Some recently erected poles are ex-Douglas street lamp standards, but new ones have also been bought, the most recent British Steel examples being galvanised.

Problems at ground level are matched near the top of the poles where fittings and the "bracket" (cross) arms are attached. For much of the present century the MER overhead line used components from the British Insulated Callendars Construction Company. When the company ceased production the work went to Colton Electrical, of Upminster, which was agent for Albert and J M Anderson, of Boston, supplier of the MER trolley bases and of many of the pre-1900 overhead line components. However, Colton's ceased manufacture in the early Eighties and materials now come from a variety of sources.*

The majority of the overhead line technology is "pure 1900" and necessarily relies heavily on sustaining established skills. Painting is a continuous exercise and, over the period under review, went from dark green to black, "inherited" grey and (once again) green.

As described in Chapter 7, in the midst of the political upheavals of 1975, the Board did secure the purchase of five miles of excellent "Manx Northern"** track (and a portion of the Douglas-Peel line) and successfully lifted this material during April and May. A tractor drew rails into Ramsey, and further out the Ramsey Pier's "Planet" loco retrieved rail and established a "permanent way yard" at Lezayre station. The pier tramway's Wickham railcar was in use beyond Lezayre, and later went to Ballaugh whence it worked as far as Bishopscourt, then to a half-mile section near Crosby on the Peel line. The plot at Queens Drive, Ramsey, which was for many years the MER's chief rail store, was to be sold by early 1977, so that in future all rail storage was centred on Laxey (apart from some smaller stocks at Dhoon Quarry).

By winter 1975 the Fell rail renewal on the downhill section of the Snaefell line was almost complete, but the now imminent consultant's report outlined in Chapter 7 would make any renewal of the uphill line Fell rail unnecessary, and work since has been concerned with the running rails. The extraordinary Fell rail point at the depot was removed in 1981 and replaced by plain track. Late in the year, an excellent MER relay from Douglas to Port Jack used "Manx Northern" rails and pointwork, the latter retrieved from Northern Ireland.

---

* A pole carrying double overhead lines is illustrated in A M Goodwyn's All about the Manx Electric Railway, page 50. He labels 20 different items, several of which appear in twos or fours — Mr Goodwyn treats the subject in considerable depth.

** Actually track relaid by the Isle of Man Railway in the 1930s.

The workload undertaken in 1977 in re-opening the Ramsey line has been outlined in Chapter 7. Since that time, the Board has, logically, pursued a policy of progressive renewal of the most worn sections as resources permit. One episode which turned out rather badly was the May 1979 arrival "on exercise" of an Army Royal Corps of Transport team, which undertook to relay the Majestic-Braeside-Howstrake stretch of track, but departed after a somewhat uneven performance, with the job only about 40 per cent complete.

With both railways under common control from 1978, work on the steam line also became of concern, having its own priorities, duly assessed with those of the MER.

Exceptional to the pattern of piecemeal renewal, a major continuing operation to relay the Snaefell running rails was sustained. Over the three Board years 1978-81 some £32,000 was budgeted annually for this task (the preceding two years had each cost £26,500). By May 1978 some 220 rail lengths were targeted. To assist in permanent way operations the newly unified railways were reported to have acquired a Matisa tamper, duly regauged to 3ft. In practice, its ability to handle the very mixed ballast common in the Island proved limited — present day ballasting improvements may yet permit its use.

The budget requirement for a "single and loops" conversion for the Ramsey line kept sliding back in the Board priorities of the era — it last appeared as a "prospect" for 1979/80. Experimentally, the Snaefell overhead line was left in situ on the uppermost sections (beyond the Bungalow) in winter 1978-9. However, ice formation brought down much of the wire and the earlier practice of winter removal was resumed, except when work on the summit radar station required "winter service".

In what was to be the last winter without electric car operation, Laxey station received a major relay in the winter of 1978-80, a task completed by the end of March. Though not strictly a "track" subject, that month also saw the demolition by Douglas Corporation of the still impressive (though much simplified) IOMT & EP station canopy over the terminal horse car tracks at Derby Castle, in what most external observers saw as a short-sighted exercise in cost-cutting.

Two years later, on the night of August 5, 1982, the Board lost a major building when the Snaefell summit hotel (by now leased off) burned down. No cars ran until August 9, and temporary accommodation had to suffice until a "new" building opened in May 1984. The fire eliminated the railway's radio telephone system (newly installed in 1982) for two days, and the building work necessitated the construction of a trailing-connected siding at the Bungalow (on the mountain side of the crossing) so SMR works vehicles could load road-borne materials bound for the summit.

Although (as described in Chapter 7) the Government's attitude to the railways was, by the Eighties, to prove a more consistently supportive one, the economic restraints imposed by the decline in the number of visitors to the Island had some impact. A Snaefell track scheme for 1981-4 was a casualty of the early part of 1981, being "refused" (deferred) by the Finance Board, although substantial funds were allowed for steam railway trackwork. There were suggestions that the Walpole Road "reserved track" grooved rails were to be removed in the near future (much of the flange had already worn away) but in the event this section was still in place in 1992. At the northern end of the Bulgham shelf (where in 1903 the partially cantilevered 1898 tramway had been moved inland to a position over the original road) the retaining wall was known to be bulging. This substantial "rectification" job confronted the newly-appointed Chief Engineer, Maurice Faragher, in 1983. Loose material was taken out and holes drilled down into sound rock before a "wall" of old rails (as reinforcement) and concrete was reconstructed. The problems caused by coastal erosion at Ballure cliffs (already mentioned in Chapter 8) had by now been dealt with.

The section of Snaefell Fell rail from the depot down to Laxey saw renewal in 1986-7. This piece of track was still used for the daily trial of Fell brakes, en route for Laxey station, and was worn as a result. One of the consequences of overall rheostatic braking on the mountain line has been an incidence of "rail creep", dealt with by bolting inverted running rail to the rail foot, abutting against the uphill face of every ninth or tenth sleeper. Traffic lights at the Bungalow (to be given manual control) were under discussion at this date, but have not yet installed.

The changes at Derby Castle from 1988/89 onwards have considerably

The new castellated Summit Hotel of 1906 was a much more pleasing structure than its predecessor, but was destined to become a fire casualty in 1982. (NTM)

revised the works layout. By removing a section of the one-time goods shed's platform (including the section outside the building) the track running into the shed (hitherto used for storage) could be moved to the west so as to give additional working space, in which the erection of a raised staging enabled the creation of a proper paint shop. The two-road car shed to the east now became the joiners' shop, and is no longer connected by rail, although the two former tracks now have a single replacement which ends just outside the building (a dead-end spur, in effect, from the paint shop road). In the yard, the former Bonner Wagon siding was lifted, and two new staff buildings and a works office were erected on a (broadly) NW-SE orientation across the site of the former joiners' shop.

The period has also seen a reversion to very much the traditional "MER Green" for buildings and overhead poles (technically, the present colour is "beetle green").

The "rolling programme" of half-mile relays continued to make progress — for the 1989/90 winter this was again on Snaefell, and the Inspecting Officer has expressed satisfaction at the progressive improvement on both the steam and the electric railways. The success of a German built 90cm gauge diesel loco on the IMR has led to current consideration of other second-hand works vehicles of this gauge, obtainable through European contacts. These will much assist the PW department in its work, and reduce the use of passenger cars.

The wooden mascot, "Tommy Milner", atop Derby Castle works, went back up again in 1990, following repair. His absence during the previous few years apparently undermined his reputed "potency", since it was always reckoned that the railway would "expire" were he lost from his perch atop No 1 car shed.

The Cars

The Seventies began badly: while Snaefell car No 5 stood at the summit on August 16, 1970, an underfloor short circuit (on the overhead side of the breakers) started a fire which rapidly reduced the vehicle to a bulkhead panel and a floor. Local joiner, H D Kinnin, of Ramsey, was brought in and, in only 11 months, produced a remarkably close copy of a car in its 1895 state, that is without clerestory, but with modern windows set into its side framing. Its inaugural journey was on July 8, 1971. A change of appearance to the fleet as a whole came with the removal of the giant roof-mounted advertisement boards in winter 1970-71.

Had it not been for the at first unperceived onset of Snaefell motor problems it is apparent that the one-car-a-winter overhaul routine for the six-car fleet might have continued indefinitely. Until the late

Sixties, the Snaefell cars' running gear had resembled the machinery of a traditional ship's engine room in its spotless condition — the "newly wiped with a slightly oily rag look" was universal. The car shed was an unbelievably primitive place but the pride in the fleet displayed by men like the late Allan McMullen overrode such minor considerations. Even the lubricants looked more like golden olive oil than a mere engineering product... However, as already implied in Chapter 7, this idyllic situation was to change as the decade drew to a close.

By 1973 it had become painfully obvious that a serious malaise afflicted the Snaefell fleet — according to Mr Clucas, in that year the "between rewinds" motor mileage fell to an average of 1,068. A year later the figure was down to 501, and by 1975 an abysmal 363. At about this time, the more elderly of London Transport's traction motors were managing 632,000.* The steps taken in autumn 1975 to deal with this situation have been heavily criticised by others but the operational success — and retained visual identity— of the re-equipped Snaefell cars seems to fully vindicate them.

Some more general "events" included the 1973 appearance of an air whistle on car No 20 — a practical and successful innovation later applied to all the air-braked cars. Derby Castle had enjoyed something of a "painter's orgy" the preceding winter — car numbers 5, 19 , 20, 25, and 26 all received repaints and Snaefell 3 enjoyed a full overhaul. Unfortunately this treatment did not include a panacea for decaying motors. The next Snaefell car to go down to Derby Castle, on October 18, 1973, was No 6, while in winter 1974 significant overhaul work was in hand on numbers 20, 21 and 22, along with Snaefell 2. The last "traditional" overhaul of a Snaefell car was to be of No 4 in the winter of 1975.

By October 1975, after a season which had seen 55 Snaefell motor failures, the London Transport consultancy was in place and, having obtained Tynwald approval for a scheme inside the £150,000 ceiling imposed, by May of 1976, the consultants had found a batch of modern (1956-7) tramcars for sale in Aachen, Germany. There were 11 of these, but by accepting the task of removing them complete, the consultants persuaded the Germans to sell just seven. Each car had four motors of about 61 horsepower (46Kw), with a 24-volt control circuit operating electro-pneumatic contact gear. The control system was able to utilise the regenerative capacity of the compound-wound motors for service braking, dissipating the energy through rheostats. It was this capability which had most significance. Other additional braking systems included magnetic track brakes, but these were not retained. The Board Chairman and Mr Gilmore went to Aachen in June, with London Transport personnel, and the deal was struck for a total of £17,500. There was a

---

* There are some discrepancies between the SMR mileages here quoted and those in Transmark

slight hitch when "the car full of spares" (1010) arrived in Douglas on November 12 and turned out to be empty. The material concerned was inside one of the other cars (Nos 1003-5, 1008 and 1011) which arrived at London Transport's Lots Road Power Station two weeks later. Here, the intended stripping and scrapping routine was put in hand and MER staff rescued the misdirected spares. Car 1010 served at Derby Castle as a rather incongruous mess room until 1985.

As the end of the 1976 season approached, there had been even more Snaefell motor failures and sometimes only one car was available for use. Snaefell car No 1's bogies had by now been sent to Derby Castle and were forwarded to London Transport in September. There, it soon emerged that the position of the new motors raised complex problems and it would be simpler to produce replacement frames with an altered layout. Acton Works produced a pair, visually near-replicas, and later a price of £58,000 was agreed for a further five sets of frames.

By early the following June, the new bogies for car No 1 were at Laxey, and the car was to be ready for trials by the 17th. At this point in time the Fell brake (still fitted as an emergency "back-up") was intended to continue in partial use on the steepest sections of track, but a sixfold improvement in shoe life was confidently expected. Car 1's body had meanwhile been fitted with the revised wiring and quite complex equipment of an Aachen car (including electric gongs), making use of the original Aachen resistors, now roof-mounted above suitable shielding. It was intended to run the cars on series notches only, but in practice parallel operation has been permitted above the Bungalow — the resultant acceleration makes for an extraordinary experience when surrounded by Mr Milnes' late Victorian coachbuilding.

The wiring of No 1 provided a set of working circuit plans for the other five cars, and over the next three years these were duly dealt with (Nos 2 and 3 in 1977-8, 4-6 in 1978-9). In 1979 a further £15,000 was to be spent on the provision of special high capacity roof-mounted resistances. The ex-Aachen units had a full load duration of about ten minutes, explaining the need for continued partial use of the Fell brake, but with these new units Fell-braking became unnecessary. Pole markings are used to indicate optimum controller settings during descent.

Car No 1's plain axle box bearings were to be converted to the otherwise standard roller bearing type in 1980, and all the cars were to be scheduled to receive larger profile wheelsets from 1988, until which time they would continue to use the ex-Aachen "street tramway" profile, with an appreciably narrower tread.

Following the installation of the resistors, and the later work on the car bodies ending in 1987, the rehabilitation programme was effectively complete. The resulting set of cars continue to provide a distinctive part of the Island's attractions and should offer reliable service for many years.

Returning to 1976, with winter closure on September 30, the fleet faced a second winter of hibernation. Indeed, through 1976, a total of nine motor cars (and ten trailers) had stood completely idle. To help avoid the lengthy electrical drying out process, cars whose 1977 use seemed certain were now "exercised" from Douglas to Groudle and back (late in 1975 a number of cars had been withdrawn with faults and it is quite possible some remained unattended to by winter 1976). However, the new climate attending the decision to reopen to Ramsey saw Derby Castle hard at work to provide a larger usable fleet — the works, before reopening in 1977, saw Nos 1, 2, 5, 6, 7, 9 and 29 all in "departmental use".

Also in 1977, the Wickham railcar fleet on Snaefell received a further addition, a near-duplicate of that of 1957. A table listing these railcars appears in Chapter 9, where the incidental change from Air Ministry to Civil Aviation Authority ownership will be noted. The 1951 car now passed to MER ownership.

After June's reopening, the heavy traffic saw the appearance of three of the eight 1898 equipped ECC (Electric Construction Company) cars in regular service (Nos 14, 18 and 29) but by late summer No 18 had minor faults, as already had 17 and 31. By this date No 15 had more significant problems and 28 and 30 had been used as a source of spares. The Board, in offering for sale (ultimately) 15, 17, 28, and 31 was obviously (by the following year) able to overcome these problems within existing resources. As noted in Chapter 7, the various offers received were to prove insubstantial.

The Ramsey line works had seen extensive use of the three overhead line tower wagons. Two were "originals" numbered 1 and 3 in no apparent relation to any other stock, while the third was an adaption of van No 12, which provided convenient "indoor" storage at the same time.

Royal saloon No 59 had spent summer 1977 as an "advertisement" at the Sea Terminal but returned safely that autumn. IMR coach F12 turned up at Derby Castle as a store during that winter, but was later to be broken up.

On taking office as the new Chief Executive, one of William Jackson's first engineering concerns was with the motor equipment of the coast line cars. Given the recent experience of Snaefell motor repairs, the sub-contracting of winding repairs to a Liverpool firm, Rewinds and J Windsor & Son, was perhaps to be seen as a reasoned choice. Incidentally, at the time of writing, some 1890s armatures survive "untouched", thus demonstrating their remarkable longevity. From an engineering point of view these must have been "perfect" when manufactured.

At the same time, efforts were made to improve the mechanical elements of the motors (other than ECCs) and roller bearing armatures now (1977-8) made their appearance, beginning with one motor on car 32. There were some teething troubles but eventually the process was successfully applied to all but Nos 1 and 2 and the Brush-bogied cross bench cars.

Concurrently, efforts were made to obtain permission for a new central workshop facility at Laxey, but opposition on residential amenity grounds seems to have blocked the proposal. Staff were to continue to "enjoy" the largely unrepaired "amenities" of Derby Castle until the thorough reconstruction begun in 1988, which was still in progress in 1992.

Car No 25, in silver livery since 1977, now reverted to normal style, and the new "Isle of Man Railways" titling now appeared on Nos 7, 16, 19-22 and 55. All the saloon cars had received their air whistles by August 1978.

In some respects the visual condition of the cars had become poorer, but now the approach of Millennium Year gave impetus to a series of restorations which was to transform visually much of the fleet. At this date the Board had a number of apprentices and their enthusiasm was appropriately harnessed to the restoration of car No 1 and (later) No 2, while other repaints (detailed in Chapter 9) began to bring a succession of visual delights. The ongoing motor rehabilitation scheme saw No 33 with all four motors "done" by summer 1978, with No 19 an early candidate for the next set. The July reappearance of Snaefell 2 and 3 had seen them fitted with roof-mounted headlights so that evening working was now possible, when required. It was about this date that MER No 9 lost its twin end windows so that the 1894 G F Milnes "end aspect" temporarily became history. No 57 spent some time as a "shop" at Laxey, but this was not particularly successful and its partially stripped interior was then restored.

With the coming of Millennium Year in 1979, the new museum project mentioned previously was realised at the Ramsey car shed. This was largely stimulated (and later operated) by the Isle of Man Railway Society. The Society also bought the MER locomotive No 23 (alias "The Kruger") and freight trailer 26. These were cleaned up and given repaints in grey* and were duly installed in time for the joint opening by Mrs Elaine Hendry and Chairman Christian on May 31, 1979. Both vehicles were used as part of the Centenary of Electric Traction procession at Laxey on that day. The work on No 23 provided for later motorisation and this was to be achieved for demonstration purposes in both 1983 and 1984. The overall level of activity at Derby Castle must have been unprecedented. Snaefell Nos 4 and 6 were to be available by mid-May and the

concurrent restorations and repaints of 1, 9, 19 and 32 were ready for the Centenary procession. No 1 was lettered as for "Douglas and Laxey Coast Electric Tramway", No 9 for "Douglas Laxey and Ramsey Electric Railway" (as in about 1902), No 19 as "The Manx Electric Railway Co Ltd" and No 32 (and 62) appeared in the green livery of 1957.

Snaefell No 5 was now able to go down to Derby Castle works, being the very last Mather & Platt equipped car, and meanwhile the new resistors had appeared on sister car No 6. The Board next agreed to provide a further £15,000 for this additional work on Nos 1-5 (so that the final Snaefell line re-equipment cost rose to £27,500 per car). A new tower wagon for Snaefell was also constructed.

On Snaefell, the Fell brake shoe life had already ascended to about 12 or 13 trips before the fitting of the new resistor units. MER Nos 20-22 were now in line for roller bearing motors and this was achieved by December 1979. The Board's budget by then provided £90,000 for the coast line motor equipment, spread over four years (slightly later figures quoted £30,000 per year). The Snaefell resistors were all to be in place by 1980; in subsequent body repair programmes, completed by 1987, the car clerestories were reinforced to accommodate the significant additional load.

After 1980, the future of the ECC cars and surplus trailers remained uncertain. Storage space was still available and the non-operable cars were thus simply left aside. The 1990-1 position was that four (15, 17, 28 and 30) were electrically incomplete, and trailers 36, 50, 53 and 54 were also regarded as "out of use".

After its protracted rebuild, No 2 was completed in time for the 1981 season, appearing much as No 1 but with its "DL & RER" lettering in a new "curly"

The excellent results of co-operation between the Island Railways and the Isle of Man Railway Society are exemplified by this view of No 23 as remotored in 1983.

---

* No 23's cab is dark green.

style, also now shared by No 21 (see Chapter 9). No 5 emerged in August with full "The Manx Electric Railway Co Ltd" titling but surprisingly using a yellow letter face, and for 1982 No 6 was (as stated previously) to emerge as for "Isle of Man Passenger Transport", broadly in MER Co style.

A September 1981 casualty, while still "on active service", was that of the Hurst Nelson Snaefell wagon, which had decayed to the point of collapse. "Royal saloon" 59 was by now a Ramsey museum exhibit but has since been extricated when required for "special" service. By this season, too, SMR 1 had reappeared in May with its roller bearing axleboxes.

The next major renewal work on the cars consisted of the 1985-6 re-upholstery of all four winter cars (Nos 19-22) and their "associate" No 5. The green cars (32/62) also now reverted to traditional red and white livery but the remaining styles introduced from 1979 can still be seen — the only surviving "Isle of Man Railways" titling was, by 1992, that on Nos 25, 27 and 55. A year later, with encouragement from the IoMRS, the erstwhile No 51 shed its bulkheads and roof and re-emerged with an 1894 roof canopy* (in MER parlance an "umbrella") and number 13, with dashes in a dark maroon and lettered in 1894 style. This breezy vehicle has appeared on a number of special workings since that date, its first outing being on May 23, 1987. As already mentioned, the year also saw the completion of a three-year body overhaul programme for the Snaefell fleet.

With the visual impact of No 13 as inspiration, in winter 1987-8 trailer 43 was given similar varnished posts in line with 1903 precedent. The surviving operable ECCs currently included No 14, seen on passenger service in summer 1988. By winter, the much abused rail carrier No 52 received a major repair, its surviving dash now a strong yellow, numbered in black. Reference has already been made to the new wheels being fitted to the Snaefell cars — these are of a larger diameter so that the cars now stand about two inches taller.

The new Wickham Rail Ltd. railcar delivered to the Civil Aviation Authority for use on the Snaefell line in January 1991 represented a combination of experience gained from the construction and operation of its three predecessors and the latest technology in the field. The result is a unique vehicle. Its 81 HP Perkins diesel engine drives through a hydraulic transmission (using Linde components) both axles being powered and infinitely variable speeds being obtainable in both directions. The cab can accommodate a maximum of eight persons whilst a load platform (at the uphill end as delivered) can carry 1500kg, having its own crane. Particular attention had been given to sanding provision, and hydraulic braking is obtainable from the transmission system. There are in addition hand

and "fail safe" air brakes, the former using the Fell rail. The main dimensions are 3.886 metres in length, 2.350 metres wide and 2.580 metres high. (As in Chapter 9's table, the 1957 car was resold to Wickham Rail.)

The latest winter car heavy overhaul had been of car 22, emerging for service in summer 1990 with full "The Manx Electric Railway Co Ltd" lettering. Sadly, a depot fire originating in a resistance overheating episode destroyed virtually all the car body on the evening of September 30, but a typical MER phoenix has arisen and the resulting new car was "ex paint shops" in 1991, and in service from 1992. The lettering is now just "Manx Electric Railway". The bodywork was executed in entirely traditional style by MacArds' Joinery of Port Erin, the rest of the work by the railway workshops. Meanwhile, Snaefell 6 had spent most of 1990 in shops for a major repaint, but the other five cars had sustained service without undue delays arising.

The death of the Isle of Man Railway Society's Chairman, Dr R Preston Hendry, in October 1991, brought numerous suggestions that he be commemorated in some way. In view of his society's role in the preservation of locomotive 23 it was appropriately arranged to provide cast nameplates for the locomotive and these were duly mounted in time for a naming ceremony on May 25, 1992. The society has been occupied in commissioning the return to service of IMR No 8, Fenella and happily the supplier of nameplates for No 8 was able to offer to produce these for No 23. (For other recent changes affecting car No 6, see page 139.)

Electrical Supply

Substantial repairs in 1980, costing about £15 000, were to be followed by major revisions eight years later. The obsolescence of mercury arc rectification, combined with the increasing decrepitude of the 1903 6.6 kV (originally 7kV) underground feeder from Laxey to Douglas and Groudle substations, made such a reconstruction a priority.

Another abandonment was of the 1894 underground DC feeders, disused from the early 70s. They are now being reused as part of the earth return circuits.

A new transformer was installed in the existing building at Groudle, supplied by the Manx Electricity Authority at 11kV, with a step down to 6.6. The "emergency" 3.3kV supply available at Douglas (at one time ex Douglas Corporation) now became the feed-in to a new solid state GEC/Alsthom rectification unit, fed from the MEA sub-station at the Summer Hill end of Blackberry Lane.

For the moment, Groudle, Laxey, Snaefell and Bellevue continue to use mercury arc plant, as spare "bulbs" are still on hand.

---

* This has a boarded roof, not (as originally) canvas.

The leased-back section of the one-time Ballaglass power station, housing the MER sub-station, shared in the building's general decay and, early in 1989, the new solid state replacement installation by GEC/Alsthom, housed under the seaward span of the Ballagorry overbridge, came into use. "For the record", the new units have capacities of 150kW (Douglas) and 300kW (Ballagorry).

In summer 1992, Ballaglass was seen to be under reconstruction for residential use, with an approach road consisting largely of material from the demolished Ramsey Plaza.

Operation and Staffing

Although various references to operating practice and management changes appear in Chapter 7, the following additional information is perhaps necessary to present an overall picture. Timetabling in the early years of the period under discussion underwent little obvious change (as seen by the tourist), such reductions as there were affecting the early morning and late evening runs.

From September 13, 1971 the traditional 7.15am ex Ramsey "Boat Car" was deleted from the timetable (at various times up to three had operated). Daily journeys now fell to 14 from a one-time 20, evening runs being major casualties, and from September 29, 1973 there were further curtailments. By September 30, 1974 a mere skeleton

remained of past winter schedules with only ten journeys, of which two were on school days only, four were short workings and two only ran on Tuesdays and Fridays. The line closed completely on Saturdays and Sundays. So far as the seasonal timetable is concerned, the 7am Douglas-Ramsey disappeared in 1973 (instead running at 7.30 from Laxey) and evening departures were reduced to 7.15 and 9pm to Ramsey, and 10.30 to Laxey only. The author's early Sixties recollections of journeys on the 11pm Douglas-Ramsey (at that date well filled by Ramsey-based holidaymakers) were by now so much history. Most of the earlier Sunday morning runs also disappeared. Operationally speaking, 1973 was to prove a successful year, with higher Island visitor totals, especially in September. However, the public inquiry into the Summerland disaster which followed left a "cloud" over the Island which may well have accounted for some of the acute fall in visitor numbers in 1974. The winter of 1973-4 was of course overshadowed by the imminence of the Transmark report, but the good figures for 1973 provided useful material for the pro-MER faction in the public debates already reported. External to the Island, however, lay the oil crisis, which raised steamer fares and indeed (for 1974) those of the MER, which went up 25 per cent. The Douglas horse tramway's 100 per cent fare increase at the same time is less easily explained! Road transport was now expensive, the mountainous haul from Ramsey to Douglas in particular, and easily handled bagged traffic like potatoes and laundry kept the MER goods stock busy.

Attention has been given to the 1975 season in Chapter 7 and the consequences of the September 30 closure were of course to include the end of the line's Isle of Man Post Office Authority contract. The contract had already been severely curtailed by timetable cuts in autumn 1972, such that the MER's late afternoon collection from post boxes at Laxey, Baldrine, Half Way House, Groudle and Onchan Harbour (Majestic) ceased after September 9. However, the 11.50am out of Ramsey still collected from Belle Vue, Ballajora and Glen Mona until the last journey of September 30, 1975. The Belle Vue and Glen Mona boxes were then closed. Before the closure, a rather special private occasion on September 13 had seen HRH Princess Alice, then aged 92, as a VIP passenger from Laxey to Ramsey aboard saloon trailer No 59, accompanied by the Lieutenant Governor and Lady Paul and other distinguished guests.

The 1976 operations described in Chapter 7 were of course as dismal in their results as critics predicted. Another fare increase of 25 per cent and the absence of Rover tickets were hardly constructive elements. The Board's station property in Ramsey was made available to let in spring 1976, and the outside "facilities" were taken in hand by the Town Commissioners.

```
        M A N X   E L E C T R I C   R A I L W A Y
            1, Strathallan Crescent Douglas
            Tel. Douglas (STD 0624) 4549
            General Manager: H. GILMORE

                    Tickets from:
            Douglas Terminal Station
                 (Derby Castle)
            Sefton Booking Office
            Harris Promenade Douglas
                Laxey Station
                Ramsey Station
        ─────────────────────────────────────
    DOUGLAS - LAXEY - RAMSEY  TIMETABLE 1977
    Commencing Sun.26th June and daily until
                 further notice
        DEPART DOUGLAS TO LAXEY AND RAMSEY
    10.00am, 10.30(A), 11.00, 12noon(A), 1.00pm,
       2.00pm, 2.30pm, 3.10, 4.00, 5.00(B), 5.30,
                    7.15(C)
          DEPART DOUGLAS TO LAXEY ONLY
         6.00pm(D), 7.00(C), 8.15(C), 10.30(C)
          DEPART DOUGLAS TO GROUDLE ONLY
                    9.40pm(C)
        DEPART RAMSEY TO LAXEY AND DOUGLAS
   10.30am(A), 11.30, 12noon(A), 12.30pm, 1.45
     2.30, 3.30, 4.00, 4.35, 5.30, 6.30(B), 9.00(C)
          DEPART LAXEY TO DOUGLAS ONLY
         9.15am(C), 10.15, 7.35pm(C), 9.00(C)
         DEPART GROUDLE TO DOUGLAS ONLY
                    9.55pm(C)

 "A"  Not Sundays.  "B"  Not Sundays before July 17 and
 not after August 14.  "C"  From 11 July until 19 August
 "D"  Until 10 July and after 19 August
 Travelling time from Douglas, Groudle 12 minutes, Laxey 30
 Minutes, Dhoon 45 minutes, Ballaglass 55 minutes, Ramsey 75
 minutes.  Extra cars will also run as required by traffic


        S N A E F E L L   M O U N T A I N   R A I L W A Y

   Commencing Monday 16th May and until Friday 30th
                    September
   (Note - No cars operate on Sundays before 1,00pm)
   Departures from Laxey as required by traffic.
   JOURNEY TIME - 30 minutes each way from Laxey
```

1977 timetable. (MER)

While the 1977 Ramsey line reconstruction forged ahead, the newly-resumed Douglas-Laxey service was publicised in an interim printed timetable. The rapid completion of the work north of Laxey seems to have at first pre-empted a new printed issue for the reopening, a typewritten timetable next making its appearance (reproduced on page 119).

Not on the new timetable was the surprise appearance of a wedding party at Belle Vue on Saturday June 25, which enlivened the official first car's journey by travelling on to Ramsey, indulging in some "traditional folk customs" and stopping for photographs at Queens Drive, which held back the Ramsey arrival by some minutes. The first week's 60p Douglas-Ramsey return saw virtually every car filled to capacity. Late in the summer the Board had Douglas Tramway's advertising horse car (No 31) placed in operation on its behalf, making two return trips each day and remaining parked outside the horse tramway depot in the interval.

With the appointment of the new Chief Executive in 1977, a revised management structure evolved, in due course jointly administering both steam and electric railways. John Gordon became overall Operations Superintendent, Roy Cannell Chief Engineer and Graham Warhurst and Maurice Faragher deputies to the two last named (both succeeded to the senior posts following retirements). The late Jack Oates's arrival as General Manager was to follow in 1981 (when the operation became tripartite).

A typical illustration of the drastic effects of poor weather on the line's patronage arose in 1978 when, although 56 per cent of tourists still rode on the line, the numbers on departures from Douglas fell by 11 per cent, and Snaefell passengers by 22 per cent. The happier results of 1979's better weather, special events and more socially varied visitor population have already been implied (Chapter 7). There were 476,191 staying visitors (plus nearly 200,000 "day trippers"). The MER service began on April 9, Snaefell on the 30th, and both ran until the end of September. An "unlimited rides" MER/IMR ticket at £5 was a bestseller.

A Royal tram driver had made a brief appearance on May 23, in the person of Prince Richard, Duke of Gloucester.

The 1980 season began ominously quietly, yet by the end of the year the Board's Snaefell operation had attained its "best ever" passenger figure of 71,971. By as early as August 16, Laxey-Ramsey had attained a healthy 40,000. Fares had risen a modest ten per cent. On September 1, a winter service of relatively skeletal form (it required one car set) recommenced. This was intended both for residents and to provide for the winter tourist traffic generated by special package holidays (Sealink offered a two-day facility from October 1980 to the following May and had generated 5,000 bookings by February). The line even operated one "special"

in this connection on a Sunday. The timings (Monday-Friday) were:

Douglas	-	-	1.30	4.40
Laxey	8.45	10.45	2.00	5.10
Ramsey	9.30	11.30	2.45	-
Ramsey	9.45	11.40	3.00	
Laxey	10.30	12.25	3.45	
Douglas	-	12.55	4.15	

While the service offered was operationally convenient, it left something to be desired in terms of giving reasonable shopping times in Ramsey, for example. From December 8, by cutting the Douglas mid-day layover from 35 to five minutes, better Ramsey "shopping times" were offered, as below:

Douglas	-	-	1.30	4.30
Laxey	8.45	10.45	2.00	5.10
Ramsey	9.30	11.30	2.45	-
Ramsey	9.45		12.10	3.00
Laxey	10.30		12.55	3.45
Douglas			1.25	4.15

In view of the changes in Island visitor patronage which were to take place during the Eighties, it is fortunate that, at the beginning of the decade, careful assessments of passenger levels and fare structures were put in hand and sustained. The most "graphic" illustration of this policy follows:

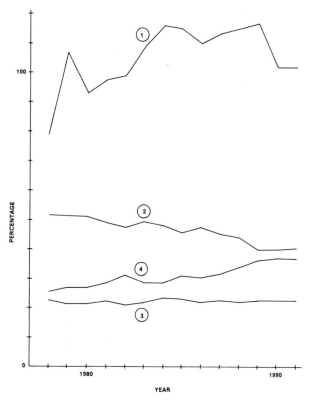

1 = % ridership of island railways as to May-September visitor arrivals, 1978-91
2 = % riders (of railways total) using MER 1978-91
3 = % riders (of railways total using SMR 1978-91
4 = % riders (of railway total) using IMR 1978-91
(2 +3 + 4 =100%)   (SB)

The preceding graph carries the story forward to 1991 — the railways' continued hold on the visitor's affection is self evident. The Port Erin hotels' "success story" is reflected in the IMR's gains — similar energetic management and promotion will surely bring equal benefits north of Douglas.

Through the Eighties a number of long-established MER lineside features were to disappear or be replaced. A summary of these changes has been added to the maps section of this book, to which readers are referred.

Family ridership in the early Eighties was encouraged by a generous concession structure applicable to both return and Rover-type tickets — when two adults' and one half fare had been paid, all other children (up to a total of four) travelled free. For the 1981 season residents were still offered generous terms — a seasonal ticket from April 13 to October 2 was to be offered at £5.50 (the season was originally planned to end on October 25). The high season was still given some late runs — the last Laxey-bound car out of Douglas was at 10.30pm, and the last from Ramsey at 9.00.

As noted in Chapter 7, in spring 1981 (following the unification of both the railways and Isle of Man National Transport's bus network) Jack Oates became deputy to Mr Jackson and General Manager of all three operations. Sadly, Mr Oates later died "in office", in 1990.

Electric line car crews were now (summer 1981) given "Setright Speed" ticket machines. About the same time, one of the enthusiasts' magazines reported (rather uncertainly) renewed carriage of

bagged mail from Ramsey using vans 11 and 14, but during the same year the IoMRS mentioned, more convincingly, the carriage of beer barrels. An innovation was the operation of evening cars on Snaefell, in concert with pre-booked tours. The car(s) left Laxey about 7pm, returning about 11.00, and were, of course, normally Nos 2 and 3, which had been fitted with headlights.

All this effort was expended against a background of drastic falls in visitor arrivals — for 1981 the numbers fell by 20 per cent to 518,239. 1982 saw an equally acute drop, to 413,089. With the Island nearly empty of tourists, the winter 1981-2 service was begun on October 5. The Snaefell hotel fire had earlier stopped all service on that line for three days in August and a sub-station fault had also closed the line for a day. At Douglas, the semi-complete body of horse car 49 reappeared, acting as a passenger shelter, until its removal in May 1982 to become a further exhibit at the Ramsey museum.

The use of a four-section summer timetable was by now firmly established — in summary form, that for 1983 was follows:

Departures from:

Period (incl.)	Douglas	Ramsey	Laxey	Groudle
28 March-28 May 19-30 Sep	5	5	-	-
29 May- 18 Sep.	12	13	(Plus a Thursday "extra" in both directions)	
11 July-19 August EVENINGS	5	1	2	1
			(Douglas)	

(extra cars May - September as usual)

By summer 1984 events concerning Island passenger steamship services were to have a further serious long-term impact on the tourist industry and (thereby) the MER . Briefly, in July, Sealink (the Heysham operator) became the property of a Bermuda-based group (using American capital). Following this takeover, Sealink acquired 40 per cent of the Isle of Man Steam Packet Company's capital and half of the seats on the board and set about radically altering the whole pattern of sea connections with the Island. In return, the Steam Packet Company was "given" the Heysham route, and in turn it ceased the 155-year-old Liverpool service on April Fools' Day, 1985, although there has since been a seasonal partial resumption of services. By the end of 1985 seasonal arrivals had dropped by 39,000 and the Fleetwood and Ardrossan services were to be abandoned (again, there has since been a resumption of minor traffic from Fleetwood), and the Scottish link moved to Stranraer. The various purchases and sales of vessels seem equally arbitrary and ill-conceived. Steam Packet shareholders, whose eager acceptance of these mergers had its origin in anticipated "bonanza" earnings, were to

---

ISLE OF MAN TRANSPORT

MANX ELECTRIC RAILWAY
WINTER TIMETABLE
COMMENCING MONDAY, 5th OCTOBER, 1981
AND UNTIL FURTHER NOTICE
MONDAY TO FRIDAY ONLY

Connecting Bus departs Central Bus Station			11.10	1.10	4.30
DOUGLAS Dep. Derby Castle	8.45 a.m.		11.20	1.30	4.40
" Laxey		10.35	11.50	2.00	5.10
Arr. Ramsey	9.30	11.20	STOP	2.45	STOP
Dep. Ramsey	9.45		noon	3.15	
" Laxey	10.30	noon	12.40	4.00	
Arr. Derby Castle DOUGLAS	STOP	12.30 p.m.	1.10	4.30	
Connection Bus departs Derby Castle		12.37	1.17	4.37	

No service Saturday and Sunday, also 25th and 28th December, 1st and 4th January, 1982.

The winter service for 1981-2 now saw the use of two cars. A year later it expanded further by adding a Tuesday morning journey from Douglas to Laxey and return.

continue somewhat disappointed for some time.

In 1984 sea passengers totalled almost 358,000, in 1985, just over 310,000. More hopefully, much improved air services restored around 50 per cent of the implied loss. The steamship operation for 1985 had planned to achieve a profit of some £2m, but instead managed to lose £3m. Remarks at the beginning of Chapter 7 make further reference to this topic and the increasing importance of business visitors: air travel accounted for 24 per cent of tourist arrivals by 1989 and residents used air services even more intensively, giving rise to a 59 per cent traffic increase over the four years 1985-9. As stated in the last chapter, the Isle of Man Seaways fleet in 1992 consisted of just two ships.

apprentices left the Board, on completion of their training, for other employment.

Passenger fares were still not unreasonable, especially for the northern line — the Douglas-Laxey return was £1.75, Douglas-Ramsey only £2.30. The seven-day Joint Rail Ticket now included both electric and steam railways and a Snaefell journey for £3.50. There were also a three-day Rail Rover and two-day MER Rovers, both with Snaefell included, and a rail-bus five-day ticket, excluding the Snaefell line.

In winter 1987-88 the Snaefell line "top section" overhead remained in place until December 1, as there were considerable volumes of building material to be conveyed from the Bungalow siding for

A flashback to the 1900s showing the prominence of the Douglas Bay Hotel (demolished 1988-9) and the carefree self-pedestrianisation of King Edward Road. If only a really good successor could arise on the still-marvellous site. (Manx National Heritage)

However, the high fares (which were by now the norm), assured shareholders of a dividend of 10 per cent. This policy has been the source of much criticism. Typically, a summer 1992 BBC TV holiday programme specifically mentioned the high cost of sea travel in an otherwise sympathetic broadcast. Coupled with the prospect of an often boisterous crossing, this can only serve as a deterrent to visitors.

The railways meanwhile kept a very tight rein on their expenditure, cutting back on winter staff levels for winter 1986-7 to such effect that a number of

new summit aerial masts. When the wire was later taken down (beyond pole 164 to the summit's 179) cars carried personnel to this point, the men then being ferried by a CAA railcar, running a shuttle service. The fate of the footbridge over the TT course at the Bungalow (a passenger amenity) which dated from 1964/5 was under discussion, and it has since been rebuilt twice, the second time after partial demolition by a road vehicle!

Robert Smith's December 1987 appointment as Chief Executive has been referred to in Chapter 7. An innovation from this date was the re-training of existing staff in new skills, producing specialists in the various trades more rapidly than by apprentice recruitment.

Another link with "company days" was broken in September 1989 with the death of former Chief Engineer, Roy Cannell. After a pre-war apprenticeship, Mr Cannell had come back to the MER in 1957 and thereafter greatly assisted the present writer in research for *Isle of Man Tramways*, and acted as a genial host to a number of enthusiast visits until his 1983 retirement.

By December 1987, major improvements to the Derby Castle premises had already been put in hand — their effect is outlined in the "track" section of this chapter (layout changes were involved). In previous reference to fares the writer made the point that they were still modest (in relation to the scenic value offered). By 1987 the Board's recognition of this had suggested that a rise of, say, ten per cent for several consecutive seasons would (although above inflation levels) provide improved revenue without deterring the average passenger, and this was again to apply for 1990. In June 1990, John Gordon, Operations Superintendent for the MER since the late Sixties came to retire. A Laxey man, Mr Gordon was much involved in village life and had in large part contrived the 90th anniversary event held in Laxey in 1984, when many of 1894's "junketings" were re-enacted.

The erection of a staff amenity block at the Snaefell depot had been completed in February 1990 and a subsequent doubling in width of part the Snaefell car shed was in prospect, at the time of writing, to provide an on-site workshop. Following its completion, the journeys of Snaefell cars to Derby Castle for body overhaul should come to an end.

The seasonal traffic by now regularly featured "special" cars for a variety of local organisations and No 19 was fitted with a public address system for use on these trips.

In 1991, the railways administration came to grapple with the once-in-a-lifetime assignment of planning of the Island's *Year of Railways*, centred on 1993's "Douglas and Laxey Coast" centenary. The writer fondly hopes that this text will have reached many readers by that date, and that in telling the moderately complex story of the MER he has neither bored the majority nor left the abnormally curious unsatisfied.

Among long-term preparations for the 1993's special events was the experimental propulsion of the IMR loco Fenella's chassis from Laxey to the Dhoon in July 1991. No problems arose, so on December 5, the railways staged a special "live" demonstration with loco No 4 Loch in steam. No 4 ran on the landward track, electric car No 1 on the seaward, the trailers 57 and 58 being used as Loch's "train", and both reached the Dhoon without any problems (there had been some experimentation a couple of days previously). All in all, 1993 promises to be as memorable as 1893!

Department of Tourism and Transport					
PASSENGER TRANSPORT RAILWAYS					
MANX ELECTRIC RAILWAY					
Commencing 5th October, 1987 and until 25th March, 1988					
From DOUGLAS					
Connecting bus departs					
Lord Street Bus Depot		9.50am		1.10pm	4.45pm
From Douglas		A	B		
Dep. Derby Castle	--	10.00	--	1.30	4.55
Laxey	8.45	10.30	10.35	2.00	5.25
Arr. Ramsey	9.30	11.15	11.20	2.45	--
From Ramsey	B	A			
Dep. Ramsey	9.45	9.55	12.00	3.25	--
Laxey	10.30	10.40	12.40	4.10	--
Arr. Douglas	--	11.10	1.10	4.40	--
Derby Castle					
Connecting bus departs					
from Derby Castle	--	11.17	1.17	4.47	--

No Service on Saturdays or Sundays

A Operates MONDAY to FRIDAY October, November & March
   Operates TUESDAY ONLY December, January & February
B Operates MONDAY, WEDNESDAY, THURSDAY & FRIDAY December, January & February
The service will cease after Thursday 24th December and recommence on Monday, 4th January, 1988

J.R. OATES,
General Manager

Winter service, 1987-8, its timings reflecting experience over the past few years. (MER)

In 1992, GEC/Alsthom activity at Dick Kerr works continues a long tradition. Here are MER stock transfers of 1904, 1906 and 1930 — each 9.625ins overall, black on gold. (JCC)

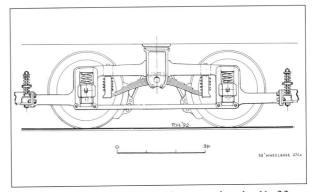

Drawing of the Brill 27Cx trucks re-used under No 22 (and still in service under 11 other cars). (PH)

Chapter 9

Manx Electric Rolling Stock

This chapter has been the subject of revision, especially in an effort to provide a reasonable summary of the liveries question, and to add some account of more recent events since its original 1968 dateline. The latter is attempted via three "tailpieces".

The material on liveries has been reassessed and gathered into a more compact whole, leaving minimal references in the car notes only where these are visually conspicuous "change points" from previous practice.

Essentially, the use of red or maroon, white and varnished teak is certain — recent restorations of pre-1900 cars opting for maroon. Assumedly the late Seventies saw some evidence for this choice from discoveries during restoration work, but the question was not the subject of any wide debate. More recently, a dark red chosen for trailer 13's restoration again has some "uncertainties" although the dark livery of older trailers was very conspicuous and assumedly continued a long established tradition (as the author commented at the time). USA readers will recognise "eaves board" as letter board!

Readers may not appreciate that when a vehicle was painted white, it nearly always acquired subsequent layers of varnish which immediately "yellowed" to produce a gradually darkening ivory, often made photographically apparent by contrast with the white clothing of bystanders. The persistently "white" white of MER cars seems to suggest an absence of varnish on the white areas.

The current position with respect to the ECC cars (14, 15, 17, 18 and 28-31) has been outlined in Chapter 8, as has 51's re-emergence as 13.

IN 1893, ELECTRIC TRACTION WAS IN ITS infancy and no clear tradition had been established in the design of its cars. Two-axle electric cars still tended to follow horse-car practice, but the Manx line required long bogie vehicles, and the nearest equivalents at the time were the large trailer cars used on steam tramways. Contemporary steam tramway trailers were of both top-covered and single-deck types and of considerable length, using a channel-steel underframe with pitch pine cross-members, plate-frame bogies placed at the extreme ends, and (in consequence of this) a high-level platform with corner access, usually closed off by a gate.

For the new line from Douglas to Groudle, cars were ordered from G F Milnes, of Birkenhead. This concern was the successor to George Starbuck, an American who had the honour of being the first tramcar builder in Britain (from 1860) and whose

venture became a limited company in 1872. In 1886 Starbuck was bought out by his secretary, George F Milnes, who carried on the business at Birkenhead until 1902, latterly in association with German interests which opened a second and much larger works at Hadley, Shropshire, in 1900. G F Milnes & Co Ltd failed in 1904, but meanwhile Milnes's son, George Comer Milnes, established in 1902 a separate business at the other end of Cleveland Street (in partnership with Thomas Voss) to supply tramcar accessories and top covers. This concern, G C Milnes, Voss & Co, later built complete cars for Douglas tramways, until closure in 1913.

The first two batches of electric cars (three in 1893, six in 1894) were effectively elongated Milnes single-deck steam tramway trailer cars, with deepened plate-frame bogies of otherwise typical design, into which the two electric motors could conveniently be fitted, one in each bogie. The internal body styling was the same as that of horse cars 27, 28 and 29 of the Douglas Bay line, and the oddly-shaped five-arc roof sticks provided the otherwise traditional turtleback construction with good watershedding properties. Dr John Hopkinson's patent bow collectors were mounted rigidly on the roof close to each bulkhead.

With these electric cars came some open trailers which were in effect lengthened open horse cars on light plate-frame bogies. The corner entrances of the motor cars allowed the conductor to pass to and from the trailer footboard and this layout was retained in subsequent deliveries. The first trailers were open "toastrack" vehicles, but they were soon fitted with roofs — perhaps reflecting the fear of broken overhead lines — and all subsequent open trailers had roofs when delivered. By 1895 the company, in collaboration with G F Milnes, had evolved its own design of saloon motor tram, with a wider underframe and straight sides to permit cross-seats for better viewing. The popularity of the open trailers made it advisable to add some cross-bench motor cars to the fleet, and several batches were brought in, from 1898 to 1906.

By 1900, the rapid adoption of electric tramways elsewhere had brought on to the British market more sophisticated types of electric car truck; these were featured in the new cars of 1903-6 and also replaced the older plate-frame type under some earlier cars. Similarly, new motors and control equipment replaced the original (largely experimental) types. The original car bodies, however, continued in use, and the fleet has survived the ensuing nine decades with surprisingly little change, apart from the rebuilding of 1893's six trailers. Seven trailers and four motor cars were destroyed in the Laxey depot fire of April 5, 1930, and three new trailers of traditional open design were ordered to replace them. Modifications have been carried out in recent years to the control equipment and to the springing of some of the trucks, and the opportunity was taken to buy modern air-brake equipment from Sheffield and Glasgow when those tramways closed in 1960 and 1962.

Little provision was made for goods at first, but after 1903 goods traffic became much more important, requiring new vehicles and the adaptation of some obsolescent passenger vehicles. With the growth of motor traffic this business declined again, and the surviving goods vehicles are now (1992) only used for between-stations parcels traffic, some of it quite bulky. The goods stock has always been numbered separately from the passenger cars, which are here dealt with first. For fuller details of the Snaefell cars, the reader is referred to Chapters 2 and 8, though for completeness these vehicles are included in the 1968 fleet tables, and in the new livery notes (1992).

The cars are listed in the order of their present-day (or final) numbers, which are not in all cases those they bore when delivered.

Motor Cars

Nos 1 to 3, G F Milnes & Co Ltd, 1893

These were the original electric cars supplied for the line from Douglas to Groudle, and were built as unvestibuled single-deck saloons with longitudinal seats for 38 (later rerated 34). They were 34ft 9ins long* and 6ft 6ins wide, and ran on two Milnes plate-frame bogies set at 23ft 8ins between centres. Each bogie had one Mather & Platt 25hp 250-volt series motor, giving a total tractive effort of 3,000lbs. The motors were nose and centre-of-gravity suspended, and drove the outer axle only, via unshrouded double helical gears — a very unusual type for so early a date. A Hughes patent coupler was fitted at each end of the car, and these are still the MER standard. Internally, the cars were attractively detailed: each window head had a mirror panel above it, and the bulkhead panelling resembled that of the 1893 bay tramway saloon horse cars, save for the external lamp-box. The traditional eye-window flap of the bulkhead carried a Milnes builder's plate of the early type.

Service braking was by hand, the brakestaff being placed outside the dash and applied by a wheel. For emergency use the cars had a Milnes patent auxiliary "scotch" brake, applied through a second brakestaff to the left of the platform door, close to the bulkhead. This applied a triangular scotch to the inner pair of the leading bogie's wheels, against the possibility of a run-back. In the opposite corner stood the Mather & Platt controller, whose handle's swing required the cutting of an aperture in the side weatherboard, now partly obscured on No 2, and only surviving at the Ramsey

end on No 1.

The control equipment was described as "experimental". A tall drum on the platform carried a handle as just described, but on the twin (resistance grid?) guard plates which hung below the car (off-centre) appear sloping rods whose function is totally obscure. A 1968 interpretation saw it as carrying bevel gearing to operate various resistance connections, but a revised examination seems less conclusive. There were two such "grids" and rods so that the function was available from either end of the cars. These unique (and baffling) arrangements also included a third resistance grid, transversely linking the others at the Douglas end of the cars. Central on the car's underframe a brass plate proclaimed "Mather & Platt, Engineers, Manchester".

In 1903, these and other early cars were retrucked and reequipped by the new MER company, using Brush type 'D' equal-wheel bogies of 5ft wheelbase; No 1 was completed on July 4, 1903, No 2 on July 20, and No 3 on August 2. Each new bogie had two 25hp motors made by the Société l'Électricité et l'Hydraulique, of Charleroi, Belgium, supplied by its agents, Witting, Eborall & Co. New American-built controllers of General Electric's type 'K 11' were fitted, with matching resistors, and the cars were given air brakes made by the Christensen Engineering Co, of Milwaukee, and supplied by R W Blackwell & Co. Each equipment consisted of a type 'A 5' motor-driven compressor set operating at 200 rpm with three-way valves, gauges, and a single reservoir. The working pressure was 90lbs per square inch.

The original axlebox springing of the Brush trucks comprised small semi-elliptical springs whose ends supported round suspension links going direct into the solid bosses on the frame. By 1906 these links had been fitted with coil springs, much softening the ride, and earlier (in 1904) the design of the motor suspension had also been altered. The maker's plates showed the works numbers, the batch being Nos 974 to 999.

No 3 was destroyed in the Laxey fire of April 5, 1930, and was not replaced, but Nos 1 and 2 still exist and are possibly the oldest electric cars at work anywhere in the world. Before their late 70's restoration, they returned to passenger service for the peak period each summer, and spent the rest of the year on maintenance duties! No 1 had removable windscreens for use in winter, first fitted in 1963-4. The Brush bogies (Nos 979 and 980) under No 2 were fitted with new axlebox coil springing in 1962, those under No 1 (Nos 984 and 991) remain as modified in 1906. By 1964, both cars had received ex-Sheffield Maley & Taunton compressor sets. In October 1947 the K11 controllers of both cars were rewired to the K12 control system, giving reduced sensitivity to maximum loading and less critical motor balance requirements; with the K11 type, even wheel diameter relationships were important.

---

*Over the body extremes, not couplers. This dimension is standard for ALL motor car descriptions in this chapter unless otherwise stated.

Nos 4 to 9, G F Milnes & Co Ltd, 1894

With the coming of all-the-year service in 1894, six more cars (Nos 4-9) were bought, with vestibuled ends more suited to winter service. Vestibuled variants of Nos 1-3, they had offset saloon doors that required a shortening of the adjacent longitudinal seat, reducing capacity by two to 36 (later rerated to 32). An iron gate again hung from the cab-front corner pillar, and outer half-doors were now provided on each side of the entrance. Internal detail was as before, but the finish of the bulkheads was especially fine, with panelling in oak and ash. As built, these cars had a double guard rail outside their full-drop windows, and similar rails were fitted to Nos 1-3. In post war years the "drop" of windows was reduced and the bars removed.

The bogies were like those of 1893, but the resistance grids were now hung transversely below the underframe, without the visible "mechanical actuation" of the 1893 cars. Again, no details survive of the controllers, though they were still admitted to be experimental. The two motors were Mather & Platt 25hp, as on Nos 1-3. Dimensions were 34ft 8ins long, 6ft 3ins wide, and 23ft 8ins between bogie centres. The long, narrow interior gave rise to the name "tunnel cars". The unsprung (rigid) bow collectors originally fitted to the three 1893 cars were by now replaced by a sprung type designed by Dr Edward Hopkinson, developed during winter of 1893-4. The new cars (Nos 4-9) were fitted with yet a third type as, by August, was car No 2. A fourth type was to appear by 1895.

In 1899 car No 4 exchanged trucks and equipment with open car No 16, receiving a later type of Milnes plate-frame bogie with four 20hp motors, built by the Electric Construction Company, of Wolverhampton. The other cars received Brush type 'D' bogies in July and August 1903, and were reequipped in similar fashion to Nos 1-3, with four 25hp Belgian motors,

K11 controllers, and Christensen air brakes. Nos 4 and 8 were lost in the 1930 Laxey depot fire, and were not replaced. In 1932, the longitudinal seats of No 5 were replaced by new cast framed reversible upholstered seats for 32 by W S Laycock, of Sheffield, forming eight rows of two-and-one seats and eight bulkhead seats (the moquette used in No 5's Fifties reupholstering was particularly pleasing). A centre partition was added at the same time.

Nos 5, 6, 7 and 9 still exist; 5 and 6 now have a centre partition, 7 and 9 are unaltered. All these cars came to lose their twin end windows by 1978. All four received ex-Sheffield Maley & Taunton compressors by 1964. No 5 received K12 controllers from No 14 in 1963, Nos 6 and 7 were changed to K12 in January 1946, but No 9 still "has" K11*. Nos 5-7 have trailer air-cocks. Brush bogies 977 and 978 under No 6 have been given modified axlebox coil springs, bogies 974 and 976 under No 7 have shock absorbers, and bogies 982 and 997 under No 5 have both these modifications, while bogies 987 and 993 under No 9 are unaltered. No 9 has served at various dates as the snowplough car and the other members of the class have at different times served as works cars (as have various "ECC's"). The implied somewhat harsh treatment is today seen as undesirable, bearing in mind the higher visual standards now applying — the possible acquisition of 90cm gauge works vehicles mentioned in Chapter 8 is a probable solution to the problem.

Nos 10-13, G F Milnes & Co Ltd, 1895

Nos 10-13 were essentially similar cars to those for the Snaefell Mountain Tramway, described in Chapter 6, but the body sides had very prominent 'D' beading down each post (below the waist). Both types were basically derived from Nos 4-9, but a major step forward was that instead of facing inward on longitudinal seats, passengers could now view the scenery from transverse seats, with double reversible seats for 40 and a triple fixed seat at each bulkhead. A prototype drawing by Milnes survives and shows the sides canted to give maximum width at the waist-rail, but in the event the cars had straight sides built out to a width of 6ft 9ins; overall length was 37ft 9ins**, height 10ft, and the cars weighed about $5\frac{1}{2}$ tons without the motors.

Nos 10-13 were less expensively finished, and cost only £260 without equipment; the interiors were of

Left: In this 1955 photograph, Mr W G S Hyde secured this close-up of a pair of demotored 1893/4 bogies, by then relics of a dismembered stone wagon at Dhoon quarry.

---

*A change may be unrecorded on this and other "K11" vehicles.

* *This dimension exceptionally includes the Milnes couplers. The similar Snaefell cars are 2ft $1\frac{1}{2}$in "shorter" due to their different coupling provision.

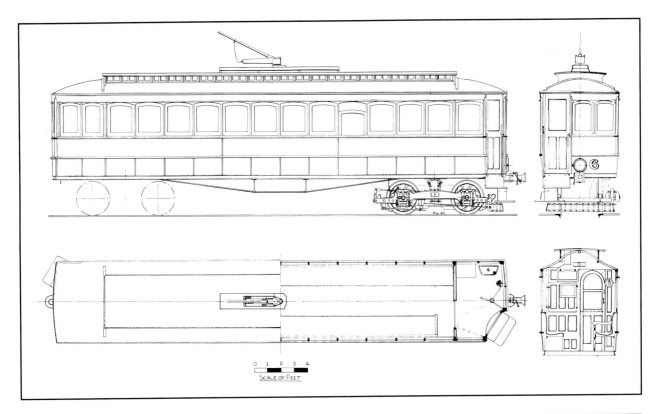

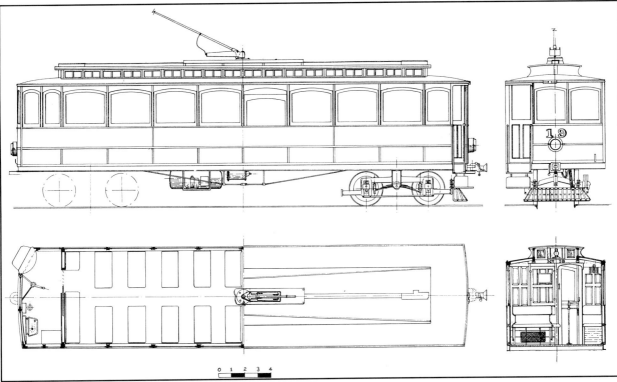

Top: *MER 5-9 class car as now running, but without bogie modifications. (PH)*

Above: *MER 19-22 class. (PH)*

Right: *The extraordinary motor suspension of an ECC bogie. The staggered suspension beam lies parallel to the truck frame, (one at each side) and hangs from three springs — two from the bottom of the motors' axle bearings, one from a stirrup attached to the bogie cross members (points A and C on the diagram). Meanwhile, the motor casings bear down on the beams via lugs B, these lying virtually below the armature centre. (The sketch is appreciably foreshortened). (FKP)*

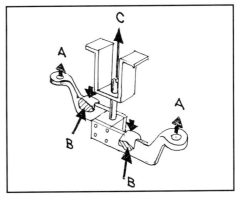

127

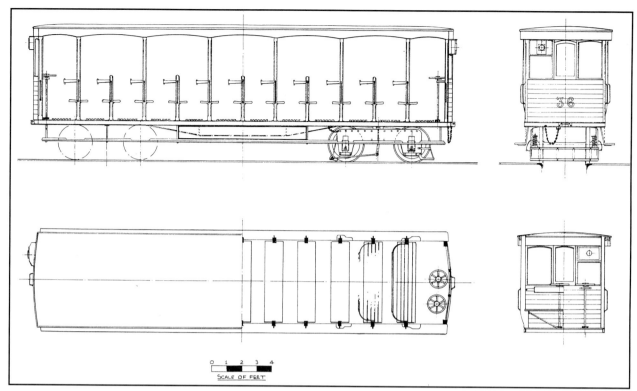

Trailer of 1894 series (34-39). (PH)

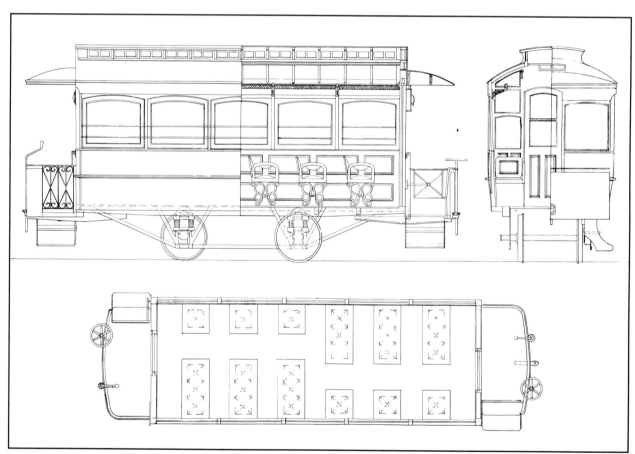

Builder's drawing of MER saloon trailer 59. To scale this drawing, wheelbase =6ft. (MER)

pitchpine. They had plain shallow-arched roofs, and were glazed only in the vestibules, the six side windows having only striped linen roller blinds. The metalwork was of "Best Staffordshire Bright" iron, and again included steam-tramway type platform gates. The bogies were of the standard Milnes plate-frame type,

with two 25hp Mather & Platt motors as before; brake equipment was as on the earlier cars, but they had a newer type of Mather & Platt controller, with a pedestal-type cast-iron case. The electrical equipment and the improved spring bow collectors of the 1895 type were installed by the IOMT & EP at Derby Castle. On

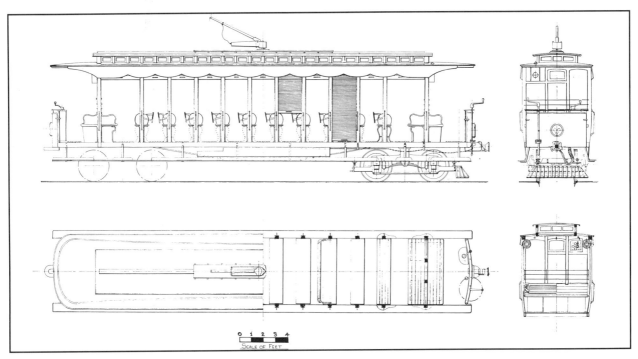

Car of 32-33 class, 1960's condition. (PH)

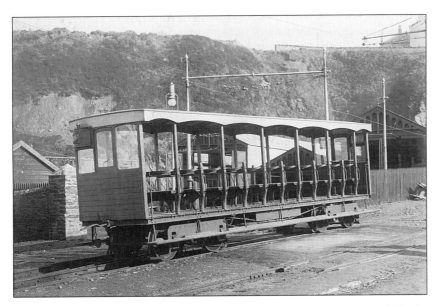

Above*: trailer 17 (?) as renumbered to 34 circa 1903/4. (Manx National Heritage)* ***Top right****: Part of No 44 showing the 1899 livery. (NTM)* ***Bottom right****: Author's partial reconstruction (from faulty image) of G F Milnes 1903 numbering.*

these cars and those of 1895, straight spur gears were probably used from the start.

Nos 10-13 remained unaltered until 1902, but were then effectively withdrawn from passenger service; two were stored (perhaps as potential extra vehicles for the Snaefell line) and two were used to augment the goods fleet. No 12 reappeared in March 1903 as a cattle car, and another became a "goods motor" in 1904, though a tentative drawing was prepared in 1904 showing one in hybrid mixed traffic form, with 16 removable seats in a centre compartment. The two stored cars languished in Laxey depot until 1918, officially withdrawn, and then became "freight" trail-

ers. (For livery notes see page 137)

Nos 14 to 18, G F Milnes & Co, 1898

The initial requirement for the Ramsey extension was apparently assessed at nine motor cars and some additional trailers. The attraction of open cars was now evident, and an order was placed with G F Milnes for nine American-style cross-bench cars with glazed bulkheads and a clerestory roof. Each car was 35ft 0ins long, and 6ft 3ins wide over the grab-rails, with projecting footboards. Seating was for 56 on 14 cross-benches, including a fixed bench on each platform. A

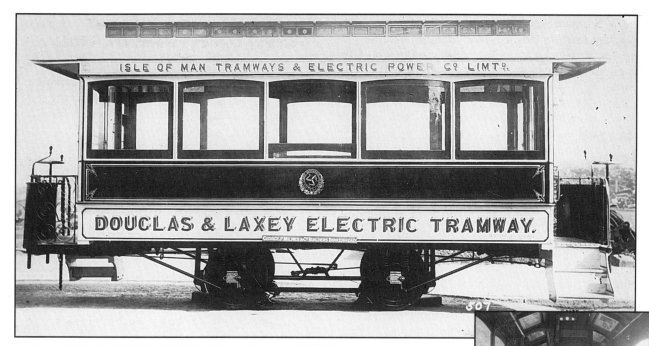

No 59 at Birkenhead, 1895, (MER), with interior inset. (FKP)

note on a later Milnes specification reveals that the numbers allocated to these cars were 14 to 22, but initially only Nos 14 to 18 were placed in service as motor cars.

It was decided to use four-motor equipment of increased output, and nine sets of four totally-enclosed 20hp motors (Nos 4389 to 4424) were obtained from the Electric Construction Company, of Wolverhampton, together with General Electric K11 controllers. The Milnes plate-frame bogies were of a more fully developed type to take two motors each, having an odd centre-of-gravity motor suspension and open spur gears. The Milnes auxiliary brake and the wheel brakes were both operated from hand-wheels, and involved a special drilling in the plate frame of the bogie; they are known as "ECC bogies", from the type of motor.

In 1899, No 16 exchanged trucks and equipment with 1894 saloon car No 4, probably because a higher powered enclosed car was needed on the Ramsey service. After 1903, Nos 14-18 were fitted with side roller shutters for use in bad weather. When the 1893-4 trucks and equipment on other cars were replaced by the new company, No 16 received Brush type 'D' bogies (now Nos 990 and 992), running on these from July 11, 1903. The footboards of all cars in this class were lengthened about 1906-8. No 15 received K12 controllers from No 25 in 1936, and Nos 16, 17 and 18 were converted to K12 from 1939; No 14 still has K11. No 17 has a non-standard scotch brake mounting with a sub-frame, as on the Brill-type trucks. All five cars still exist. (For livery notes see page 137.)

Nos 19 to 22, G F Milnes & Co Ltd, 1899

The last four sets of 1898 ECC equipment had been held back for use under these new and luxuriously finished cars, which thus received ECC 20hp motors (four per car) and K11 controllers. The bogies and brake equipment were as for Nos 14-22 but with an elegant brass handle to the brakestaff instead of a wheel. Earlier cars were so modified later.

Nos 19 to 22, known as the "winter saloons", were delivered in the summer of 1899 as fully glazed vestibuled eight-window saloons, having transverse slatted seats for 48 in pitchpine and sequoia. They are 35ft long and 7ft 4ins wide, and seat 40 on double seats, with a triple and single seat at each end bulkhead. The centre partitions now fitted may not be original; the style is in keeping, but the construction is different. Body weight is about 6^1/$_2$ tons. They were given oak and ash lining timbers and a generally deluxe finish throughout, though the ceilings were unlined.

The new company found after 1903 that the winter service cars needed better running gear, and in September 1904 No 21 received Brill type 27Cx trucks from new open car No 30. Nos 19 and 22 followed suit in October, taking the trucks of Nos 29 and 31, and No 20 exchanged trucks with No 28 in November. These 27Cx trucks were a narrow-gauge variant of the most familiar form of the Brill No 27 truck, on which the bolster embraces the side frames. They had the same four 25hp Belgian motors as the contemporarily reequipped older saloons, and as a result of this changeover 19-22 received Christensen air brakes, again taken from Nos 28-31. The saloons became taller and the cross bench cars shorter following this exchange! Four Westinghouse compressors were obtained and fitted to these cars in 1947-51, and four Maley & Taunton compressors, bought in 1962 from Glasgow, are held as spares.

At a later date, probably about 1932, 19 to 22 were given upholstered seating, with moquette covering. Three cars received new cast framed reversible seats by W S Laycock, of Sheffield, but No 20 retains its original seat frames. All four cars have trailer air-cocks, and each car originally enjoyed a total of ten makers' plates. Nos 19 to 22 are still hard at work throughout the year, and are the mainstay of the MER service, covering between 30,000 and 35,000 miles every year. Their cumulative mileage (even with less intensive use since 1975) seems likely to reach 1,000,000 per car by 1993. The loss of No 22 as a result of a fire, and its 1991-2 reconstruction are dealt with in the preceding chapter. (See page 137 for livery notes.)

No 23, Isle of Man Tramways & Electric Power Co Ltd, 1900

No 23, built at Derby Castle sheds to the design of Frank Edmondson, was a centre-cab electric locomotive for use in winter. It then borrowed the bogies and equipment from passenger car No 17, hauling goods and stone traffic. A collision at "Bonner Corner", just north of Bulgham Bay on January 24, 1914, damaged No 23 severely and eliminated it from the scene for 11 years, until it was rebuilt in the winter of 1925-6 using the old cab and two newly-built wagon bodies, as detailed under goods stock.

Nos 24 to 27, G F Milnes & Co Ltd, 1898

To work the Ramsey extension, the company had ordered nine 56-seat cross-bench cars from G F Milnes for delivery in 1898, but only five of these (Nos 14-18) entered service as powered cars on delivery. The other four (Nos 19 to 22) were instead used as motorless trailers and were renumbered as 40-43 on the arrival of the new 1899 saloons, which took their 1898 numbers.

In 1903, the new company decided to motorise these cars, using Brush type 'D' trucks, Belgian motors, K11 controllers and Christensen air brakes. No 42 re-entered service as a motor car on June 19, 1903, followed by No 43 on July 9, No 41 on July 18, and No 40 on July 27. All four cars were given roller shutters by Clark, Burnett & Sons, "of London, Paris and New York", and similar blinds were fitted to Nos 14-18 and trailers Nos 44-48. Soon after being motorised, Nos 40-43 were renumbered res-pectively 24-27, forming a class with similarly-equipped open car No 16; these five were known as "paddlebox" cars, from the shape of their foot-boards, modified to clear the Brush bogies.

No 24 was destroyed in the Laxey depot fire, and was not replaced. Nos 25-27 still exist, and were fitted in 1964 with ex-Sheffield Maley & Taunton compressors, replacing the Christensen sets. Their Brush bogies were modified in 1906 as described elsewhere, but have escaped the more recent changes; truck numbers are 988/989 for car No 25, 981/995 for car No 26, and 985/986 for car No 27. No 27 received K12 controllers in 1939, and No 26 in 1948; No 25 still "has" K11 controllers, taken from car No15. Dimensional details are as for Nos 14-18.

Nos 28 to 31, Electric Railway & Tramway Carriage Works Ltd, 1904

The new company made inquiries to several builders for new cars, although G F Milnes prepared a drawing (dated January 7, 1904) showing cars similar to the 1898 batch. The firm was already facing closure and an order was placed instead with the Electric Railway & Tramway Carriage Works Ltd, at Preston, for four motor cars and four trailers. The motor cars, Nos 28 to 31, were 56-seat cross-bench vehicles owing much to the earlier Milnes designs, and were 35ft long over dash plates, 6ft 3ins wide over grab-rails, and 10ft 6ins high from rail to clerestory. Each car had two Brill type 27Cx bogies set at 23ft 6ins centres, and each bogie was fitted with two Belgian 25hp motors by the Société l'Électricité et l'Hydraulique. These were the first MER cars to use the Brill type of truck, with its outside-hung motors. It retained the Milnes "scotch" brake, in suitably modified form.

The cars came with white painted posts and bulkhead framing, and had red eaves boards — the new MER "standard".

Nos 28 to 31 arrived in July 1904, and later that year exchanged trucks with winter saloons Nos 19-22 , as already described, receiving Milnes 1898 trucks and ECC 20hp motors. They also lost their Christensen air brakes, being now referred to by the staff as "ratchet" cars. Roller shutters were fitted from the outset. All four cars still exist, the only recorded modification of recent years being the conversion of No 28's controllers to type K12 in 1954. The other three nominally have K11 control, but it is doubtful how many K11 circuits now re-main, if any; recording of rolling-stock changes has not always been fully maintained.

Nos 32 and 33, United Electric Car Company Ltd, 1906

Motor cars Nos 32 and 33 were built by the UEC Company at Preston, successor to the Electric Railway & Tramway Carriage Works Ltd. They were 14-bench 56-seat cross-bench cars built to the same style as Nos 28-31, with roller shutters. The dimensions given for Nos 28-31 apply also to Nos 32 and 33.

These two cars each received four $27^1/_2$hp GE60 motors, thus having 110hp available. From 1928 to 1939, the bogies of No 33 were used in winter under the rebuilt locomotive, No 23. As built, the two cars had K11 controllers, but No 32 was changed to type K12 in February 1948. Their Christensen air brakes were replaced by ex-Sheffield Maley & Taunton sets by 1964, and there are now no Christensen sets in use.

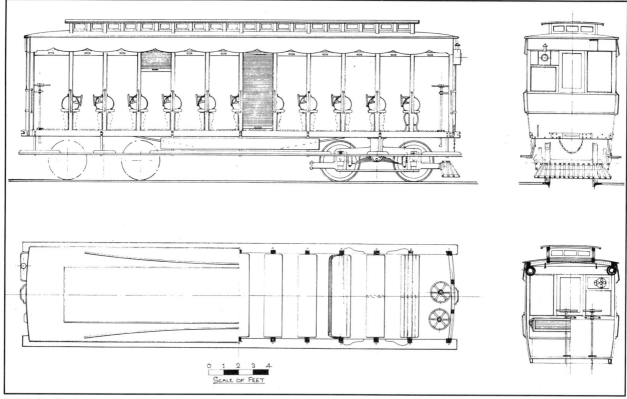

MER 61-62 class trailer. (PH)

Passenger trailers

The motor trams are numbered approximately in order of building but this does not apply to the trailers. These have always followed on from the highest-numbered motor tram and, as the fleet expanded, the trailers were renumbered several times. The present numbers are those carried from 1906, when the fleet reached its maximum, with Nos 1-33 for the motor cars and Nos 34-62 for the trailers. The classes are listed here in order of delivery. Trailer lengths are taken over their coupling bar jaws.

Nos 49 to 54, G F Milnes & Co Ltd, 1893

Although the first three motor cars each had only 50 horsepower, their designers may have thought that they could haul two loaded trailers up the 1 in 24 gradients, and this would explain the initial order for three motor cars and six trailers. Experience doubtless showed quickly that the available power would only suffice to haul one trailer, and after the first year, deliveries of power cars and trailers were in approximately equal numbers.

The six original trailers of 1893 were effectively elongated 11-bench open horse cars on light plate-frame bogies. They were 28ft 9ins long, 6ft 3ins wide over grab-rails, 6ft 9ins wide over foot-boards (this is a standard dimension for all open trailers) and seated 44. As delivered, the end benches had elongated pillars carrying iron lamphouse arches, though lamps were not carried during the 1893 season. By the following year, light canvas roofs on wooden frames had been added, supported by the two (now occupied)

lamp arches and by new full height pillars at the fourth and eighth positions.

An ingenious (and effective) emergency brake was adopted for the trailers. Each trailer had hand wheel brakes and the Milnes patent auxiliary scotch brake, giving two wheel-operated brakestaffs within each dash, plus a further safety feature — a chain attached to the scotch brake linkage with a ratchet action on the pull rod. This chain is secured to an anchor point on the motor car, and contains a weakened link, so that in the event of a breakaway the trailer would be automatically braked and its rigging remain undamaged in the process.

It seems that these 1893 trailers were at first numbered from 11 to 16, though only Nos 15 and 16 are known from photographs. When motor cars Nos 10-13 arrived in 1895, trailers Nos 11-13 are thought to have become Nos 23-25; in 1898, the class apparently became Nos 28-33 (views exist of Nos 32 and 33), and in 1903 or 1904 they were moved up to occupy Nos 49 to 54, leaving Nos 28-33 free for new motor cars. At about the same time, their 1894 canvas roofs were replaced by light wooden roofs, still without end bulkheads. By 1903 some had the roof edge in white. Later rebuilding included the addition of panelled bulkheads, and detail differences exist in the class, Nos 49, 51, 53 and 54 having six posts, while No 50 has only four; the extra posts were fitted in 1947-8. No 52 was less favoured, and became a rail carrier, mounted on ECC bogies for added strength. In 1970 the other five were still used in mid-summer, Nos 50, 51 and 53 having lost their scotch brake and its staffs, the emergency brake chain being now connected directly to the wheel brakes. (See livery notes, page 137.)

Nos 34 to 39, G F Milnes & Co Ltd, 1894

These trailers had fixed roofs, horizontally boarded end bulkheads with a centre drop-light, and canvas side curtains. They were thus able to offer considerably wider scope for year-round use. These cars again had 11 four-seat benches, and were 29ft long, and 6ft 1in wide over the grab-rails. Metal "safety rail" hooks were fitted to the pillars, as on the 1893 version. They were finished in a dark varnish with maroon painted dashes.

As delivered, these cars were very probably numbered from 17 to 22; photographs exist of Nos 17 and 19. In the 1898 renumbering they became (permanently) Nos 34 to 39. Two of the class, Nos 36 and 37, still exist, and are used in mid-summer; they retain their scotch brakes as originally fitted. (The others were Laxey fire casualties.)

No 59, G F Milnes & Co Ltd, 1895

This was a special saloon car to be used by the directors and their guests. As built, it was a four-wheel car with Milnes trunnion running gear and 28ins wheels; the 3½ins axles turned in gunmetal bushes. It was 22ft 2ins long and 6ft 9ins wide (see drawing), and seated 18 on red Utrecht velvet reversible seats with armrests. A carpet by Spence of Douglas was fitted over the linoleum floor, the bulkheads carried mirrors and the ceiling, G B Cowen photographs of local scenes. As delivered, the car weighed 60 cwt.

The original Milnes specification for this car survives in the MER records (blueprint 3,374 of 29 January 1895). The body length was to be 16ft 6ins inside, 17ft 2ins outside, plus two platforms of 2ft 6ins each; the width was 6ft 3ins over side pillars and 6ft 9ins over steps, platform height above rail 2ft 4 ins, wheelbase 6ft. The underframe was to be of thoroughly seasoned pitchpine of suitable strength, put together with knees and framing bolts and strongly trussed, the floor of Baltic pine boards tongued and grooved and properly secured to the side sills and cross rails. The end platforms were supported by strong arms hung from the headstocks and rails and had a railing, a dash plate, a step with grab handles, two spindles for ordinary and auxiliary brake, a hinged gate to close the platform on one side, and an ornamental iron railing to enclose it on the other. A strong wrought-iron jaw with pin was provided for coupling up to the motor car. The side, corner and door pillars, panel backers, and car frame were to be of white States ash, side panels from floor to waist of teak, roof similar to motor cars with swinging ventilator frames glazed with ornamental glass, and inside walls panelled with fancy woods. The price quoted was £150, with delivery in three months.

A possible number allocation was 26, but no definite evidence exists and the records refer only to "Mr Bruce's Special Trailer". In 1903 this number was required for a motor car and the saloon trailer may have become No 32, but by 1906 it had become No 59. In August 1902 it served as the royal saloon for the

Summary of M E R passenger fleet, 1968

Motor Cars Nos	Type	Seats	Date	Builder	Trucks	Motors	HP
1, 2	Unvestibuled saloon	34	1893	Milnes	Brush	S E H	25
5, 6, 7, 9	Vestibuled saloon	32	1894	Milnes	Brush	S E H	25
14, 15, 17, 18	Cross-bench	56	1898	Milnes	Milnes	E C C	20
16	Cross-bench	56	1898	Milnes	Brush	S E H	25
19-22	Winter saloons	48	1899	Milnes	Brill 27	S E H	25
23	Locomotive (body only)	–	1925	M E R	–	–	–
25-27	Cross-bench	56	1898	Milnes	Brush	S E H	25
28-31	Cross-bench	56	1904	E R & T C W	Milnes	E C C	20
32, 33	Cross-bench	56	1906	U E C	Brill 27	G E 60	27½
Trailer Cars							
36, 37	Cross-bench	44	1894	Milnes	Milnes (B)	–	–
40, 41, 44	Cross-bench	44	1930	E E	Milnes (A)	–	–
42, 43	Cross-bench	44	1903	Milnes	Milnes (C)	–	–
45, 48	Cross-bench	44	1899	Milnes	Milnes (B)	–	–
46, 47	Cross-bench	44	1899	Milnes	Milnes (A)	–	–
49-51, 53, 54	Cross-bench	44	1893	Milnes	Milnes (A)	–	–
55, 56	Cross-bench	44	1904	E R & T C W	Brill 27	–	–
57, 58	Saloon	32	1904	E R & T C W	Brill 27	–	–
59	Short saloon	18	1895	Milnes	Milnes (B)	–	–
60	Cross-bench	44	1896	Milnes	Milnes (A)	–	–
61, 62	Cross-bench	44	1906	U E C	Brill 27	–	–

Air brakes are fitted to Nos 1, 2, 5, 6, 7, 9, 16, 19-22, 32, 33, 57 and 58.
Roller shutters are fitted to Nos 14-18, 25-33, 40-48, 55, 56, 61 and 62.

Snaefell Cars							
1-6	Vestibuled saloon	48	1895	Milnes	Milnes	M & P	25

Key to Manufacturers and Builders

Brill	—	J. G. Brill Co, Philadelphia, USA
Brush	—	Brush Electrical Engineering Co Ltd, Loughborough
E C C	—	The Electric Construction Co Ltd, Wolverhampton
E E	—	English Electric Co Ltd, Preston
E R & T C W	—	The Electric Railway and Tramway Carriage Works Ltd, Preston
G E C	—	General Electric Company, Schenectady, USA
M & P	—	Mather & Platt, Manchester
M E R	—	Manx Electric Railway Co Ltd
Milnes	—	G. F. Milnes & Co Ltd, Birkenhead (later at Hadley, Shropshire)
S E H	—	Société l'Électricité et l'Hydraulique, Charleroi, Belgium (later A C E C)
U E C	—	United Electric Car Company Ltd, Preston

Key to Milnes bogie types
Three types of plate-frame trailer bogie exist and are here designated by letters. Type A appeared with the 1893 and 1894 cars and have five rivets securing the bolster to the side plates, later variants used four rivets and are shown as type B. These two types are interchangeable; allocations are those of 1967. Type C are motorless E C C 1898 bogies, with deeper side frames than those of types A and B.

MER rolling stock table as of 1968 — the "bolster" mentioned in the Milnes bogie types footnote should more correctly be referred to as a cross member. For convenience, Snaefell stock is included — these cars now have "LT" trucks and four 61hp Kiepe motors. No 22 is now "by MER" rather than Milnes!

journey of King Edward and Queen Alexandra. Previously, in 1900, it had been remounted on spare lightweight plate-frame bogies, though the bolt holes for the original wheel trunnions still show on the sills. No 59 still exists, with its original seats and interior fittings, and was only used in regular service from 1933, when the platform entrances were transposed to coincide with those of the adjacent motor car. Its elaborate lettering is seen in the early photograph reproduced.

No 60, G F Milnes & Co Ltd 1896

In 1896 a fourteenth trailer arrived, basically of the 1894 type, but with teak-and-white horizontally divided end panelling; its drawing of June 8, 1896, survives in the MER records. Seating was for 44 on 11 benches, length 28ft 9ins, width over posts 5ft 9ins. Its original number may well have been 27, since the conjectural renumbering of trailers Nos 11-13 would by this time have created a continuous series from 1 to 25, or 26 with the 1895 saloon. Finally, at some date between 1903 and 1906, it became No 60. Damaged in the Laxey fire of 1930, it was repaired, and still has the distinctive feature of brass seat-end grab-rails, as on contemporary Douglas horse and cable cars. Its bogies and brake gear are unaltered. (1970)

Nos 44 to 48, G F Milnes & Co Ltd, 1899

For the Ramsey extension, the last four cross-bench motor cars, ordered as Nos 14-22, had entered service as trailers and become 40-43, "the first". They acquired their electrical equipment in 1903. In 1899, the remaining imbalance was redressed by five new cross-bench trailers, Nos 44 to 48. These were of a more substantial design than those of 1893-6, with a clerestory roof, and were mounted on the standard type of Milnes plate-frame bogie with the usual combination of wheel brake, auxiliary scotch brake, and emergency brake linkage. Seating was again for 44 on 11 benches, and dimensions were 28ft 8ins long, and

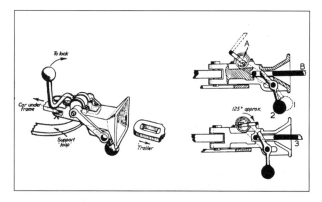

The Hughes' patent coupler as fitted to MER motor cars. This combined buffer/coupling was devised for use on steam tramways by Albert Hughes, a partner in G F Milnes & Co. The trailer coupling bar B is locked in position by the action of a swinging catch and by rotating the control lever. When uncoupling, the control lever is raised to position A and the catch weight then moved manually from position 2 to position 1. (FKP)

Trailer 60 in 1955, finished in the dark livery commonly applied to pre-1899 trailers. (Author's collection)

6ft 5ins wide over grab-rails. The clerestory ends were unglazed, and the centre bulkhead windows had a drop-light as on the 1894 and 1896 cars. These trailers again had the white lower bulkhead panel, introduced with No 60, and retained varnished posts, but had white "eaves boards" (continued across the top of the bulkheads) duly lined out and with a white lamp box. The bulkhead window frames were varnished to match the posts. They thus matched the new "ECC" motor cars exactly.

Nos 44-48 were never renumbered. They were fitted with side roller shutters after 1903, and then remained intact as a class until 1930, when No 44 was destroyed in the Laxey depot fire. Nos 45 to 48 still exist, and amass a considerable mileage. No 45 has lost its scotch brakes and staffs, being re-equipped in the same way as Nos 50, 51 and 53. (1970)

Nos 40 to 43, G F Milnes & Co Ltd, 1903

The new Manx Electric Railway Company ordered four cross-bench trailers for delivery late in 1903, from the Hadley Castle Car Works of G F Milnes. Almost identical to the five built by the same company's former Birkenhead works in 1899, they were 28ft 6ins long, 6ft 5ins wide over the grab-rails, and seated 44 on 11 cross-benches. These cars took the numbers 40-43 which had just been vacated by the 1899 cars, lately motorised and re-numbered 24-27. They were mounted on the heavier "motor" type of Milnes plate-frame bogie, presumably from re-bogied 1893-4 cars. Their paint style introduced "white" bulkhead framing (externally) for the first time, but varnished posts were still retained (see Ballure viaduct view of two car train).

Nos 40-43 (11) were among the first MER trailer cars to be fitted as new with the familiar roller shutters, which work on the principle of a roll-top desk. A letter of December 17, 1903, from Mr Edmondson, of the

MER to H D Eshelby, receiver and manager of Milnes, reveals that the MER had undertaken to fit these shutters to the cars on Milnes' behalf. One had been done, but the acute 'S' bend at the bottom of the pillars, peculiar to these cars, had caused great difficulty, whereas the company's staff had successfully fitted many such shutters to earlier cars. Nos 40 and 41 were destroyed in the Laxey fire, but Nos 42 and 43 still exist, although No 42 has lost its scotch brake and staffs, and has the emergency linkage connected to the wheel brakes.

Nos 55 and 56, Electric Railway & Tramway Carriage Works Ltd, 1904

Two more open trailers were obtained in 1904, under the same order as motor cars Nos 28-31; Milnes was on the point of closure, and the order went to the ER & TCW, at Preston. Although the new 44-seat trailers (Nos 55 and 56) owed much to earlier Milnes cars, they showed several refinements, such as glazed clerestory ends and wood panelled sills. They are 29ft 4ins long, 6ft 5ins wide over grab-rails, and 10ft 6ins high over the clerestory. Roller shutters were fitted as built. Designed to match Nos 28-31, they were mounted on the same Brill type 27Cx trucks, and shared their high floor level. Both cars still exist; the scotch brakes have been removed in recent years, and one brake-staff at each end is thus disconnected, pending removal, the emergency brake being connected to the wheel brakes. (1970)

Nos 57 and 58, Electric Railway & Tramway Carriage Works Ltd, 1904

A letter of January 28, 1904 from Mr Edmondson reveals that two saloon cars had been in use as winter trailers, with their air brakes removed. To avoid this practice, an order was placed with the Preston works for two eight-wheel saloon trailers, Nos 57 and 58. With their high clerestory and rattan seating, they were quite unlike any Milnes product. They seated 32 on reversible transverse seats, and were 32ft 9ins long and 6ft 9ins wide. The bogies were again of the Brill 27Cx type, fitted with the scotch brake; this was removed in 1943 but later reinstated.

In addition to the hand wheel brake, scotch brake and emergency brake linkage, Nos 57 and 58 were fitted with air wheel brakes operated from the motor car, and thought was also given to extending this to other passenger trailer cars. This was not carried out, although all the surviving closed motor cars except No 9 have air-cocks. The original rattan seating served for nearly 60 years, and was then replaced by blue plush; No 57 was reseated in 1960-61 and No 58 a year later. Both cars have received major attention since 1990.

Nos 61 and 62, United Electric Car Company Ltd, 1906

In 1906 two more trailers were bought from the Preston works under the same order as motor cars Nos 32 and 33, the total outlay being £2,843 15s 4d. They were identical to Nos 55 and 56 save for rod-operated, rather than rope, bells. Dimensions, capacity (44) and trucks (Brill type 27Cx) are as for Nos 55 and 56; the scotch brakes are now removed, but the twin brakestaffs remain, both connected to the wheel brakes. These cars normally run paired with the 1906 motor cars, No 61 with No 33, and No 62 with No 32, and shared their paint style.

With the delivery of Nos 32-33 and 61-62 the fleet attained its maximum of 30 motor cars (15 open, 15 saloon) and 29 trailers (26 open, three saloon), plus the locomotive and two goods motor cars. This total applied from 1906 to 1920. (1970)

Nos 40, 41 and 44 (11), English Electric Co Ltd, 1930

The 1930 fire at Laxey destroyed seven trailers (Nos 34, 35, 38, 39, 40, 41 and 44) and four motors (Nos 3, 4, 8, and 24). Three new cross-bench trailers were at once ordered from English Electric at Preston and became Nos 40, 41 and 44. They were put on the lightweight type of 4ft 9ins wheelbase bogie, salvaged from the burned trailers of 1894. These cars have strap bells, but are otherwise broadly the same as those of 1899 and 1903, which they effectively replaced; dimensions are 28ft 8ins long and 6ft 5ins wide over grab-rails, and seating is for 44. No 41 has lost its scotch brakes and staffs and has the correspondingly modified run-back provision. (1970)

General Notes

Certain general features of the MER passenger fleet need to be described before passing on to the goods stock. The four types of Hopkinson bow collector originally fitted to cars 1-13 are described in Chapter 1; these were replaced about 1897 by fixed-head trolley poles, with 4½-inch wheels. The trolley base used is the Boston Pivotal, marketed by the Anderson Co, and is noted for its compensated springing which gives virtually constant line pressure; despite the many sharp curves, dewirements are quite rare. All cars, except Nos 32 and 33, are wired trolley to south end breaker.

Interior lighting on the motor cars has always been electric, but the head and tail lights were at first oil-lamps in bulkhead lamp-boxes; the original red leading and green rear lights were replaced by orthodox white leading and red tail lights during the last war (the same change was made on the horse tramway, from which, by legislation, the earlier practice originated). Some of the older cars rarely used at night still have pre-1939 red and green bulkhead lenses. Most lamp-boxes have lost their oil-lamps, but separate railway-type bracket-mounted lamps were still (1970) carried at night for emergency use. All motor cars have jumper sockets for trailer lighting, but not all trailers have full ceiling lights; those of 1893-4 only have bulkhead lamp-box lighting. Electric headlamps were fitted to all earlier cars by about 1903, and in pre-war years an extra spotlight was mounted on cars used in

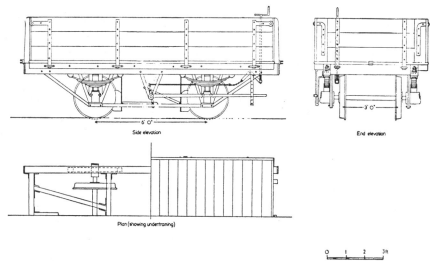

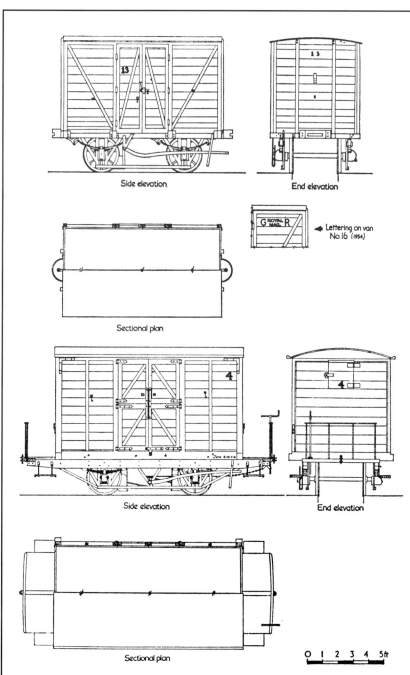

Top: IoMT&EP open wagon of about 1897. (MER)
Above: *Manx Electric covered vans. (J N Slater) See page 139 et seq*

winter; this was reintroduced in 1966-7.

In summer, cars run with their brush access covers removed so that atmospheric moisture taken up by the windings during the winter can be freely driven off, and before any car is used a lengthy drying-out on a booster is necessary. A new plant for this purpose is in hand (1992).

Car wheels are generally reprofiled at 60,000 miles. Until about 1970, motor cars used 32ins (81cms) spoked (forged) wheels, which were sent in batches to Sheffield when in need of re-tyring, but thereafter rolled steel "one piece" wheels from British Steel were adopted, and when their reprofiling allowance has been used are changed "complete". Nearly all trailers (excluding 61-2 and 57-8) had chilled iron wheels until their obsolescence saw the arrival of cast steel substitutes early in the Sixties. Axles are tested ultrasonically at intervals, as are replacement 4ft 8½ins axles bought from British Railways and shortened for MER use. Warning of approach was originally by a foot gong, and internal car signalling is by G F Milnes's rather archaic rod-operated bells. Bell connections on trailers are now out of use.

Liveries

As mentioned in the introduction to this chapter, the electric line's cars have always appeared in a combination of red or maroon, "white" and teak, with, in addition, the use of varnished or (later) grained posts on cars with cross-bench seating. The seats themselves are often in a dark varnish, excluding those outside bulkheads which commonly appear in a light oak scrumble. The alternative to varnished or grained posts is white paint, which was used at various times, increasingly from 1930.

The first closed cars had varnished teak upper panels above white rocker panels, the latter lined out in yellow and red, but 10-13, of 1895, seem to have been teak from sill to eaves board. From 1894, a beautifully coloured Three Legs of

Man appeared as a crest on the side panels of the saloon cars. The early trailers had their ash posts varnished and their chamfers picked out in red — all cars with dashes assumedly shared the same red or maroon of the period. The 1893 cars were lettered as for "Douglas and Laxey Coast Electric Tramway", those of 1894 "Douglas and Laxey Electric Tramway".

Reverting for a moment to the line's 1893 inception, the question of the alternative use of straw or gold lining on the (maroon) dashes and teak side panels of Nos 1-3 (paralleled by fine white lining) cannot now be resolved. Number shading and form are reflected in the restored state of Douglas cable tram 72/73 though here toned to different base colours.

The short-lived DL&RET livery of 1899. (MER)

The Snaefell cars (pre-1902) were similar in their livery to the coastal line's Nos 4-9 but with a garter-surrounded fleet number, rather than a crest. Their side panelling lining had more subdivisions and lacked cornerpieces of the elaborate type first used (this simpler format also appeared on the ends of 4-9). The lettering was of course "Snaefell Mountain Tramway". Under MER ownership the present style appeared, itself an echo of the "M E R Co Ltd" styling of coast line cars.

So far as the 1898 ECC cars are concerned, the original paint style appears to have included white eaves boards (see Ballure 1898 view), with the posts and the bulkhead varnished as far as the crown piece — the cars seen at Ballure in 1898 had a white lamp box, duly lined out. The varnished (or stained) area of the bulkhead had, by the Thirties, come to extend as far as the roof stick — at least one of the 1904 cars (No 31) had by then "reverted" to the 1898 style.

The bulkhead interior faces and their middle pillars have always been varnished, but a variety of styles using different areas of white paint are on record so far as cross-bench cars are concerned. The chosen illustrations show the main variants. Cross-bench cars bought in 1904 and 1906 came with white posts and framing.

Returning to 1899, the new winter saloons bore on their lower panels the new title "Douglas, Laxey and Ramsey Electric Tramway" but the word "tramway" was shortly to be replaced by "Railway". This latter title had appeared by 1904 on Nos 4, 9 and 19-22.

The new MER Company's paint scheme was somewhat darker overall (eaves boards were now red edged white on four sides) and used a definite red and white which (as earlier) seemed more immune to "yellowing". Detail painting of the above-window area was now more elaborate — the varnished drop-frames continued, although for many years now they have been grained to provide a more durable finish. The red lower panel (edged with white) which carried the

company title was mirrored by the lower panel of the repainted (and new) trailers, which bore the fleet number. The upper teak panel carried the Manx crest, as before. As in a later note, the 1950's saw a gradual adoption of "austerity" styles, using "MER" as a title.

After nationalisation, the first board adopted a "new look" colour scheme of green and white externally, grey and white inside. By 1958, 14 cars had been so treated; these were motor cars Nos 1, 20, 21, 22, 25, 27, 29, 32 and 33, trailers Nos 50, 61 and 62, and Snaefell Nos 2 and 4. The practice thereafter lapsed, the last green car being Snaefell No 4 (until September 1963), and the traditional red, cream and teak being fully restored. The only surviving part of the 1957 livery is in the white ceilings of some Snaefell cars, a definite improvement to the rather dark interiors.

Other details

The best-riding cars are, of course, those on type 27cx Brill trucks to which no substantial modification has ever had to be made. The motor sound on both these cars and the Brush-bogied ones is relatively unobtrusive. The Brush bogie as supplied had a characteristic roll, due to the generous lateral limits inherent in its bolster design, but when resprung and given shock absorbers, as on No 5, it offers a superb ride. The ECC bogies provide a much more solid ride, and with their open gearing produce a strident tramcar gear sound; the body (due to the lack of a sprung bolster) constantly adapts itself to track contours, the front visibly responding to super-elevation before the rear. Since this has continued for almost 100 years, the process appears to be harmless.

Trailer noise varies with the type of bogie frame and wheels fitted; those using steel wheels and plate frames give a particularly ringing note, the others less so. The MER's most characteristic "personal" sounds are the rapid rail beats of fast-running cars on the long down grades, the swish of the trolley wheel, and the musical ring of flanges on reverse curves.

Additional notes on MER liveries, 1992 (including Snaefell cars)

As previously stated, by the Fifties an "austerity" livery had been applied to many of the MER saloon cars, devoid of lining and with drop windows now painted white on some cars (1 & 2 are known).

On cars which had lost their transfer crest the letters "M.E.R" (no third full stop) now appeared on the upper (waist) panel with the rocker panel in plain red. Cars which retained a crest (No 5 was among the last) received this lettering on the lower (rocker) panel on the red ground. Pre-1904 cross-bench trailer cars had long ago been given red (on white) lower bulkhead panels, the upper remaining in teak, some with a surviving crest. The end "panels" of cars with boarded ends were dark red overall and by 1945 had grained posts (No 37, for example). The fleet numbers of trailers still appeared on the lower panel (or centrally in the last mentioned class). Numbers were by now quite different from their Milnes originals, retaining the basic shape but often reduced in size and without the extremely elaborate graduated shading the Birkenhead works employed. Numbers on the cross-bench cars began to reappear below their headlights — they have occupied both possible positions at different times.

After nationalisation (and the "green car" era) the Board came to acquire a smaller version of the original (1894) transfer crest and cars re-acquired traditional panel lining. Rocker panels were painted red and lined out and carried the words "Manx Electric Railway" in a not unpleasing style — the below-underframe board on cross-bench cars had continued to display this wording (or "MER"). Small fleet numbers appeared just below the roof line on the sides of the cars, to assist depot staff. At least two cars (7 and 19) displayed "MER" and "Manx Electric Railway" for a while. The use of the title "Isle of Man Railways" from 1977 introduced a more modernist lettering style, using self-adhesive techniques, but the size and colour (yellow on red) were not (in the author's view) too incongruous. A two part crest derived from the IMR's was perhaps a less happy innovation. Following the introduction of "historic" liveries in 1979, the restored 1893 cars emerged in more or less maroon shade so far as the dashes were concerned, with a decidedly "creamier" ivory paint in use for the hitherto white areas of rocker panel and window surrounds. No 1's repaint was overall a pretty accurate reconstruction, though with some lining detail differences and a rather over-spaced lettering display — it lacks waist panel transfers but these seem not to have appeared until 1894 so this is "correct".

Later repaints used the title "Douglas Laxey and Ramsey Electric Railway" — on one car (No 9) in the correct (1894) lettering style applied to some of its class around 1900, on other cars in a "curly" but simplified version of that of 1899's Nos 19-22. The original is illustrated and shows its extreme complexity, so that a simplification was perhaps inevitable. Its appearance on No 2 (the revised style, that is) is more ornamental than accurate. Car No 19, re-lettered as for "The Manx Electric Railway Co Ltd" is quite accurate, the quality being excellent. In 1982 No 6 emerged sporting "Isle of Man Passenger Transport" broadly in the MER Company styling, but was repainted in 1991. In February 1992, the 1894 title (Douglas and Laxey Electric Tramway) and that of 1899 (Douglas Laxey and Ramsey Electric Tramway) remained unrepresented. The "Isle of Man Railways" title survives only on cars 25 27 and 55.

This discussion of paint styles is not exhaustive — there have been a number of transient variations!

Additional general notes on rolling stock, 1970-92

On car No 1 a new side screen board has omitted the hand aperture which related to the 1893 controller position earlier mentioned. No 1 has carried a temporary vestibule at various times to improve the lot of winter drivers. The different floor heights of various cars result in the use of "personalised" coupling bars with varying degrees of "cranking". These are kept on a wall rack and painted with the relevant car pair's numbers. Some cross-bench cars have carried temporary windscreens at different times, but their use was never protracted. Air-operated whistles are now standard on all air brake cars.

Where restorations have restored full drop windows, window bars have (of necessity) been reinstated. By 1968 all 4-9 class cars had one-piece driver's windows and thus had only one movable vestibule window left (to the driver's left) out of an original five. The loss of the twin end-windows was an aesthetic misfortune — however, bearing in mind the then carefree habits of some Island motorists with respect to road crossings, maximum visibility was a "must". No 9 was among the last to lose this feature. In 1992, the reconstruction of car 6 has seen the twin end windows restored. Improved traffic light discipline permits this welcome reversion to original style. Additional headlights have been fitted to various cars for winter use (both pre- and post-war) and these also appeared on Snaefell from 1978, so that evening "specials" could be run. Previously, the cars had only had bulkhead oil lamps.

Goods rolling stock

In 1894, the legislature imposed on the company the duty to carry goods, mails, merchandise and parcels. Two six-ton open wagons were ordered from G F Milnes & Co, and arrived in the Island on November 30, 1894, followed soon afterwards by two six-ton closed vans with end platforms. A separate series of numbers was adopted for goods stock, the wagons becoming Nos 1 and 2, the vans 3 and 4. Another six-ton open wagon (No 5) had arrived by February 1896, again from G F Milnes.

The extension to Ramsey resulted in the addition of

five more six-ton open wagons (Nos 6 to 10). which probably arrived during the construction period of 1897-8, and two six-ton vans with end platforms (Nos 11 and 12) for the Ramsey parcels traffic which began in 1899. All these probably came from G F Milnes & Co, of which Mr Bruce was then a director. There were also the three Bonner wagons, which were apparently regarded as road vehicles and were thus not numbered in the goods stock. By 1900, there were thus four rail-borne vans and eight wagons, plus the engineering vehicles, which at that time comprised 12 platelayers' bogies, three tower wagons, one wire bogie and one cable bogie. The steam locomotive, later named Injebreck, had been sold to Douglas Corporation Water Department, and the contractors' wagons from the Ramsey extension accompanied it to West Baldwin; during the sale negotiations, the water committee was given a steam-hauled trip from Derby Castle to Laxey and back, perhaps the only steam passenger train ever to run on the line (until December, 1991).

Four pre-1900 drawings of goods stock survive in MER records. They comprise a G F Milnes side-door wagon with drop-type door; one by IOMT & EP dated December 10, 1895, of a similar wagon with lifting door; another of a wagon with removable sides, internal screw brake column and lever brake (as always, on the seaward side only); and one of a motor goods wagon similar to the 1898 ECC motor cars, but with plain arch roof, two intermediate posts each side, and drop-sides to the three sections thus formed. This last vehicle was never built.

In 1900, Derby Castle works built an electric locomotive which was numbered 23 in the passenger stock list and has already been described. Passenger car No 12 of 1895 retained its number when rebuilt to a motor cattle car early in 1903, as did the further car of this class (No 11 or 13) which was rebuilt as a freight motor in July 1904. In September 1904 the new company commenced an office record book which, together with the balance sheets and a list printed in a "weekly returns" book, has formed the basis of this account.

On March 16, 1903, F Hughes Caley, of Milnes, quoted for light parcels or luggage vans at £55 each, with detachable bodies; open wagon bodies could be substituted when required. If supplied without wheels and axles, the price dropped to £45 10s. Two new vans, Nos 13 and 14, arrived during 1903-4, possibly from Milnes; No 13 was a "small mail van" and No 14 was listed as "luggage van". Neither had end-platforms. The September 1904 returns also showed two un-numbered "freight trailers", which are thought to have been high slatted-side bogie wagons built at Derby Castle and mounted on de-motored 1893-4 bogies displaced in the 1903 re-equipment. The staff called these "sheep trucks".

The next additions were two "large mail vans" in 1908, Nos 15 and 16, built by the MER at Derby Castle, originally with end-platforms. The fleet then stood at eight four-wheel wagons, eight four-wheel vans, two unnumbered bogie trailers, one motor freight van and one motor cattle van. In the year ended September 1911, the goods motor disappears from the record book and re-emerges as a third bogie trailer; in fact, it was simply de-motored. Only the original purpose-built wagons and vans (Nos 1-16) are shown with numbers in the weekly returns book.

In 1912, the motor cattle car was converted to a trailer, and four more open wagons were placed in service. Of these, Nos 17 and 18 were standard six-ton open wagons built by G C Milnes, Voss & Co in March 1912, while Nos 19 and 20 were 12-ton stone wagons on 1893-4 ex-motor bogies, built by the MER and known by the staff as "dreadnoughts". No 19 entered service in February 1912, No 20 in March. This brought the goods stock to its pre-1914 maximum of 25 vehicles, as follows:

Open wagons (10) — 1, 2, 5, 6, 7, 8, 9, 10, 17, 18
Bogie stone wagons (2) — 19 and 20
Vans (6) — 3, 4, 11,12, and parcels vans, 13, 14
Mail vans (2) — 15 and 16
Unnumbered bogie trailers (two slatted-side trucks and two ex-passenger vehicles) — 4
Locomotive (1) — No 23
25 vehicles in all

The Bonner road-rail wagons are never mentioned in the office records, but were certainly purchased by the MER and used for at least a few years.

The crash of January 24, 1914, eliminated the locomotive from the scene for 11 years, and probably accounted for two of the three Bonner wagons as well. The next changes occur in 1918, when the other two withdrawn passenger cars of the 10-13 class (then still languishing in Laxey depot) were transferred to the freight stock as trailers. The numbers 21-26 were allotted to these and the four unnumbered bogie vehicles, probably as follows:

No 21 (?) — Freight motor rebuilt July 1904 from passenger car No 11 or 13 and de-motored since 1911.

No 22 — Motor cattle car rebuilt early 1903 from passenger car No 12 and de-motored 1912.

No 23 (?) — Freight trailer rebuilt from passenger car No 13 or 11 in 1918, retaining scotch brake and two brakestaffs.

Nos 24, 25 — Bogie trailers built by MER in 1904.

No 26 — Freight trailer rebuilt from passenger car No 10 in 1918, and given air brakes in January 1920.

By 1924, cattle and sheep traffic by rail had largely ceased, and sheep trucks Nos 24 and 25 were rebuilt in March and April 1924 as 12-ton "dreadnought" stone wagons. The locomotive was brought back to life late in 1925, using the cab of the original 1900 locomotive (No 23) and two new wagon bodies; when in use, it borrowed the trucks of passenger car No 33. In February 1926, freight trailer No 21 re-emerged as a fifth dreadnought stone wagon, distinguished by a

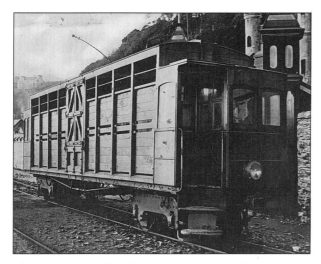

The impressive rebuild of No 12 as a specialist cattle vehicle circa 1909. (MER)

A Bonner wagon seen at the Derby Castle siding in 1899. The wagon has just been drawn off its rail-borne "undertrack".

steel underframe, and in March 1927 the ex-motor cattle car No 22 (formerly No 12) was scrapped; trailer No 23 of 1918 now became No 22 and allowed the locomotive to regain its former number. In 1926, the company bought its first motor lorry.

One open wagon disappeared in 1930, reducing the goods fleet to 25 vehicles, but much of the fleet now stood semi-derelict at the Dhoon where, by the mid-Thirties, rail-borne quarry traffic had finally ceased. All 25 vehicles survived on the books until 1941, after which regular annual reporting of stock temporarily ceased. The war years saw all serviceable goods stock in use again, particularly on airport construction; stone waste traffic from Laxey reached such a level that on September 9, 1941 the late W E Kerruish was able to book 291 tons in a single day. In 1944 van No 15 was wrecked in a run-back at Ballaglass, and freight trailers 22 and 26 were also written off; No 22 remained derelict for some years at Dhoon, and No 26 (ex 10) still existed as a store in Laxey depot, in quite good condition. It saw restoration to its trailer state in 1979, sponsored by the IoM Railway Society.

Ownership of road vehicles had risen to two in 1930, three in 1948 and four in 1949, but rail-borne goods traffic fell again after the war to "one van load" level, and in 1952 ten open wagons were written off, including (nominally) all five dreadnoughts. Dreadnought 21, which had been retrucked in April 1942 with Brush bogies, was kept for engineering purposes, and is still in good order; it was further altered in 1958-9, and more drastically in 1977 (see notes below). The official wagon stock was now down to four, but the remains of the others stood at Dhoon quarry sidings until after 1957. No 10 still existed, derelict, at Derby Castle in 1965.

Following nationalisation, the MER Board refurbished the remaining goods stock (open wagons Nos

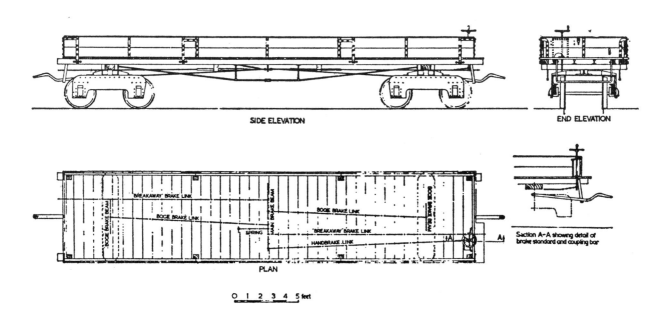

SIDE ELEVATION

END ELEVATION

BOGIE BRAKE BEAM
BREAKAWAY BRAKE LINK
BOGIE BRAKE LINK
MAIN BRAKE BEAM
SPRING
BOGIE BRAKE LINK
BOGIE BRAKE BEAM
"BREAKAWAY" BRAKE LINK
HANDBRAKE .LINK

PLAN

Section A-A showing detail of
brake standard and coupling bar

0 1 2 3 4 5 feet

MER Dreadnought stone wagon No 24. (J N Slater)

Wickham Railcars for Snaefell

Prepared with the assistance of Wickham Rail Ltd., Successors to D Wickham Ltd

	Years	Operators	Works No	Engine	Approx wt, (Unladen)	Remarks
1	1951	Air Ministry	5864	Ford V8 petrol	2.5T	Given Diesel engine 1964-5, sold to MER 1977, currently out of use
2	1957/8	Civil Aviation Authority	7642	Ford 28hp diesel	2.5T	Purchased by Wickham Rail Ltd.,1991 for future use elsewhere after rebuild
3	1977	" "	10956	Perkins 4.203 litre normally aspirated diesel	3T	
4	1991	" "	11730	Perkins 4.236 litre N A diesel	4T	Replaced 2

Nos 1-3 were built by D Wickham Ltd, Ware, Herts; No 4 by Wickham Rail, Suckley, Worcester.

1, 5, 7 and 8, and vans Nos 3, 4, 12, 13, 14 and 16), later adopting a pleasing olive green livery. The Board's parcels traffic continued to be well supported, and the mail contract assured full van loads to and from Ramsey several times daily. However, life expiry of road vehicles caused collection and delivery of MER-hauled goods to cease from March 31, 1966, though mail traffic continued (until 1975), as does some substantial parcels traffic between stations. The surviving vehicles, although fewer in number, are a representative collection of all periods, and are listed below.

MER goods stock, 1968

No	Description	Empty weight (tons, cwt, lbs)	Built
1	6 ton open wagon	2 8 33	1894
3	6 ton van with platforms	2 10 3	1894-5
4	6 ton van with platforms	2 10 3	1894-5
5	6 ton open wagon	not stated	1895-6
7	6 ton open wagon	2 7 0	1897-8
8	6 ton open wagon	2 8 3	1897-8
11	6 ton van with platforms removed	not stated	1898-9
12	6 ton van with platforms	2 11 0	1898-9
14	Small vans, no platforms	not stated	1904
16	Large mail van, platforms removed	not stated	1908
21	Bogie engineers wagon	4 16 0	1926
26	Large freight trailer used as store, ex-passenger car 10	not stated	1895

All wagons and vans (except Nos 21 and 26) have side lever brakes on the seaward side only, plus screw brakes. The original livery comprised grey ironwork, with white numbers.

There are also two rail tower wagons on the coastal tramway, and one on the Snaefell line. The other two non-passenger vehicles on the Snaefell line (coal car 7 and the 1895 open wagon) are described in Chapter 2.

1992 Postscript

Wagon 5 had been scrapped by 1992, and freight loco 23 became a museum exhibit at Ramsey in 1979, motorised for demonstration runs in both 1983 and 1984. Van 12 now carries a tower platform, while Dreadnought 21 was rebuilt in 1977, with two hydraulic cranes added. Of the original coast line tower wagons two survive, while that on Snaefell now rides on a former Milnes bogie. The 1895 Hurst Nelson open wagon built for Snaefell failed in service in 1981 and there are now two open wagons constructed on former Snaefell bogie frames and two interconnected rail bogies. These are without brakes and two interconnected rail bogies. These are without brakes but are always pushed uphill. "Coal car" No 7 has remained unused, and since the Aachen re-equipment cannot be "resuscitated". The Air Ministry railcar of 1951 was sold to the railways in 1977 and replaced by a new Wickham (No 10956) powered by a Perkins engine (the owners by now being the Civil Aviation Authority). This closely resembled that of 1957. Isle of Man Railways itself owns two 3ft gauge Wickhams, bought secondhand in 1978, their works numbers being 7442 and 8849. They have been used by both electric and steam railways. The new Wickham of 1991, and the departure of that of 1957 are referred to in Chapter 8 (see table, also).

Appendix I
East Coast Railways

As late as 1893, the fare from Douglas to Laxey was 8s per horse-drawn car, such a vehicle holding but four passengers; excursion brakes carried seven. Likewise, to Ramsey the alternatives were an earlier-established coach via Kirk Michael, the steam railway (opened in 1879), and the steamers. By the latter years of the century, the Mona Steamship Company was running the Fairy Queen, Lancelot, Manx Fairy and Minnow between Douglas and Ramsey, making two return trips daily, one starting from Douglas in the morning and one after lunch, with calls at both Laxey and Dhoon Glen. Other facilities were offered by steamers proceeding to or from Glasgow, Belfast or Ardrossan and on cruises round the Island.

Meanwhile, schemes for railways were put forward. The first known evidence is letter of January 6, 1874 from William Lewis to G W Dumbell, which proposed an extension from the Douglas-Peel railway, and described the route as following the river Glass to below Glenville, then running north-eastwards up a side valley to Hillberry and down the southern side to the Groudle valley to Port Groudle. Nothing came of the proposal.

On March 1, 1882 there appeared the Douglas, Laxey & Ramsey Railway Co Ltd, with a capital of £130,000 in £5 shares. Of the eight subscribers, three were Manxmen, four hailed from Manchester and district, and one from Flint. The engineer appears to have been Daniel Cregeen. A manuscript of 1883 exists on the costs of working a line to Laxey, followed in 1885 by an elegantly written manuscript estimate of working expenses for the same Douglas, Laxey and Ramsey Railway, the detailed costing even including lamp oil! Agreement had been reached with the IMR for joint use of Douglas station and for a station and junction at Quarter Bridge, the other intended stations being at Ballaquayle, Falcon Cliff, Summer Hill, Onchan, Ballameanagh, Glen Gawne and Laxey; those from Douglas to Onchan were rated suburban. New articles of association were drawn up on August 22,1885 and a prospectus issued by Chadwick, Boardman & Co, of Manchester, on November 17, 1885, but the scheme failed for lack of support.

George Noble Fell undertook surveys during 1887-8 for an east coast line with the title Douglas, Laxey & Snaefell Railway, though the application lodged was for Douglas-Laxey only. To secure land purchase powers, Fell appeared in November 1888 before a special committee of Tynwald Court, his ambitious proposals involving expert witnesses on an unusual scale. One mile of the eight would have been on viaducts (of Fell's own design), and the land costs were estimated by the court at £62,000 if the line had a separate quayside terminal, or £37,000 if the line ran into Douglas alongside the IMR. Plans for the Douglas-Laxey section had been lodged in the Rolls office on September 19, 1888, and the inquiry began on November 6; the chief

technical witness was James Whitestone, who had been an articled pupil of W H Barlow on the Midland Railway. The line was approved, but work was never started.

A further company, the Douglas, Laxey & Maughold Head Marine Drive and Tramway Company Ltd, was registered on September 8, 1890 with a capital of £100,000 and an address c/o F Browne, Advocate, of Athol Street, Douglas. All seven subscribers had London addresses. Joint working with the Isle of Man Tramways Ltd (the horse tramway operator) was proposed, though with no details of motive power.

In 1891, Fell's scheme of 1887-8 was revived with a new title, Manx East Coast Railways. A book of lithographed plans survives, showing a line from Douglas to Laxey. Starting at Douglas with a station just north of the IMR locomotive shed, the line paralleled the IMR to Quarter Bridge and then followed the river Glass, crossed the road to Tromode, and climbed by sinuous reverse curves to cross the Glencrutchery stream beyond the then Douglas waterworks. The next station was to be close to Onchan's central crossroads, after which the line descended towards Groudle, crossing the stream by a 44ft high bridge. A summit height of 325ft 6ins was reached just over six miles from Douglas, the route thereafter being virtually that of the electric line as built in 1893-4, but ending at the Queen's Hotel, Laxey, 150ft above datum. The total distance was eight miles seven furlongs.

Daniel Cregeen's lithographed plans for the Douglas, Laxey & Dhoon Railway exist in the Manx Museum, and although probably post-1890, are the culmination of much earlier field work dating back at least to November 1883. From a full-scale separate terminus near the North Quay (and fronting the IMR station), it tunnelled under the Peel Road/Athol Street junction to emerge alongside the IMR , which it followed to Quarter Bridge. The line then turned north-east to Ballaquayle Cottage, Glencrutchery and Onchan, with no gradient steeper then 1 in 50 and with bridges at all road crossings, save for a level crossing at Summer Hill Road. After a station at Onchan, close to the centre of the village, the line was to parallel the road to Laxey, crossing the Groudle river by four 80ft spans with a maximum height of 68ft. From here, the route followed was that of the later electric line, but with a girder bridge to cross the main Laxey road, a viaduct of three 50ft spans across Glen Gawne (Garwick), and a summit level of 319ft, reached after five miles five furlongs. The Laxey station was again just to seaward of the Queen's hotel, on the 150ft contour line.

The ensuing section was much more dramatic. A seven-arch viaduct 99ft high with spans of 43ft was to cross the Laxey valley on a curve of $6^1/_2$ chains radius, forming a virtually complete semi-circle. A mineral branch to the washing floors was to

form a trailing connection just beyond the viaduct. From here until the Dhoon terminus (at 442ft) the line was to climb at an almost constant 1 in 31. The intended terminus, ten miles form Douglas, was on the southern shoulder of Bulgham Bay, where, no doubt, railhead development was envisaged.

After part of Fell's 1887-8 survey was used by Saunderson for the electric line in 1893-4, Fell's Snaefell survey was kept alive until 1895 by a separate Snaefell Railway Company, whose office was in Athol Street. The Douglas, Laxey & Ramsey scheme of Cregeen and associates had its office in 1893-4 at 1 Gellings Court, but Cregeen died on April 19, 1894, after a career largely spent with HM Commissioners of Works in London.

The last east coast steam railway proposed was a direct rival of the electric line. On April 9, 1896 a Mr Mylchreest sought leave to introduce into Tynwald a Bill for a railway from Laxey to Ramsey, and a first reading followed on May 13. His backers were a London syndicate, R Blackie, J Templeton Slade and A T Green, with G Noble Fell as its surveyor. The IOMT & EP petitioned Tynwald on October 28 for leave to present its own Bill, and by December 10, the steam railway scheme had been 'withdrawn by consent'.

The Groudle Glen Railway

In 1895 the services of Frederick Saunderson were engaged by the proprietors of Groudle Glen to create what some have argued to be the first "miniature" railway in the British Isles. The railway however was more accurately "narrow gauge" in its concept. Work was commenced during 1895 (Saunderson's beautifully drawn and coloured plan was among documents seen by the present author during the Sixties) and advanced at such a pace that passengers were carried from May 23, 1896, with a formal opening on July 20. The total length was $^3/_4$-mile, with (ultimately) two locomotives and eight cross-bench carriages.

The line finally closed after summer 1962 and was later dismantled, but volunteer effort and generous sponsorship have seen the widely scattered mechanical "constituents" substantially either preserved or brought back for renewed service on an ultimately fully reconstructed line, progressively re-opened from May 1986. The Groudle Glen Railway (David H Smith, the Plateway Press, 1989) contains an excellent history of the line, and the present operating company, Groudle Glen Railway Ltd* produces a guide book which relates the restoration story and (on a less lavish scale) the overall pre-history. The restored line will be an attractive "adjacent feature" to 1993's events at Groudle.

_____
* 19 Ballabrooie Grove, Douglas, Isle of Man

Appendix 2
Other lines closely related the the Manx Electric

(i) Lines actually constructed

The Ramsey Pier Tramway

The author's account of this line in Isle of Man Tramways derived from a number of sources, and it now appears that the originating date quoted is incorrect. The following account should correct this:

Ramsey's 2,300ft Queen's Pier belongs to the Department of Highways, Ports and Properties (a successor the the Harbour Board). Regrettably, it was closed to the public in May 1991, following vandalism. Its future was being looked into at the time of writing.

Its construction and opening by the Lord Bishop of Sodor and Man on July 22, 1886 were matters of great rejoicing — Ramsey seemed poised on the brink of an expansion parallel to that already being experienced by Douglas. It seems likely the structure included provision for a tramway track (first mooted 1882) as a mid-Nineties photograph by Keig shows it without rails but apparently with longitudinal decking timbers where the rails were later added. By the mid-Nineties a tramway and provision for steamer landing were matters of serious intent — Mr G S Hearse has found an order date of 1895 for the rails. The pierhead added at the seaward end finally saw completion in 1899, and the Press now (August 1899) reported the arrival of a passenger car, hand-propelled, which is the subject of the accompanying sketch. This vehicle apparently conveyed Edward VII and Queen Alexandra in August 1902. It must be assumed that the formerly existing luggage trunks (there were seven in all, plus a flat truck for heavy articles) were obtained at about the same date, and that the tramway had been under construction for some time — it would obviously have been of some use during the pierhead's construction. The track diagram shows the layout as evidenced by actual observation in about 1950, but early photographs which feature the pier entrance (after the pierhead's addition) show the track running straight out on to the pier approach

with a curved branch diverging to the south, only. The tramway's siding (just after the entrance kiosk, left) necessitated structural additions to the pier.

Steamer traffic in pre-war years was still significant (typically 17 calls per week) and in May 1937 the Board purchased a Hibberd *Planet* locomotive (No 2037) and a bogie cross-bench trailer (numbered 2038) from the same firm — the actual construction was at Park Royal Coachworks in north London. This petrol-driven combination was joined in 1950 by a Wickham petrol-engined railcar, No 5763, with seats for 11. The by-now 'Y' tracks at the entrance were buried in 1955-6 and a straight spur on to the pier approach substituted, using ex-Douglas Cable Tramway rails. A Royal patron again rode the tramway on July 4, 1963 in the person of Queen Elizabeth the Queen Mother, using the Hibberd combination, with tasteful decorations added. During the Fifties and Sixties the Wickham car was the most used, although the Hibberd loco was "dual purpose" in that it sometimes hauled luggage trucks.

Even by the late Sixties all still seemed much "as ever" — the pier was kept in good visual order and was a pleasant place to while away a sunny afternoon. However, radical changes were in the offing. The condition of the pier head (used by Steam Packet steamers on both Ardrossan and Belfast routes) had by now rapidly deteriorated and the last (Belfast) steamers were to call in 1970. With reduced patronage, the Board ran the tramway for the last time in September 1970 — it is uncertain what operation (if any) took place in 1971, but by 1972 the then lessee of the pier café, Mr J Maisey had also run the tramway — 7,000 of the year's 40,000 entrants had used the line. The lessees for 1973 were a Mr and Mrs Venables. Of the luggage trucks (which were of two main sizes and had various detail differences) six were removed and presumably scrapped following the end of the Board operation in

The original hand-propelled Ramsey Pier passenger car. The original livery was white (cream?) overall. (FKP)

1950's views of Pier rolling stock. The livery was dark green with aluminium roofs. (W G S Hyde)

September 1970 — one survivor and a permanent way trolley remained at the pier in 1992. The 1899 passenger car suffered an arson attack during 1973 and the remains were then disposed of.

In 1974 no-one appeared to want to run the tramway until, late in the summer, members of the Manx Electric Railway Society undertook the operation with volunteer crews. The Harbour Board had, meanwhile, made some repairs to the decking and rails. The Society began to operate on August 5 (weekends only from September 21) and by October 13 had carried some 5,670 passengers.

This encouraging result again saw the MERS as operators for 1975 and 1976 (June 28 to October 5, approximately

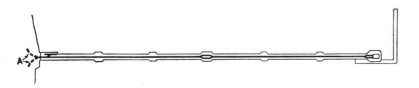

Track diagram, Ramsey Pier Tramway. Tracks A were removed in 1955-6. (JCC)

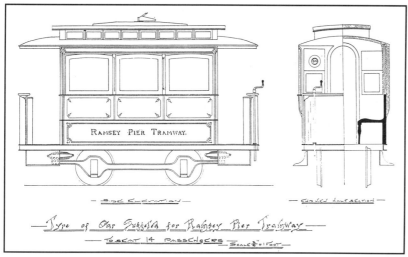

Electric car design produced by the MER circa 1906.

6,000 passengers; May 30 to October 17, 4,315) but for 1977 only the café operator, a Mrs Sayle, made use of the tramway, primarily to transport foodstuffs and sales goods (though occasionally some passengers may have been carried). However, on May 27, 1979 the tramway reopened in the charge of Mr G S Hearse and his son, and continued to operate for another two seasons. The final season lasted for 96 operating days and saw 900 miles run, with a passenger figure of 7,000, the last public journeys being on September 9, 1981. Operation had, since 1976, been entirely by the Planet combination, as the Wickham car had been loaned to the MER Board early in 1976 (along with the Hibberd loco) for use in the track-lifting work described elsewhere in this book. The Wickham vehicle then went to the Isle of Man Railway and was kept at Castletown until 1969 or so — it was noted as in store at Douglas in July 1980. The Hibberd loco acquired "steam outline" "boiler" fittings in January 1981.

So far as the pier operation was concerned, the Board's closure decision apparently related to deterioration of the timber rail supporting members about which concern had been first expressed in 1974-5.

As stated, the last service train ran on September 9, 1981. At the time it seemed possible that the surviving stock might see re-use on a line in the Mooragh Park, and for the moment it remained in store in the Harbour Board yard. By 1982 "weathering" of the trailer had become significant, and (having established contact with the IOMRS) the several parties came to agree that the loco and trailer should go on loan exhibition as part of the Ramsey museum display. The stock was delivered on September 30. Restoration work on the trailer by IOMRS members and further help by Mr Hearse saw the train re-emerge to run on the MER tracks along Walpole Drive on May 25, 1985, as part of an "enthusiasts' weekend", and there were further similar operations later. The last operation was in May, 1991. At the time of writing the Ramsey museum is closed pending revised (seasonal) operating arrangements

(August 1992). Especial thanks are due to Mr G S Hearse for help with this text and to the Department of Harbours, Ports and Properties.

Laxey Wheel Incline Railway ("Browside Tramway")

This little-known line connected Laxey Wheel with the roadway below. It was built about 1890, and comprised a double track with two 20-seat toastrack cars having dissimilar diameter wheels. The line was worked on the water counterbalance method, taking water from a cistern filled from the mine tailrace. A braked drum acted as a controlling windlass at the upper end.

The line was initially owned and operated by the Faragher family of Cronk e Chule farm, who later sold it to the mining company. Spasmodic Press advertisements appeared; one of 1895 specifies the return fare as 1d, but another source gives the original fare as 1d up and 1d down, later reduced to 1d up, ¹/₂d down. An old employee of the mine, living in 1964 in Laxey, was employed as a "tout"

for the lift and sometimes as "bung boy" at the lower station, emptying the tank of the car that had just descended.

By 1910 the line had shown itself unprofitable, and it was dismantled; the remains of the head gear still existed in 1968.

Section (ii) Proposed lines

Ramsey: tramway proposals, 1882-99

According to a map of 1882, the already projected 3ft gauge freight tramway on the future Ramsey pier (as earlier, the pier itself was constructed in 1886) was originally to have extended into the town, assumedly with horse traction. In 1897, during negotiations for bringing the electric line into Ramsey, the Ramsey Commissioners proposed a horse tramway to link the electric line's terminus with the steam railway, and in the 1899 *The Courier* was pressing the Harbour Board to build an electric tramway from the pier to the town.

(Acknowledgements to Stan Basnett)

Dhoon Glen, 1895

In 1895, correspondence took place between a Mr Drinkwater and Governor Ridgeway concerning an undefined tramway along Dhoon Glen. It should here be noted that the West Baldwin reservoir line, which is described in the Journal of the Stephenson Locomotive Society, May 1963, and subsequently in the Journal of the Manx Museum, was considered for retention as a passenger line according to a contemporary Ward Lock guidebook, but this did not occur and the line was removed.

Below: A car arrives at the upper terminus, of the Browside line, sans customers! (G R Peake)

Appendix 3
Tickets of the MER
(including the Ramsey pier tramway)

Introduction

The Author's original text included an extensive appendix on this topic by a noted authority, the late Mr W H Bett. It was at first thought possible to reprint Mr Bett's 1968 text and update this by notes on the more recent changes, but the present Author lacks the detailed knowledge necessary to add a tailpiece of the necessary quality to preserve a balanced treatment overall. For this reason, Mr Bett's text has been reduced to a less detailed form (students of this particular topic can obviously refer back to the 1970's text where more detail is sought).

The Manx Electric's Practice

Ticket and fare collection systems have a long and complex history, much effort having gone into ensuring that the operator (rather than the platform staff!) received all the fares paid. The Manx Electric and its predecessor companies have opted always for a "pre-purchased" ticketing system - eg, a ticket is bought at a booking office and later cancelled on the car - only passengers joining at minor intermediate points obtaining a ticket direct from a conductor. Tickets from booking offices were (nominally) date stamped on issue (as was the case on ordinary railways), the earlier ones using an inked press.

The collection of all tickets at the end of the journey is scarcely practicable, although trains approaching Douglas ore often boarded by an inspector who collects all the tickets. Ticket collecting enthusiasts were often offered generous "samples" arising from this practice.

The earliest tickets were strange hybrids in design between the "Bell Punch" tickets (on fairly thin paper, usually 2.25 in by 1.25in) common on street tramways throughout Britain, and the "Edmondson" card ticket traditionally used by railways (using a stiff card always 2.25 in by 1.25 in), eg, having the "bell punch" layout but the Edmondson physique!

A specimen of these hybrids owned by Mr Bett was on a thicker card than a "bell punch" paper ticket (though rather thinner than an Edmondson) and is dated June 2 1896, having received what appears to be a machine cancellation rather than the hand nipper cancellation normal on Edmondson tickets. Another ticket (ex Mr Julian Edwards collection) is 2.75 in by 1.25 in and thus is of standard "bell punch" width but well over normal length, and was on a normal thin "bell punch" type paper. Both these are reproduced, including the advertising material on Mr Edward's ticket.

The fare quoted on the latter leads to its dating as being of 1895 (Douglas - Groudle return was then 5d, Douglas - Garwick 8d. The Edward's ticket's Groudle fare of "3d" would be for a single journey). Only Mr Bett's ticket shows its printer (Foster of Northampton.

A surviving Snaefell ticket of 1896 shows this line originally to have used an orthodox "railway ticket" layout, which points the particular contrast with those just discussed and illustrated.

The basic form of the standard MER card ticket was first introduced by Williamson of Ashton-under-Lyne, who seems to have become the printer in the late '90s. The railway still uses this ticket style, though with several successive suppliers since the demise of Williamson. Paper "ribbon" tickets also are sold on the cars from modern ticket machines. The original tickets had a date space at the head (as earlier, not always used and now effectively abandoned), a centre column where lay the title and conditions, and spaces down each side of the centre column in which appears a variety of geographical information, where a "punch" (or more correctly cutting nippers) are used to make cancellations. The use of the plural is deliberate, as generous break of journey facilities are and were accorded MER passengers.

Such interrupted journeys necessitate "fractional" cancellations, made by punching when the ticket is first presented. If the passenger is riding through, the conductor gives three or four clips down the side of the ticket from top to bottom; if break of journey is requested he punches the section or sections to be travelled on his car and leaves the remainder to be cancelled by a subsequent conductor. In the case of returns, one side relates to the outward and the other to the return journey. At one time, "break of journey" tickets existed and were used when a passenger changed his mind and decided to leave the car at an intermediate point after his ticket had been presented and cancelled. A serial number appears across the foot of the ticket, and the inscription "single" or "return" is added once or even twice. In the latter case the positions were across the top and across the bottom, above the serial number.

Most tickets issued at offices were originally white and had an overprint consisting of (a) "$^1/_2$" for half-fares, if applicable, (b) a letter, or letters, denoting which of the three routes radiating from Laxey the ticket covered — 'D' for Laxey-Douglas, 'R' for Laxey-Ramsey, 'S' or sometimes 'LS' for Laxey-Snaefell (also 'T' or 'BT' for the former Bungalow-Tholt-y-Will-Sulby Glen bus service), and

finally (c) 'S' or 'R' for single or return. Thus a Douglas to Ramsey return was overprinted "DRR", a half-fare Ramsey to Laxey Single, "$^1/_2$RS". These overprints were originally in red on singles and half-fare returns, but in green on adult returns. In latter years, they became plain black. On some tickets a statement of the journey covered (eg Douglas-Dhoon) accompanied the overprint initials (in this case DRR). The overprint initials are now largely supplanted by a statement of the actual fare paid (the practice pre-dates decimalisation).

Tickets issued on the cars originally had the fare printed in the text and had stage sections set out "fareboard" fashion. They were usually plain white or vertically parti-coloured (striped) white and blue for single and vertically parti-coloured white and pink for return, without overprints. Later, a type bearing an overprinted fare and a standardised stage-array for all values was used, having the letters "D-L-R" (for Douglas, Laxey, Ramsey) across the head and the names of the principal intermediate points in route order down the sides; both boarding point and destination were punched on issue. Returns were variously coloured (examples include orange, yellow and green cards), with overprints as necessary, (again, colouring is now largely absent, dependent on the age of the particular ticket stock).

At the once-busy Onchan Head station an 'Automaticket' counter-embedded machine issued perforated 'singles' to Douglas. Less standard issues include "name ticket" coupons in 20-ride booklets and the $3^1/_2$ins square book of tickets formerly available for a personally conducted day tour including refreshments (later versions were $3^1/_2$ x 2ins).

By 1965, the Board was offering residents winter-fare tickets in tens for the price of eight (the fares themselves were already at half the summer level), and in summer 10 journeys for 11 times the winter fare. Boarding-house keepers and hotels were offered distribution of coupon tickets at 25 per cent reduction to Laxey, Ramsey and Snaefell, for their summer guests.

Rover tickets have appeared in plain white, green or yellow, or have coloured striping. They have day spaces and a Snaefell section, all selectively punched and are issue-dated.

Since 1977 there have been changes to the line's ticketing system, which had previously altered little. These have seen a simplification of the card tickets (following Williamson's demise in the early Eighties, printers have included British Rail and, most recently, Bemrose of Derby) and the adoption of "Setright Speed" machines for platform staff (which record the transactions). These produce the usual paper "ribbon" ticket with ink-printed detail for the specific journey. As far as card tickets are concerned, there are now ten originating "stations", plus three for Snaefell, and, as earlier, the "letter" overprints (such as "DRS") have in some cases disappeared, to be replaced by a superimposition of the actual fare.

By the early Eighties, with two railways and the buses in common ownership, Rover tickets were widened in scope. A three-day variant allowed its use on <u>both</u> railways and one Snaefell journey, while one for five days now included the buses

as well, but excluded Snaefell (both were used on consecutive days). Concessions to families were (and are) generous — when one child accompanied its parents, further children up to a maximum of four were conveyed free. Residents' contracts (a typical validity might be from April to October) had unlimited use over their currency and were deservedly popular. Further references to other "Rover Ticket" variations will have been seen in Chapter 8.

Ramsey Pier Tramway Tickets

The Queen's Pier tram (IoM Harbour Board) at Ramsey was a user of stock roll

tickets (ie, the familiar cloakroom type) in conjunction with a bell-punch. Properly titled tickets suddenly appeared instead, about 1961. These were perforated at one end and made up in pads, and worded ISLE OF MAN HARBOUR/QUEENS PIER TRAM ADULT 2d (or CHILD 1d). The adult's ticket was white, and the child's blue. About 1963, fares were doubled and similar tickets at 4d, adult, 2d, child, came into use. They were sometimes unpunched, or at other times clipped with a non-registering hand-nipper; some have appeared with no fare stated. A specimen of the form used in later years is not to hand.

An 1895 ticket — see above. (Julian Edwards)

Mr W H Bett's "Foster" hybrid of 1896.

A Snaefell "return", 1896. (WHB)

MER "DRR" of 1945.

1950's single.

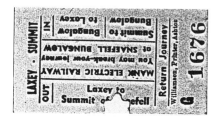

1950's Snaefell ticket without overprinting.

An early (1950's) example of a fare overprint.(WHB)

A 1960's Howstrake return, probably hand coloured (purple on white).

A "heavily used" DRR from the Sixties. The multiple clipping is typical.

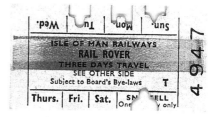

An "Exchange" ticket, issued in exchange for a Name ticket — date probably late Fifties/early Sixties.

A "Rail Rover" issued May 29, 1983.

Appendix 4
Route Maps — Manx Electric Railway

These maps are based on "Parliamentary" and other plans, but with buildings and field boundaries corrected as far as possible to the present day. Gradient profile sections do not coincide with the maps as they have to be accommodated within page width dimensions, but stations provide easy cross reference points. A solid bar across the line indicates a car stop observed in both directions; unidirectional stops are shown by a bar to the left (northbound) or right (southbound), former stops by a white bar. 'S' after a stop name indicates occasional use only (secondary status). Other standard symbols are: CR (crossover), FP (electric feeder point), P (pillar box), T (telephone access point) and WB (warning board). Detailed plans of Derby Castle, Laxey and Ramsey stations appear in Chapters 1 and 3, and of Douglas and Laxey depots in Chapter 6. Ballajora and Dhoon quarries appear in Chapter 4, and Chapter 5, respectively Station buildings at the lineside appear as a St Andrew's cross within a rectangle, positioned on the appropriate side of the tracks.

Electrical feeder system

Feeder points are shown by FP on the maps and are numbered in series from Douglas. Some are pole-mounted switch boxes, usually associated with overhead feeders, and others are the older IOMT & EP ground pillars, which served for underground feeders. Both types of feeder were normally left unbridged across the section breakers: this allows maximum localisation of faults. Most ground pillars had pull-out (fused) connections, but some contained switchgear and more elaborate internal connections, especially if linked to the trolley wires at feeder points. Their external appearance is the same, with a lifting lid to give access to the pull-out connections and a side door to the lower interior. (All 1894 feeders are now disused.)

At feeder Points 16 and 34 there is only a pole-mounted switch, at feeder points 1, 3, 8, 9, 10, 11, 12, 13, 17, 18, 27, and 29 there is only a ground pillar, and at feeder points 2, 4, 6, 7, 14, 19 to 25, 28, 30, 31, 32 and 33 there are both. At feeder points 01, 02, 5, 15, 26, 32 (partly) and 35, the switchgear is in adjacent buildings. Section breakers are at feeder points 1, 3, 5, 9, 11, 13, 15, 22, 24, 26, 28, 31 and 33 (bridged) and there were telephones at feeder points 01, 02, 1, 5, 15, 17, 18, 23, 24, 26, 28, 30, 31, 32, 33 and 35. A replacement feeder runs overhead from 26 to 27 to take the place of the underground feeder from 26 to 30, now disused. The underground feeder ran overhead from 16 to 17, and the overhead feeder runs underground from 15 to 16, with a feeder from point 15 to the Snaefell line overhead in Laxey station. The Snaefell DC underground feeder passes through one pole switch and two standard pillars (no longer connected to the wire) to reach the section gap at the former power station; on this line, the trolley wires are connected by cross wires. Some changes to the electrical system arise from the circumstances described in Chapter 8.

Map changes

The maps which follow were correct in 1968, and rather than attempt their modification the following information is given:

The last two decades have seen the disappearance of the following from the lineside features visible on the maps (the disposal of the former office and Manager's residence, earlier the property of Isle of Man Tramways Ltd has been referred to in Chapter 8, as has the demolition of the IOMT & EP canopy over the horse tracks: Derby Castle depot changes have also been dealt with earlier).

Onchan Head: shelter of about 1899 and an adjoining inspector's office/booking office demolished 1978.

Groudle: Howstrake Estate toll house of 1893 demolished (after many years as a private house) 1988.

Half Way House: building too small to be included (see below).

Garwick Glen: Substantial passenger shelter demolished in 1979 (the Glen became a private property during the Sixties). Likewise the booking office (a sales kiosk vanished in about 1968)

Laxey: Distilled water tower adjacent to track now in ruins (1895).

Laxey: Small hut used by officer in charge to regulate Snaefell car departures demolished 1987.

Laxey: Approaches to Minorca — stone test house of 1898/9 now demolished (in ruins after 1935).

Minorca: Add new shelter, being one removed from Half Way House (earlier structure thus replaced).

Ballaragh: Lineside shelter demolished 1973.

Dhoon Glen: Larger shelter/toilets demolished 1985, a new smaller building erected in 1987.

Dhoon Quarry: Former sawmill demolished 1973 (it yielded a usable traction motor), followed by the one time "creosoting house' in winter 1979-80.

Ballaglass: Power station (in now advanced decay) sold off 1968, (sub-station area leased until 1989). See Ch 8 for recent events.

Ballaglass Glen: Old shelter demolished 1985, new one completed 1990.

Ballafayle-Corteen: Lineside shelter demolished 1979.

Lewaigue: New building 1986.

Ramsey: Plaza cinema demolished 1990-91 (this long accommodated the MER's "station").

Snaefell Line: At the Bungalow, the small wooden booking office of 1895 lasted till 1984 (the TT Marshal's Office is now used).

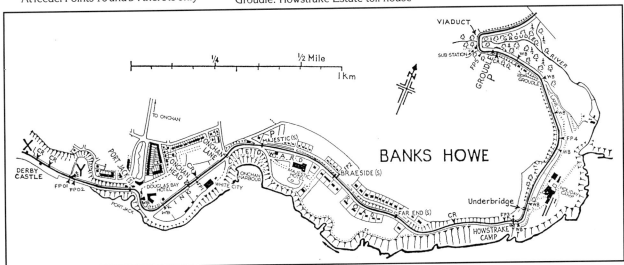

Map 1: See area plan for details at X and Y. (J C Cooke)

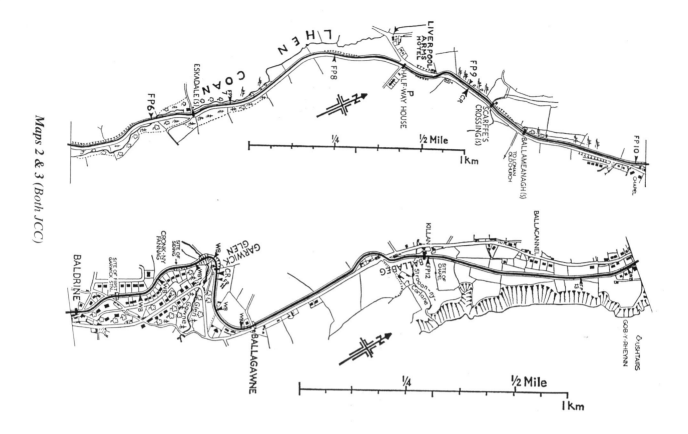

Maps 2 & 3 (Both JCC)

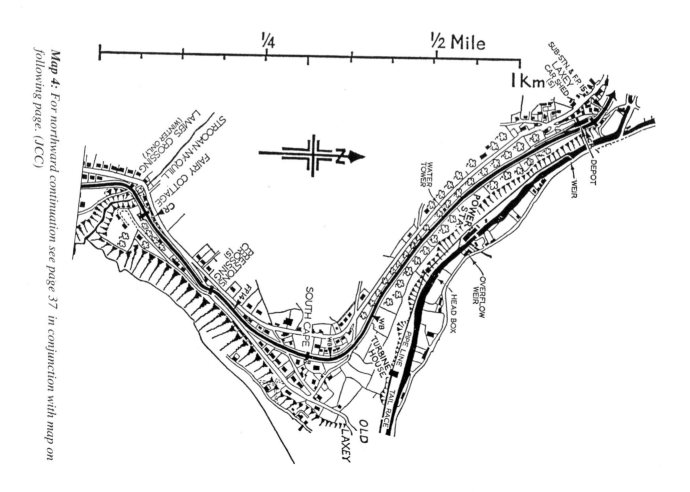

Map 4: For northward continuation see page 37 in conjunction with map on following page. (JCC)

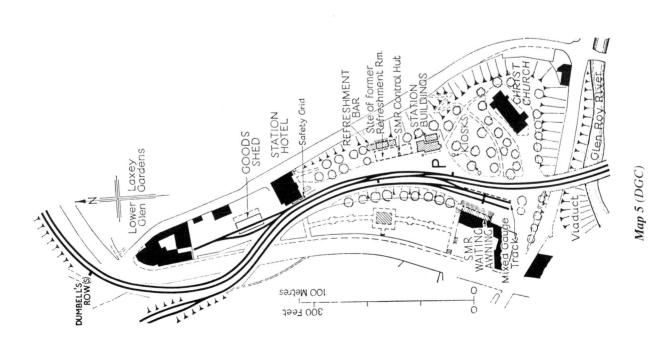

Map 6 (DGC)

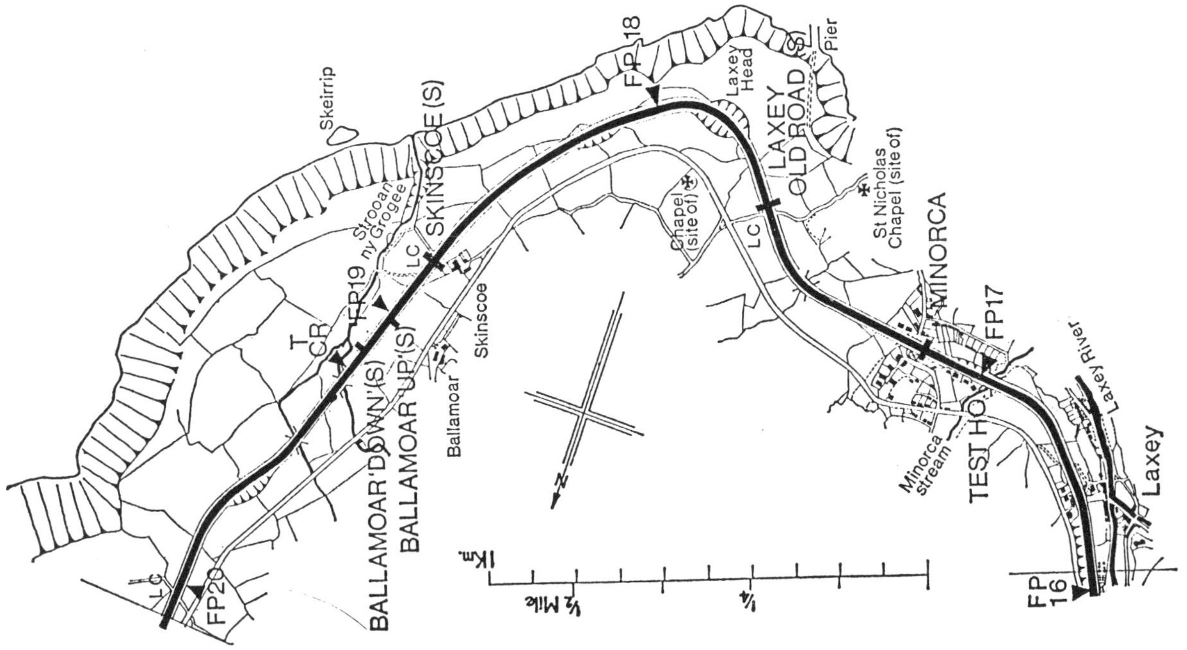

Skeirrip

Strooan ny Grogee

BALLAMOAR DOWN'S (S)

BALLAMOAR UP (S)

Ballamoar

Skinscoe

SKINSCOE (S)

FP19

CR

FP20

LC

LC

Chapel (site of)

LC

FP18

Laxey Head

LAXEY OLD ROAD (S)

Pier

St Nicholas Chapel (site of)

MINORCA

FP17

TEST HO

Minorca Stream

Laxey River

Laxey

FP 16

½ Mile

¼

1 Km.

N

Map 5 (DGC)

DUMBELL'S ROW (S)

Lower Laxey Glen Gardens

N

GOODS SHED

STATION HOTEL

Safety Grid

REFRESHMENT BAR

Site of former Refreshment Rm.

SMR Control Hut

STATION BUILDINGS

Kiosks

CHRIST CHURCH

P

SMR WAITING AWNING

Mixed Gauge Track

Viaduct

Glen Roy River

0   100 Metres
0   300 Feet

149

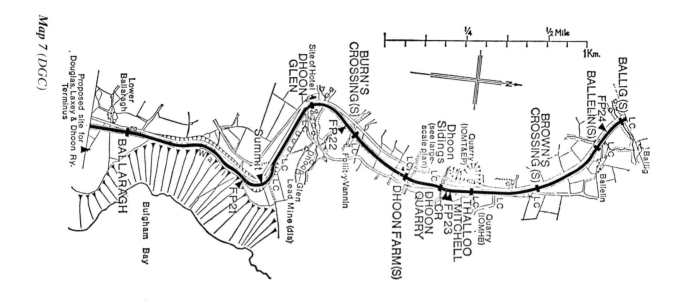

Map 7 (DGC)

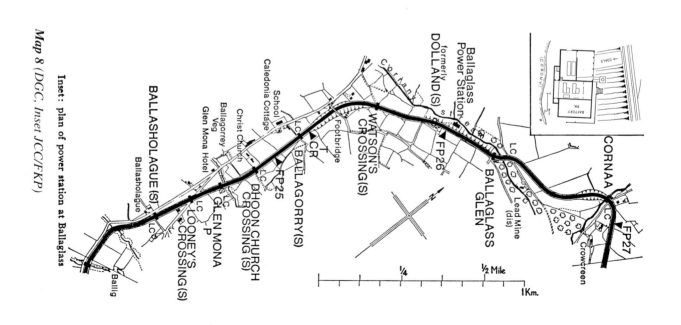

Map 8 (DGC, Inset JCC/FKP)

Inset: plan of power station at Ballaglass

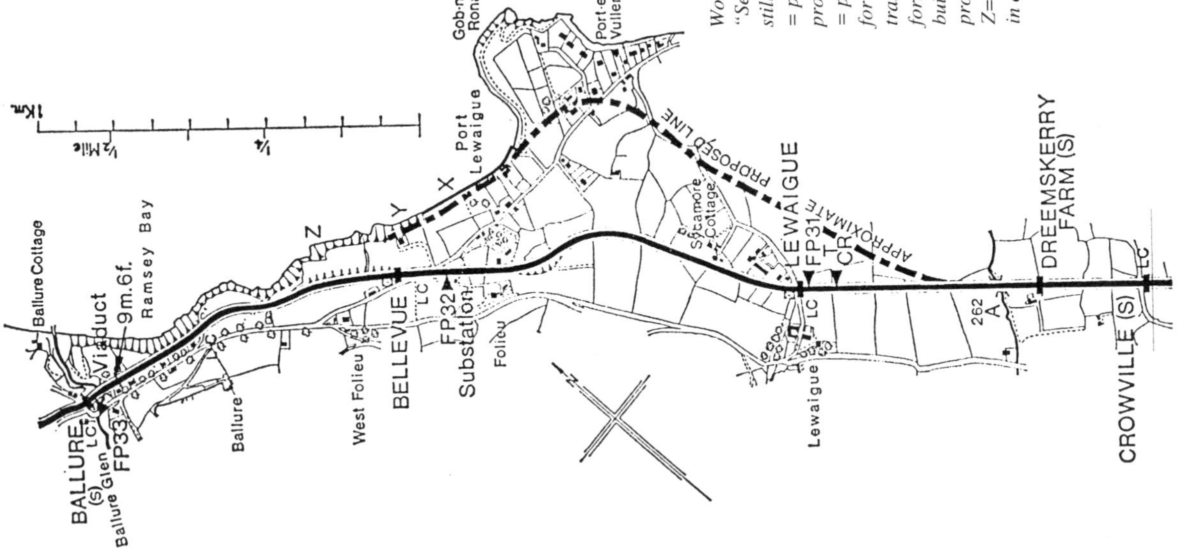

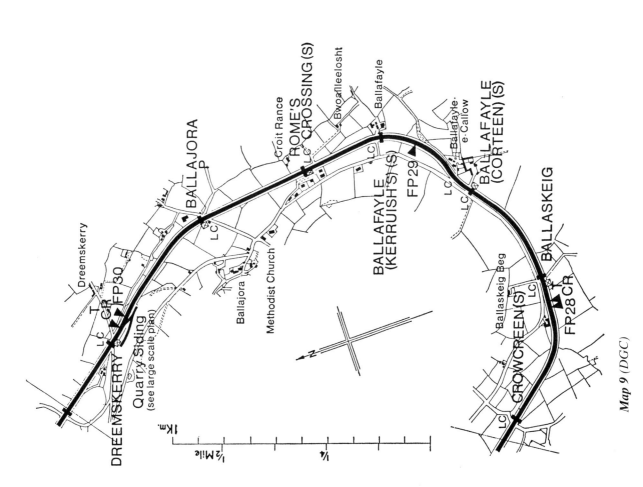

Works, etc for 1897's "Sea Level" tramway still exist as follows: A = point of divergence of proposed shore route; X = partly built sea wall for promenade tramway; Y = pair of former boarding houses built fronting proposed promenade tramway; Z = rock shelf partly cut in cliff.

Map 10 (DGC)

Map 9 (DGC)

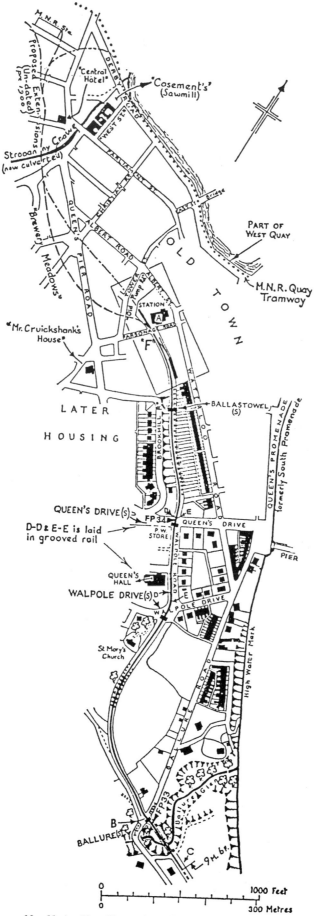

*Map 11: A = Plaza Cinema, formerly The Palace; B = road crossing
with traffic lights; C = site of 1898 depot; F = "Mr Cruikshank's
garden" (see 1899 text). Extension proposals shown here are pre-1900.
The rectangle shows the area covered by the Ramsey station plan
appearing in Chapter 3. (J C Cooke)*

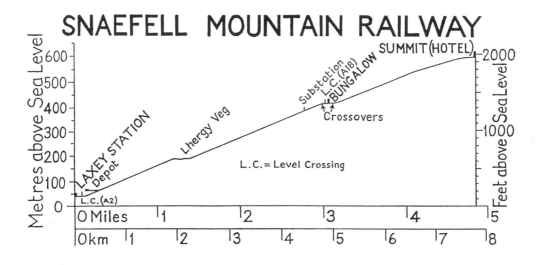

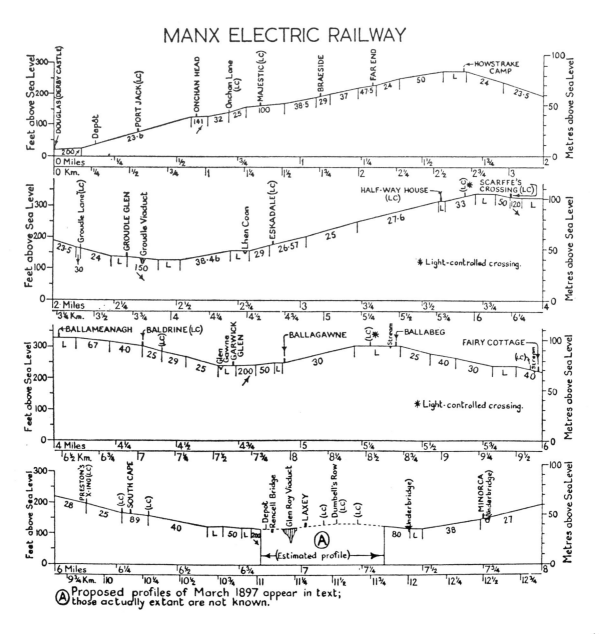

MANX ELECTRIC RAILWAY (continued)

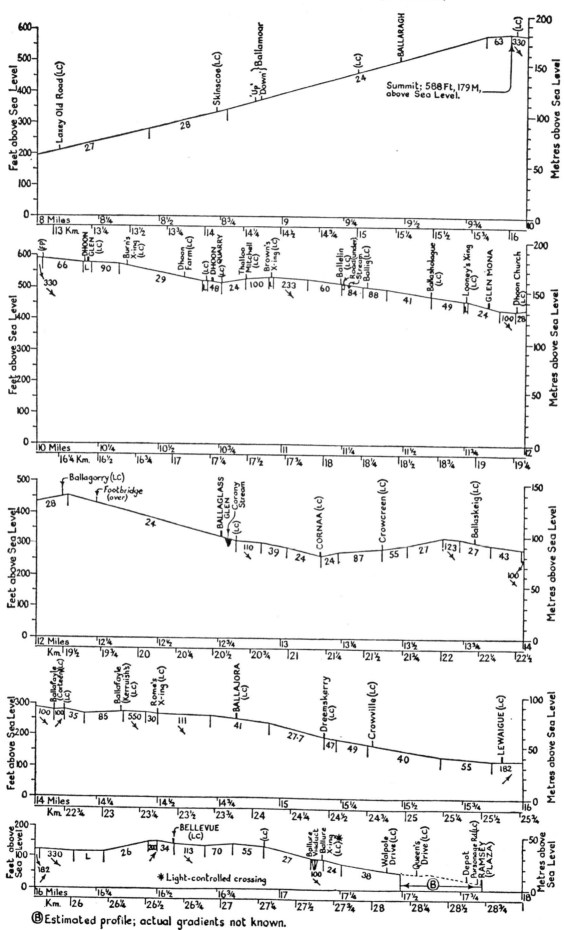

Ⓑ Estimated profile; actual gradients not known.

Appendix 5
The Island Government
(with special thanks to Martin Caley)

As the legislative background to the history of the Manx Electric group of lines is entirely Manx, and its existence under Government control after 1957 has similarly been a direct Manx responsibility, it is helpful further to explain the Island's system of government.

Tynwald

The Island is a British Crown dependency, with, as Head of State, the Queen "in Privy Council". The Crown has overall responsibility for the "good government of the Island". However, as its parliament, the Island has in its Tynwald the oldest continuously-surviving such institution in the world (from about 979AD).

The parliamentary body comprises the Sovereign (normally represented by the Lieutenant-Governor), the Legislative Council and the House of Keys. From 1866 the latter has been popularly elected — its present 24-member format dates back to 1266. The Keys elect, from among their own ranks, a Speaker, who retains his/her vote. The Legislative Council's origins go back to (at least) 1405.

Returning to more recent times, prior to 1919 the Legislative Council consisted of eight members appointed by the Crown. By virtue of its composition, it could effectively nullify Keys-originated legislation (see later). By 1975 a slow process of democratisation had led to the composition of a Council with but two members appointed by the Crown, of whom one had no vote, and eight members elected by the Keys (when a sitting member is so "elevated", a by-election is necessary).

In 1980 the Governor ceased to preside over the Council, which now elected a President from among its own members.

When sitting together the Keys and the Legislative Council comprise the High Court of Tynwald, and it is there that matters of finance and general policy are debated. Legislation is considered separately by each House, and Bills have to pass three readings in each before being submitted for Royal Assent — in recent years the Lieutenant Governor has acted in this respect for the Queen, providing the legislation concerns "domestic" matters only. The Keys has a five-year lifespan, and Tynwald meets at approximately monthly intervals from October to July.

The Executive Council

Returning to 1919, the Governor had come to be aided in his duties (he both presided over Tynwald and had overall responsibility for Island finances) by a somewhat ad hoc institution, the Executive Council. Its original composition seems indistinguishable from that of the Legislative Council of the day, but by the time the Home Office recognised its existence (in 1946) it comprised seven Tynwald Members, typically Chairmen of major Boards of Tynwald. These last institutions included two categories, Boards and Statutory Boards, the latter in charge of the equivalent of nationalised industries. By 1957, there were 16 Boards and Statutory Boards, including that of the MER.

The MacDermott Commission of 1958 saw the Executive Council at last afforded full statutory status. By 1962 it comprised the Chairman of the (newly created) Finance Board (from 1976 this Board was to assume the overall financial responsibility previously vested in the Governor), four other Board Chairmen and two Tynwald members appointed by the Governor. The latter continued to preside, and had a casting vote.

By 1968 its composition had further developed — it now comprised the Chairman of the Finance Board, two members of the Legislative Council and five members of the Keys (unless the Chairman of the Finance Board happened to be a member of Legislative Council, in which case he was treated as the second "Leg Co" member and the Keys had six places).

Although the various Boards retained their autonomy, the effects of "Exco's" deliberations were to be increasingly felt. The episode of the Transmark consultancy illustrates the seriousness with which it by that time considered controversial issues, prior to reporting to Tynwald. From 1980, the Governor ceased to preside over the Council, but still "attended and participated". After further revision in 1984, its "directions" finally became mandatory for various Boards (this was a prelude to the major Governmental changes described below — its original function had been entirely an advisory one, for the benefit of the Governor).

Ministerial Government, 1986-90

The outline given in Chapter 7 explains the new concept of the Chief Minister, whose chosen ministerial subordinates now ran "Departments", most of these being amalgamations of preexisting Boards. So as to provide continuity, coincident with the creation of "Ministers" in 1986, the Executive Council's membership was finally revised to comprise Ministers only (a prelude to its final metamorphosis four years later). Meanwhile, typically, the MER Board had been absorbed by the Isle of Man Passenger Transport Board (in 1983) and was now (December 1986) merged with the former Tourist Board to become the Department of Tourism and Transport, (Department of Tourism, Leisure and Transport from July 1990). Several of the statutory Boards continue in existence. By 1990 a Constitution Act created the office of President of Tynwald (first holder, Sir Charles Kerruish) and the holder of that office now also presides over the Legislative Council, with eight Tynwald-elected members, the Lord Bishop and the Attorney General (the latter still voteless). The President has a casting vote in both offices, and his selection from among the Keys necessitates a by-election.

"Exco" itself was to become the "egg" from which the new Council of Ministers was finally to be hatched, in 1990, and its deliberations thereafter finally excluded the Governor's personal attendance, although he is still supplied with agenda, minutes et al.

Acts and Orders relating to the M E R

Manx Electric Railway Act, 1957

Statutory Bodies (Appointment) Act, 1962

Isle of Man Passenger Transport Act, 1982

Department of Tourism and Transport Order, 1986

Government Departments Act, 1987

Department of Tourism, Leisure and Transport Order, 1990

Bibliography and Acknowledgements

The basic research for a great deal of this book was undertaken some 40 years ago, and outline histories of the Island's horse and electric lines by the writer appeared in 1954-6 in *Modern Tramway, Tramway Review,* and in the brochure issued by Douglas Corporation to mark the eightieth anniversary of the horse tramway in 1956. Apart from these, few published accounts existed of the lines described in this book and the writer is thus more than usually grateful to all those who have assisted. They have been grouped under the subjects dealt with, but it is a considerable exercise of memory to recollect all who have helped and the author here asks the understanding of whose names have inadvertently been omitted.

Manx Electric lines, specifically:

A Callister, A R Cannell, the Lady Chorley, D Clayton, R C Drinkwater, W Duggan, B Barraclough Fell, Professor H B Fell, L Gale, H Gilmore, F Henry, W E Kerruish, D Kinnell, A McMullen, A W Morley, H Quayle, T A Quilleash, J Rowe, M Saunderson, Miss Ida Shaw, C Taylor, Mrs E Tollemache, R Ward, J F Watson, the *Electrical Review,* the Librarian of the Institute of Electrical Engineers, Mather & Platt Ltd, Post Office Records Dept, station, depot and engineering staffs of the MER Board, and successive boards and their several chairmen.

Assistance in general

Government Office, Douglas, the Isle of Man Harbour Board, the Isle of Man Highway & Transport Board, the Isle of Man Tourist Board, the Rolls Office, Douglas, Miss C E Baron, W S Basnett, G Body, L Bond, W Bond, J I C Boyd, G B Claydon, the editor of the *The Courier,* T Cowley, B E Crompton, A M Cubbon, R L Eastleigh, the Right Rev the Bishop of Montreal, F R G Farrell, Mr Godwin (Isle of Man Holiday Centre), Major F C Harris, Miss Ann Harrison and colleagues at the Manx Museum. P G Hislop, W G S Hyde, the editor of the *Isle of Man Times,* D W K Jones, Rev Bertram G Kelly, F W Killip, F W Ladds, J B Matthews, J H Meredith, Ramsey B Moore, D Odabashian, R B Parr, G R Peake, J H Price, J N Slater, A Tranter, W J Wyse.

The main sources used in compiling this work, other than personal interview and correspondence, have been the Manx Press, the transport and technical Press, and official reports. The first comprise *The Courier* and its predecessor *The Ramsey Courier, The Isle of Man Examiner, The Isle of Man Times, The Manxman,* and *Mona's Herald,* the second *The Engineer, Electrical Review, The Electrician, The Light Railway and Tramway Journal, Modern Tramway, Railway Magazine, The Street Railway Journal,* and *Tramway and Railway World* (formerly *Railway World*). The reports consulted are those of Douglas Corporation, the Select Committees of

Tynwald, and the Manx Electric Railway Board, and use has also been made of papers held by the MER Board, the Isle of Man Railway Company (via W T Lambden and B E Crompton), Douglas Corporation Transport Department, the Rolls Office, Douglas Government Office, Douglas, the British Museum Newspaper Library, the Public Record Office (London), the Companies Registry of the Board of Trade, and those at the Nunnery, Douglas, by kind permission of the late Captain J W L Fry-Goldie Taubman.

Several of the tickets accompanying Appendix 3 were supplied by Mr W H Bett, and photographed by Mr F Roland Whiteside, FRSA. Other specialised help in photographic work is acknowledged to Messrs J T Chapman Ltd, S R Keig Ltd (Douglas), Mr D W K Jones and Mr R B Parr. Measurements used in the preparation of the car drawings were taken by Messrs P Hammond, S Basnett, J N Slater and the author.

In conclusion, I would express personal appreciation of the exertions of my former editor J H Price. The volume of work undertaken by Mr Price in this capacity approached that involved in compiling the original manuscript, to which he had already made major research contributions over earlier years. Retrospectively, an equal debt to the late Mrs Annie S Pearson should be recorded. Her professional skills were fully matched by her extensive participation in research on the Island, as Manx friends will recollect.

Bibliography

Since the appearance of this book in its original form, a succession of "MER" albums and booklets have emerged from other authors. It will (perhaps inevitably) be found that "echoes" of the Author's 1970 text are to be found in some of these later works! Among these, the following most deserve mention:

"Isle of Man Album" (Wyse and Joyce, 1968) has good pictorial content. *"Manx Electric Railway Album"* by Hendry and Hendry (1978) is photographically excellent. A M Goodwyn's *"Snaefell Mountain Railway"* (1987) contains its share of derivative material—his later *"All about the Manx Electric Railway"* contains some good original work but both books include some "personalities" better (in the writer's view) omitted. In connection with fundraising for the Douglas cable car, the writer and W G S Hyde produced two successive *"Isle of Man Tramway Album(s)"* and a more general work, *"Isle of Man Remembered"* all with substantial MER photographic content. A "centenary" guide produced by the MER in 1991 contains some interesting "fresh" information on various aspects of the line (Kniveton & Scarffe). Reference to the use made of magazines produced by the Manx Electric

Railway Society and the Isle of Man Railway Society has already been made in the Introduction.

Three recent texts on more general matters should be mentioned. D G Kermode's *"Evolution at Work: A Case Study of the Isle of Man"* (1979) contains substantial information on the evolution of the island Government to that date, whilst Connery Chappell's *"The Dumbell Affair"* has much excellent detail on the involvement of the affairs of IOMT & EP in the bank crash of 1900. *"A brief history of the Isle of Man"* by G V C Young is also highly commended.

Acknowledgements, 1992

Working from diverse sources, there were occasional difficulties with conflicting statistical information and it is appropriate to mention here the kind assistance of Martin Caley of the Island's Treasury, who was able to provide up-to-date official figures. Also, in providing major assistance on behalf of the Railways' administration, my thanks are due to Robert Smith and his team, especially Mssrs Faragher, Goldsmith, Ogden and Warhurst. Ms M Critchlow of the Manx Museum gave help on a number of difficult topics and effected useful introductions. Of 1970's helpers, I have again enlisted Stan Basnett, and Messrs S Broomfield, J C Cooke, J N Slater and J B Matthews, and also the Douglas horse tramway's Wilson Gibb.

Ron Hopkinson of Orrell, Lancs, has been instrumental in contacting Brian Hopkinson (one of Dr Edwards' grandsons) and a recent book edited by an American resident friend, John Stevens, conveniently provided material on Sir William Siemens. Mr J H Price kindly supplied LRTL/LRTA magazine issues with relevant content. R Powell Hendry provided valuable help with photographs, as did R M Casserley and those mentioned in the photo captions. Substantial assistance by local concern "Milnthorpe Printers" is also acknowledged.

My present wife, Mrs Majorie Pearson, has borne the impact of renewed authorship with exemplary patience!

More details about the 1930 fire at Laxey can be found in *"Mann Ablaze!",* by Stan Basnett (published by Leading Edge Press & Publishing Ltd).

Index

*Some detail figures for the ear-
lier Board years will be found in
'Isle of Man Tramways', P272-3.
** Mr Gilmore was typical of many
MER staff in following a family
tradition; his father is seen (at
Laxey) on P81.

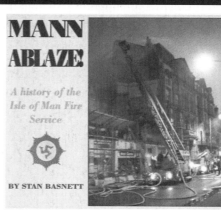

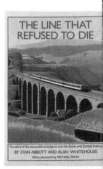